Chimpanzee Travels

Also by Dale Peterson

Visions of Caliban: On Chimpanzees and People
with Jane Goodall

The Deluge and the Ark: A Journey into Primate Worlds

CoCo Logo
with Don Inman and Ramon Zamora

Intelligent Schoolhouse: On Computers & Learning

Genesis II: Creation and Recreation with Computers

Big Things from Little Computers

A Mad People's History of Madness

Chimpanzee Travels

On and Off the Road in Africa

Dale Peterson

A WILLIAM PATRICK BOOK

ADDISON-WESLEY PUBLISHING COMPANY
Reading, Massachusetts   Menlo Park, California   New York
Don Mills, Ontario   Wokingham, England   Amsterdam   Bonn
Sydney   Singapore   Tokyo   Madrid   San Juan
Paris   Seoul   Milan   Mexico City   Taipei

Grateful acknowledgment is made to Apparition Music and songwriters Dennis Pendrith and Patrick Godfrey for permission to reprint lyrics to "Joshua Giraffe," recorded by Raffi on the *Baby Beluga* CD.

Library of Congress Cataloging-in-Publication Data

Peterson, Dale.
    Chimpanzee travels : on and off the road in Africa / Dale Peterson.
      p. cm.
    Includes bibliographical references.
    ISBN 0-201-40737-X
    1. Chimpanzees—Africa. 2. Peterson, Dale—Journeys—Africa.
I. Title.
QL737.P96P46 1995
599.88′44′096—dc20
    [B]   94-19462
                                               CIP

Jacket design by Jean Seal
Jacket illustration by Richard Geidd
Text design by Karen Savary
Set in 11-point Monotype Baskerville by Weimer Graphics, Inc.

1 2 3 4 5 6 7 8 9-MA-97969594
First printing, November 1994

To my wife and children, who wanted to come along

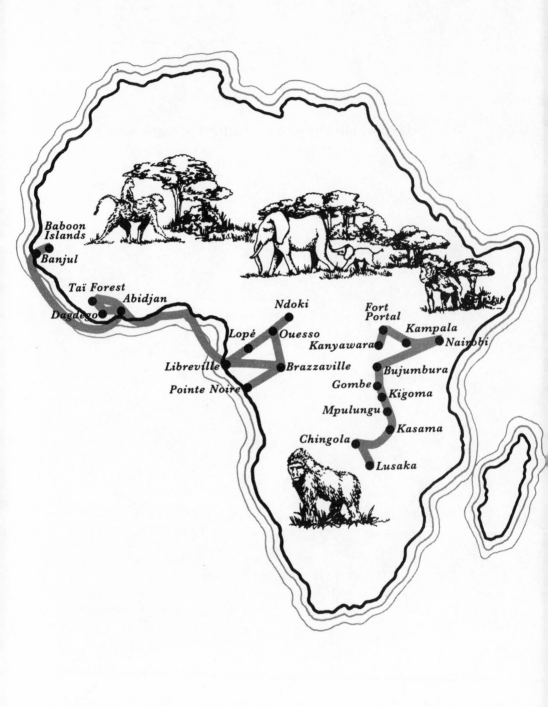

Baboon
Islands
Banjul
Taï Forest
Abidjan
Dagdego
Ndoki
Fort
Portal
Lopé
Ouesso
Kampala
Kanyawara
Nairobi
Libreville
Brazzaville
Bujumbura
Pointe Noire
Gombe
Kigoma
Mpulungu
Kasama
Chingola
Lusaka

Contents

Chimps, Cows, & Cockroaches

*Most kinds of creeping things are eatable, and are
used by the Chinese. Locusts and grasshoppers are not
at all bad. To prepare them, pull off the legs and
wings and roast them in an iron dish, like coffee.
Even the gnats that swarm on the Shiré River are
collected by natives and pressed into cakes.*

–Francis Galton, *The Art of Travel*

Once, when I was in the Brazilian Amazon, I met an American couple
who had been traveling for four years. They had done Europe. They
had done Asia and the Soviet Union. They had done Africa, top to
bottom. Now they were doing South America. "What's it like to travel
nonstop for four years?" I wondered aloud. "After a while," the man
said, "it just becomes a job. Like any other job. You wake up in the
morning and ask yourself, 'What do I have to do today?' You do it,
and then you go to bed at night."

"Do you get weekends off?" I asked.

We were on a boat going down the Amazon River—the American
couple had a cabin on the boat, I had a hammock—and somewhere in
the middle of this general conversation, a spider lowered him or herself
down from the roof of the boat almost onto my nose. That close, the
spider seemed big, and my glasses took in the hairy image and mag-
nified it, like a fish in ice, so the spider became even bigger. Surprised,
in a reflex, I violently clapped my hands at the spider but missed,
hitting my glasses instead. The force of the blow smashed the wire

frames of my glasses and knocked the twisted consequence halfway across the deck. I picked them up: useless. I threw them overboard.

The woman said she hated spiders. I said I didn't. I did hate giant cockroaches, I said.

"You mean the kind that get to be three-and-a-half-inches long and can fly?"

"That's the kind!" I said, and I told them about crushing giant cockroaches with my shoe one night while trying to sleep in a noisy brothel in Tamatave, Madagascar. The roaches hid all around the room in a crevice between the baseboard and the floor, and they would start to creep out whenever it was dark. I would turn the light off, wait five minutes until I could hear the faint scuttling across the floor—they seemed to be headed for my dirty socks—then turn the light on and attack with my shoe. When my shoe struck one, it would pop softly, like bubble gum. But they were fast. Then I recalled the giant cockroach I encountered in an American-style hamburger joint in Manaus, Amazonia. This roach, as big as a mouse, bolder than a rat, scurried along the lunch counter directly after my french fries. He knew precisely what he wanted. It was frightening.

"That's nothing," the woman said. Once, when they were in Thailand, she woke up to find five giant cockroaches congregated on her sleeping husband's face. What were they doing? They were busy eating his nosehairs.

I couldn't top that story—but I tell it and its context now to illustrate three points. First, most people exaggerate about insects. All the giant cockroaches I've seen have been closer to two-and-a-half-inches long, not three-and-a-half. Three at the most. Second, some people dramatize what they've seen and done while traveling. That was not a noisy brothel in Tamatave, Madagascar, for instance. It was an ordinary rotten hotel with several good-looking prostitutes operating out of the bar. Third, a few people actually like to travel. Those are the kind who think traveling is a form of employment and then wake up in Thailand with giant cockroaches eating their nosehairs.

I am not one of those redoubtable few. I'm more the sort who slaps at a spider, misses, and breaks his glasses instead.

The only reason I have traveled, a little, is that I am interested in primates—monkeys, apes, and lemurs. I once wrote a book about them, in fact, and in doing so I traveled around the world and entered forests in South America, Africa, India, and Southeast Asia. I looked into places where shadows swayed across my face. I watched monkeys high above quietly dive away, leaping and landing with a soft splash in the leaves and then scampering away along elevated branch highways. In Borneo, I slid into a trance (or fell asleep, I should say) inside a 100 million year old rain forest as tall as Niagara Falls and dreamed that a tennis coach was shouting: "Strike hard!" I took his advice, and my game was greatly improved. Hit three aces in a row. I woke up with a white butterfly rowing in the air above my face and a bird crying out from some invisible place: "Strike hard! Strike hard! Strike hard!" Cockroaches be damned! You go to these places to visit your own self as you lay down in a cool breeze on a flickering forest floor six million years ago; or maybe you go because you remembered that unremembered dream illuminating all wild places in the head, a cool reality hidden somewhere right behind the heat of human suffering or a blissful interior twilight where sense is woven into nonsense and words dissolve into non-words, where the lion lies truly with the lamb: The paradise we think we were promised.

That's why I went to the tropics.

And that's why I was persuaded to go back, this time to concentrate on Africa. My imagination had been stoked by the famous chimpanzee scientist Jane Goodall, whom I met in 1989, with whom I discussed the possibility of collaborating on a project of some sort, something having to do with chimpanzees. Problem was I didn't know the first thing about them. Thus, hoping to educate myself concerning the hairy apes with thumbs on their feet, during two extended trips in 1990 and 1991 I traveled in a big circle right around their home territory—into East, West, and Central Africa—and finally penetrated that circle, taking a train into central Gabon and walking, in northern Congo, into the heart of an enchanted forest known as the Ndoki.

Those were my Chimpanzee Travels, and they started in Boston on a miserably cold January day, which by the time I reached London had become merely bleak and dreary.

Changing planes in London required changing airports, from Heathrow on one side of the city to Gatwick on the other, and I transformed that necessary excursion into an unnecessary excuse to linger in my favorite city for several hours. I had arranged to meet my British editor for a late breakfast. He stood me up at the last minute, citing some standard excuse. I had also arranged to meet an old friend for a late lunch. Her familiar face appeared out of the anonymous crowd like a blossom, and we ate lunch at an Indian restaurant. I expanded on what I had mentioned in my brief letter to her: I was traveling to Africa to find chimpanzees.

After lunch, my friend handed me a folded white envelope, which, as I discovered, contained a small fragment of stone. A piece of the Berlin Wall, she said, just smashed, to provide good luck in Africa.

I put the envelope in my pocket.

My other possessions I kept, sorted according to my own patent-pending system, stuffed into a single backpack. The backpack I had just purchased, and I was pleased with the fact that it had straps for the shoulders but also a leather handle on the side; you could haul it along vertically and strapped on your back, but you could also turn it ninety degrees to the horizontal and carry it as a soft bag. I intended to carry this important object in the horizontal, right onto the plane as a legal piece of hand luggage, but the pimpled youth checking bags at Gatwick for the midnight flight to Lusaka, Zambia, saw it in vertical terms: "That's a rucksack!" And so I hastily pulled out a few essentials and then watched the bulk of my possessions tremble down a conveyor belt into a hole. I passed through a series of metal detectors and glass doors and sat down, waiting for my flight.

I opened a book—some light travel reading called *Gulliver's Travels*—and tried to concentrate on that fantasy world of travel. . . . It would be nice to pretend that I sat there with vision and equanimity, book in hand, pith helmet on head, body and heart aligned in the direction of Africa, calm and clear-eyed, that sort of thing. But the truth was less heroic. I was tired and anxious, a knot in my stomach, not enjoying the book, missing my family terribly, and doubting the purpose and logic of my travel—or of any travel. I don't even like flying on airplanes.

Nor did I have much idea what I was getting myself into. Where in Africa was I going? Well, I had a list of names and addresses, given to me by chimp expert Geza Teleki. I had written to some of the people on that list, and a few had written back. But what would the chimps be like? I had never really been up close to a chimp in my life. I couldn't even remember having seen them in zoos. Would the chimps be aggressive, easy to find, strange, friendly? I had no idea—I was just a writer, not a chimp expert.

I once asked Geza Teleki a very direct question: "What's so special about chimps? Why should anyone care about them?" Teleki, a big, strong-willed person with a bitter laugh, an Americanized Hungarian aristocrat and refugee from World War II, a well-trained anthropologist with lots of experience studying chimps, leaned over his living room table, the glass top of which contained Hungarian money, looked at me directly with his good eye, and said, "Because . . . they're people."

That was, I have since decided, a koan, slipped like a coin from a pocket into the vault of a great big couch. The thought lozenge is still dissolving, very seriously, in the stomach of my mind. But what does it mean? I was hoping to find out.

The boarding of Air Zambia flight 378 to Lusaka was announced. I squeezed into the queue, followed the person in front of me as we toddled up a gently curving ramp, obeyed directions with a bovine nod, turned a corner, and conveyed myself down the aisle until I was settled in comfortably and bolted under a seat belt. There was soft music and a low rumbling. The plane shook, shifted, and rose.

After a few hours of ordinary magic the plane descended, the door opened, and I was hit by a blast of hot air. And then I found myself standing in a hot summer morning with sweet smells flowing through the open windows and doors of a small, concrete-and-cinderblock airport. I collected my pack, passed through Zambian immigration and customs, exchanged some dollars for kwacha at the official rate, ignoring the unofficial money changers standing just outside the bank, and then climbed up through the anus of another plane, smaller, that soon lifted me and three dozen Africans over a green and flat country, grassland with patches of brush and trees and a network of dirt roads and paths spreading everywhere almost randomly, like veins. An hour or so later this second plane landed at a very small airport in a lonely place called Chingola, and I shuffled out into the late morning blast of heat and felt suddenly tired and vaguely bereft. My fellow passengers were all greeted in great warmth, with cries, shouts, kisses, hugs, handshakes, and I, dazed now from sudden changes of physical and social circumstance, spun slowly around, looking for a person I'd never seen before. Eventually I approached an older man, short and compact, with a white beard, sun-damaged face, missing teeth, and wild wispy hair, who didn't seem to be busy greeting anyone. "I'm looking for David Siddle," I said.

He said: "I'm looking for Dale Peterson." His face curled into a devilish smile, and he shook my hand. We fetched my bag and carried it out to his car, a rattletrap Datsun that required a running push by some idle bystanders before the engine turned over.

We drove along rough roads, our windows wide open, through a sun-pasted landscape of red earth and scrub trees, past a mountain of copper mine trailings, on our way to his farm. David Siddle and his wife, Sheila, are English from the old days, settlers in Zambia since 1954, when that country was still Northern Rhodesia. He and his wife and children chose to stay on after independence, and they were allowed by the new government to continue farming and ranching on ten thousand acres situated at the edge of the Kafue River, a tributary of the Zambezi, on the border with Zaire. They lease that land now but still own, with their two grown children and their families, some nine hundred head of cattle. They grow coffee and other cash crops as well as raise beef and provide employment for sixty local people.

They also now operate the single chimpanzee sanctuary in this part of Africa: Chimfunshi Wildlife Sanctuary. Chimps are not endemic to Zambia so far as anyone knows, but baby chimps are smuggled out of Zaire south into Zambia, where they are sold illegally and eventually confiscated by the Zambian government and turned over to the Siddles.

"The terrible thing about chimps," David confessed, "is that they make bloody wonderful pets. They'll cuddle right up against your breast. One slept in a bed between Sheila and me for months, wearing nappies. Then they get to be about four or five years old, and they're weaned, and people become *pudding* to them! Even then they're about as strong as you are, and *they don't like to be told what to do!*"

We drove through a town, passed villages—mud huts with tin or grass roofs—moved across miles and miles of dry woodland, here and there broken open into small plantations and on occasion punctuated with phallic termite mounds. Military roadblocks: We were waved through two and flagged down at a third. Sullen soldiers with submachine guns converged on the car. An enigmatic face behind mirrored sunglasses studied David's papers and gradually gave them back.

We turned onto a rough dirt road and battered along for several miles onto the ranch, still passing through woodland—a fork here, a gate there, and eventually, partly obscured behind some trees, a very high mud-block wall. "The Great Wall of Zambia," David pointed out without further explanation. And then we came to a clearing, a rustic cluster of buildings, some eager peacocks and geese, and a dirt drive circled around a big tree. David stopped the car. We were home. Sheila came from around a corner, smiling, with short dark hair and hazel eyes, and introduced herself. We pulled my pack out of the car. Sheila took me to the guesthouse, which included, I was happy to discover, clean bed, flush toilet, working shower with hot water, and electric light.

After washing up and changing clothes, I stood out on the stoop of the guest cottage and looked from there across the way once again to the fourteen-foot-high wall, electrical barbed wire strung around the top. I could see the tops of a couple of bare trees. I heard screaming from the other side.

Late in the afternoon, I walked down to the house, where Sheila was busy in the kitchen preparing "tea" for the chimpanzees. "Tea" was in fact industrial-strength porridge, with lots of milk, and Sheila was filling several tin buckets with the concoction.

She and I hauled the buckets out of the house along a path to the wall, then alongside the wall until we came to a large brick building: the feeding building. The slender, bright-eyed nineteen-year-old Zambian manager of the chimpanzee project, Patrick Chimbatu, was waiting for us there, holding baskets of fruit and vegetable scraps. As the three of us approached with food and buckets of porridge, the whole feeding house began to shake, inflate, and rise above the ground, with explosions of mad screams and a vast pounding excitement. It was a terrific din, awesome. I wanted to cover my ears. We entered a short concrete corridor with two separated, steel-barred cages on either side. And behind the bars of the four cages, chimpanzees appeared, screaming and pounding. Two of the cages were closed to the outside, and two were open, with steel hatches that led out into an enclosured area.

"Charlie's not here yet," Sheila said. Charlie was the biggest of the chimps, she said, weighing around 120 pounds, and he was dallying outside with one of his wives.

In one of the closed cages were five very young chimps. Four of them came right up when they saw me and reached their small hands out of the bars to touch my hands and face. They started poking my face, pulling my eyebrows. Their fingers were like little sausages. Their hands, I discovered when I clasped them, were far stronger than I expected. I had never been close to a chimpanzee before, young or old, and I was curious to touch their faces. Their faces, dark brown or light brown or freckled, had a waxen sheen, suggesting a rubbery or leathery quality, but not so: I touched a face with my hand and felt only a softness.

Sheila was ladling out porridge to any chimp who wanted it, and Patrick passed out fruit and vegetables. "Uh-oh, here comes Charlie." Sheila warned me not to move near the cage Charlie was entering. Charlie was huge, with bulging arms and bulging legs and a weight lifter's shoulders. His hair bristled on his back and shoulders, and he burst in from the outdoors through a hatchway, burst in hooting and screaming and rushing—three or four other big chimps in that area ricocheted out of his way in a panic, tumbling, dashing out of the way. Charlie swaggered up to the bars, screamed and carried on for a few minutes, and then mildly accepted his share of porridge and fruits.

Next cage over from Charlie, by himself and isolated by a closed hatch, an adult male named Chiquitto, his face wide and cream-colored, added to the commotion, making hoots and then smacks, a Bronx cheer, then long, low raspberries through loose lips. "We had to lock up Chiquitto because the river is low. He knows the escape route when the water is low," Sheila explained as Chiquitto drank his porridge and slobbered over his fruit. Patrick, meanwhile, had hauled in a water bucket, and soon Chiquitto wanted to wash. Patrick poured water into Chiquitto's cupped hands. The big ape splashed water into his face, onto his head, around his eyes. He scrubbed his hands together, then washed one foot and then the other. Then he stood up, stuck out his rear end, bent over, and reached up and washed his bottom.

Every morning Patrick takes the five baby chimps for a long walk in the woods. It's their morning exercise, important since they are not big enough to go out into the enclosure with the rest of the chimps. Did I want to go along?

After an abridged night's sleep and an extended morning wake-up to peace in the countryside (piercing whistle of birds, crying of peacocks, baying of bullmastiffs, honking of geese, squawking of parrots, screaming of chimps, hooting of an owl, cooing of a wood dove), I set out with Patrick and a local game warden, who brought his old rifle and said he was looking for poachers. Patrick opened a cage door and out climbed five young chimps. These were the little guys, perhaps two to four years old, with sweet curious faces and long leathery hands. They looked like elves. We walked into the woods, and one walked upright alongside me, holding my hand and sometimes looking up into my face.

Then suddenly the grip on my hand was tightened, and the chimp's feet turned into hands too, and she climbed right up me as if I were a tree, climbed around and onto my shoulders. The other chimps were walking, scrambling, and riding on Patrick and the game warden.

Now these five young chimps jumped down and scrambled around. They stood up on their hind legs to get a better look at the world, crouching, ridged at the brow, hairy and curious, short necks, huge ears, steady-gazing eyes. As we walked through the woods, the chimps cantered sideways or dashed into the trees and played. They wrestled. They walked on all fours in a slow, loping style—one foot synchronized with its opposite hand. I sat down on a log and watched them, and one young female came up and sat on the log next to me and began reaching into my shirt pockets and then unbuttoning my shirt.

Patrick played with them, chimpanzee style. He hooted, chased, slapped. They scampered and galloped. We walked farther into the woods, three adult humans, five young chimps.

Now the four-year-old male named Sandy, weighing perhaps thirty or forty pounds, walked right behind me, deliberately tail-gating—as we walked he batted my heels, each heel in turn just as I stepped down: slap slap slap slap slap slap slap slap. He did this. I stopped. He stopped. I started. He started: slap slap slap slap slap. Then he dashed ahead of me and climbed into a tree, and just as I was walking past and under the tree, Sandy dropped down and crashed onto my shoulders, arms around my neck, nearly knocking me over with his heavy, bony weight. He leaped onto the ground and dashed off again, this time flanking to my rear, following me, abreast of one of the other chimps. I had my eye on him by then. But Sandy ran up uninterestedly, about to move on past me again, though just as he passed he stomped hard on my foot with his foot and slapped my hip with his hand.

Sandy moved on ahead then, where I could see what he was doing, and he seemed to have forgotten about me for real this time. He was doing something with a small tree, had it bent down, was fiddling with it, bent down and bowed to the ground. Just as I walked close he let it go. The small tree whipped back up and into my face.

We stopped for a time, sat down. Patrick and I sat on a log. The game warden stood around with his rifle. We talked a little, and then Patrick pulled out a small book that he read with deep concentration:

How to Keep Your Family Happy. And the chimps rushed into the trees and fought and played, leaping, dangling, climbing. To change direction, they simply spun around a branch or a trunk.

And now just on the other side of a big tree, in a small grassy field, cows moved in. The chimps jumped out of the trees and walked up to the cows, who were noisily grinding and swallowing grass, and the chimps moved a little closer, on their hind legs now, cautious, walking upright. The chimps had started out toward the cows cautiously, but soon they waxed sanguine. They began barking, then jumping up and down, then stamping their feet, then screaming at the cows.

The cows waned phlegmatic: indifferent, grinding grass.

I thought about the chimps. Then I thought about the cows, and the cows made me think of an Oliver Sacks piece I'd read in the *New Yorker* magazine, a profile of Professor Temple Grandin, an expert on domestic animals who also happens to be autistic. She was locked up in an institution as a child, but managed finally to get out, perhaps through sheer intelligence and talent. She's still autistic, however.

"The emotion circuit's not hooked up—that's what's wrong," Professor Grandin says, by way of self-diagnosis. She has never fallen in love, for example, and finds such behavior hard to comprehend in others. Close friendships continue to elude her, and she finds people and their society remote, troubling, often confusing. She has survived in the difficult, duplicitous world of emotional human beings by operating, as she herself describes it, "like an anthropologist on Mars." Temple Grandin has studied people and their ordinary reactions, reads about them in periodicals, and through what she calls "strictly a logical process" has developed a mental library about humans and how they can be expected to react to particular circumstances. Whenever she encounters a puzzling social situation, Grandin simply refers to the data in her mental library and compares that with whatever is unfolding in the world before her.

With cows, however, she feels right at home—so much so that she has become one of the world's top designers of feedlots, humane slaughterhouses, and other environments for cattle. "When I'm with cattle," she told Oliver Sacks, "it's not at all cognitive. I know what the cow's feeling."

Pretty soon the chimps got bored with the cows, and we started walking again. Presently we came to a huge termite mound about the size of a small house and overgrown with trees and vines, like an ancient volcano. The chimps scrambled all around it, up the mound, into the vines and trees.

After an hour or two had elapsed, we returned to the feeding cages. When we got there, Patrick opened a cage door and four chimps clambered into their cage. But not Sandy. Sandy was not interested. He sat down, refused to budge. Patrick called Sandy, entreated him, promised and threatened, but Sandy would have none of it. I had no idea how to handle a chimp. Plus, I had already had enough of Sandy— who had swatted my heels, jumped onto my neck, stomped on my foot, and whipped me in the face with a tree. But I made the mistake of moving a little too close to the chimp, who was sitting and then squatting very stubbornly on the ground, and the minute I moved close enough, he climbed right up my legs and body and into my arms, snuggled his soft small face into my beard, like a child tired and ready for bed, and I carried him back inside his cage without further ado—or was it adieu?

What would an anthropologist on Mars think about this? I asked myself. But I didn't know the answer.

One thing I forgot to say about Temple Grandin. Even though she is immensely sensitive to the mentality of cows, Professor Grandin really can't relate to monkeys or apes. They are too much like people, she declares, and just as confusing.

2

A Tourist in Zambia

*Tedious journeys are apt to make companions irritable
one to another; but under hard circumstances, a traveller does his duty best who doubles his kindliness of
manner to those about him, and takes harsh words
gently, and without retort. He should make it a point
of duty to do so. It is at those times very superfluous to
show too much punctiliousness about keeping up one's
dignity, and so forth; since the difficulty lies not in
taking up quarrels, but in avoiding them.*

—Francis Galton, *The Art of Travel*

Mpulungu, it said on the map, pronounced, one could imagine, with
the first letter grace-noting the second and an accent on the combination—but those two letters still didn't make a fair syllable to my Eng-
lish-wrought brain. I practiced the correct pronunciation silently, but
every time I said the name out loud I accidentally added an extra
couple of letters at the front and placed an accent on the second syllable. Something like Mapitulungu.

Mpulungu was at the very bottom of Lake Tanganyika, yet still in
Zambia, and I knew that a boat steamed up and down the lake every
week or so and left from Mpulungu on a Friday morning. I wanted to
take the boat up Lake Tanganyika to Jane Goodall's research site in
northwestern Tanzania. It was now Tuesday, and if I left today I
thought, I should have no trouble catching the Friday morning boat: a
vessel my *Africa on a Shoestring* said was called the *Liemba*.

Mpulungu didn't look very far away on the map. An unruly piece of Zaire protruded down and dented the northern edge of Zambia—so I'd have to make a little zig and a zag to get there—but it still didn't seem far. Two hundred miles? David and Sheila had never been there themselves, but they thought it should be easy enough, and they hoped once I had done it I would write back and explain how it was done. There was probably a bus, Sheila thought. Perhaps from Kitwe or Chingola. Or I could hitchhike.

Africa on a Shoestring was not fully enthusiastic about Zambia, I began to realize as I skimmed through its brief review of the place: "This strangely shaped country . . . one of Africa's most eccentric legacies of colonialism . . . disastrous economic woes . . . occasional attack by renegade units of the Renamo bandits . . . . Don't attempt to sleep in a railway station . . . national parks nowhere near as easy to visit . . . transportation difficulties . . . cost of accommodation . . . a pity . . . must get permission from ZESCO headquarters in Lusaka . . ." *What is "ZESCO"?* I wondered. I leafed back but couldn't find the answer. I continued: "You can camp at the *Chirundu Hotel* . . . but watch out for the elephants that come to drink out of the swimming pool . . . good place to stay is the *Unity Motel* . . . It's adequate but over-priced." *Well, which is it: "good" or "adequate" and "over-priced"?* I asked myself, slapping the book shut with an immature impatience.

Still, I felt in enormously good spirits just then, and either a bus or hitchhiking sounded just fine to me. I was ready to proceed no matter what the transportational modality. I would relax, be a tourist for a while, drink some more beer, and also perhaps see something of the country.

Sheila had just returned from an excursion into town, her weekly trip to buy a few dozen sacks of rice for all the workers. She needed a government permit to purchase and transport the rice, and the government office that normally gave such permits didn't have paper, so they couldn't give her a permit. I don't know how she finally managed to get the rice; the point is that she was exhausted and aggravated. How would I get to Mpulungu? She might drive me to Chingola, where I could look for a bus, she said halfheartedly. But I saw she didn't feel like dealing with my transportation problems at all.

"You don't really want to drive me in, do you," I said.

"No, I don't," she admitted.

Her mood didn't faze me in the slightest. I had traveled enough already to know the name of the small knife required to whittle a gnarl

of this type: patience. *Obstacles to travel, in Africa, are not of place but of time.*
That's what I was thinking, and I did feel patient indeed as I sipped
on a Mchinga Lager. But patience was hardly even required, because
just a few minutes later a young German couple drove their old
Peugeot into the Siddles's driveway.

The German woman must have been twenty-five years old. She
was a giant, about six foot four, with long bright blond hair and a belly
button showing from under the bottom of a too-short red shirt, as if
she had suddenly grown so big and surprised the shirt. Her name was
Brünnhilde, she said, and she wore four copper and turquoise brace-
lets on her left arm and beaten silver hoop earrings in her ears. She
had a slender face and a curved nose, no eyebrows, peaches-and-cream
skin. Her companion was big, too, tall and powerfully built, with a
strong jaw and blue eyes, short brown hair, and white socks inside
sandals on his feet. He shook my hand and told me his name, which I
immediately forgot.

Brünnhilde had only been in Africa for two weeks. She had come
to fetch her companion. He had been in Africa for two years, trying to
set up a trading consortium between the Germans and the Zambians,
part of some foreign-aid project. David and Sheila knew them only
remotely, I realized, but they had stopped in to see the chimpanzees
before going to Lusaka to catch a flight back to Europe. Did they have
room in their Peugeot for another person? They did. There was a
Chinese train, they said, that went in the direction I was going. They
would take me to the Chinese train. It left at perhaps nine or ten that
evening from the Chinese station in Kapiri, before Lusaka. Right on
their way. It would be easy. This was a stroke of luck.

"What is the news?" the German wanted to know. "We don't get
the radio. I hear some rumors that the Berlin Wall is down, but I can't
believe it. It's impossible, is it not?"

David and Sheila didn't get news directly from Europe, either.
"But *he's* just come here last week," David said of me.

"Yes, the Berlin Wall is down," I announced, pleased to deliver the
news to a German. Suddenly I remembered the folded envelope in my
pocket. "In fact, I happen to have a piece of the Wall right here!" And
I pulled out the envelope, unfolded it, removed the small chip of stone,
and placed it right in the German's hand. I was seized by a sudden
impulse of generosity: "You can have it," I said.

The German examined it closely. "But this is just a stone!" he
said. Then, looking at me suspiciously, he added: "This could be any
stone. How do I know it's from the Wall?"

While the Germans went down to see the chimpanzees, I packed my bag. Then we climbed into the Peugeot, I in the back, and drove away. We drove through the gate, back down the long dirt road, and then off the Siddles's farm and onto a single-lane tarmac highway without traffic, through woodland and elephant grass, past squalid mud huts with thatch or rusting tin roofs, past schoolgirls walking along the road in tattered blue uniforms and carrying rough hoes, raising red dust everywhere as we went, listening to African music on the car tape player.

We were stopped at a military roadblock. A camouflaged officer leaned in the window. "Where are you from?" he wanted to know.

"Salewesi," the German said.

"Where are you going?"

"Lusaka."

"You can go on."

"Thank you very much," the German said, and then, as he put the car in gear and pulled out, he turned to me and explained: "I'm always polite. It confuses them."

We drove on, past a long, gullied mountain of burned rubble—copper trailings—through bamboo and scrub and under a sky clumped with white and gray, past women walking along the road with baskets on their heads, past rusting car bodies alongside the road, and through the lingering smells of wet grass and diesel fumes. A road sign with a picture of a red heart and black skull and crossbones said:

**AVOID TRAFFIC
ACCIDENTS AND AIDS:
THEY CAN KILL.**

And the German couple jabbered to each other in German as we drove.

I was curious about his job. What sort of trading consortium were the Germans trying to set up in Salewesi? "The Chermans are pulling out next April," he shouted above the wind rushing through the open windows.

"I thought you were setting up a trading consortium," I shouted.

"Setting up a trading consortium? Not possible here. It's impossible," he declared, tossing a look at me over his shoulder. Then he added, with an exaggerated drama in his voice: "There is no hope! There is no hope!"

The couple resumed jabbering to each other, and then a few minutes later, the German looked over his shoulder at me again and said, "Be careful. You are not allowed to photograph anything in this country. Be careful with your camera. There are no tourists here. If you take photographs, they will think you're a spy and put you in prison."

A spy? I thought, amazed at the concept.

The land turned dreary, and the sky turned into bruised flesh. We moved up behind a slow-moving, two-trailer truck spurting diesel smoke into the air and blocking our progress on this one-lane highway. A sign on the back of the truck said:

ABNORMAL.

We came to a town, bought some fruit, drinks, and cigarettes, rested for a few minutes, and then drove again until we turned onto a deeply rutted mud track and drove along that for three or four miles until we came to the Chinese train station. This railroad was built by the Chinese fifteen years ago, a gift from the proletariat of China to the proletariat of Zambia, the German informed me. (Later, I read in *Railway Across the Equator* that this railroad was built with a $230 million loan from the Chinese, a deal that included several underpowered engines and other rolling stock, and enough expertise to place 1,160 miles of steel from Kapiri to Dar es Salaam. China wanted to give Zambia a route to the sea for copper exports that would avoid unnecessary congress with South Africa.) The only trouble was, the German went on to explain, the Chinese gauge is different from the African gauge, so this train only goes to Dar. No other trains will fit on the track, and no other tracks can be connected to this one.

We parked the car in front of the station. I said goodbye to Brünnhilde, who stayed with the car while her friend walked with me into the train station. We found the ticket window and read on a sign that the train for Dar would be leaving at 9:20 P.M. that evening. That was the train I wanted, the German said, and I should buy sleeper accommodations—a first-class ticket, if I could get one, or at least a second-class ticket—and get off some time in the morning at Kasama.

Everything seemed straightforward. I said goodbye to the German. I shook his hand, genuinely grateful for his help. "Goodbye," I said. And then, with some minor embarrassment: "I'm sorry: What is your name again? I forgot your name."

He looked at me deeply. "What does it matter?" he said. "We will never see each other again. Isn't that true? We will never meet again." That was most probably true, I agreed.

•　　•　　•

There were actually two ticket windows, one for third-class, the other for second- and first-class, and in front of both windows a large and impatient crowd had already begun to form. I entered the periphery of the crowd. A woman's face appeared from behind the bars of the second- and first-class ticket window, and the crowd surged forward with expectation, but she refused to sell tickets. Reserved tickets will not be sold until one hour before the train leaves, she explained. It was almost two hours before the train left. We would have to wait.

Actually, the whole station seemed very crowded, and I looked up to see a huge portrait of Chairman Mao gazing out at us from the far end of the station. Gradually I began to realize that I was the only white person in the entire station, among perhaps five hundred or a thousand other people, Africans all, it seemed. Africans are not racist, so this observation remained interesting rather than anxiety-producing. I was more provoked by the problem of getting a ticket for the train. Anyway, pretty soon another white person appeared in the station. By the time I noticed him, he was already moving toward the ticket windows, and he was shimmying and cutting his way through the crowd, clutching in one upraised hand a wad of money. He had white hair, rectangular glasses, and thin reptilian lips. He wore gray pants, a white shirt with dark blue dots, and over that a long, baby blue cardigan. He cut in front of me, and soon he had pushed himself right up to the window. "Hello, sister!" he cried out to the woman at the ticket window. "Hello, sister! Remember me?" He was waving his money. "You remember me, yes? I have reservations for three. I telephoned, but you know how these telephones are."

She explained again that she could not sell reserved tickets yet. He would have to wait until an hour before departure, just like everyone else. But he wouldn't be deterred: "Will you take my money? We're ready, sister. We'll take three first-class, sister. I've got the money. We'll take it right now. I've got my visa stamped. I went to see the big guy in Lusaka. I'm legal. Take my money." He went on and on in this vein. She resisted. "Everybody else is waiting, too," she said. He persisted: "Sister, how are you? Don't you remember me? Can you take my money now? I'm right here. I have the money. I'm ready, sister." And eventually he had harassed her so thoroughly that she gave up and sold him three first-class tickets.

Now everyone else began demanding tickets, too. "I cannot sell tickets until one hour before the train leaves," the woman repeated several times, but the crowd pressed. One young African nearby looked at me and began complaining loudly: "What kind of a country is this? These bureaucrats do everything by the book, but who wrote the book? Why should we be standing here? This is wasteful. This is inefficient. This is why we Zambians never get ahead!" He was well-dressed, and he had a wide face with narrow eyes. I looked down to see he was holding a tan briefcase with a combination lock and wearing light gray shoes.

Fistfuls of money were waved frantically. People grimaced with frustration, complained loudly, demanded tickets. Finally the woman at the window gave in and started taking money. Meanwhile, the white man in the cardigan, three tickets in hand, was extricating himself from the crowd. I was still on the edge of this crowd, getting worried and frustrated myself, and he paused to speak to me on his way out.

"Are you a priest?" he asked. "You look like a priest."

"No," I said. "I'm just a tourist."

"Tourist? By yourself? What are you going to see? People will think you're CIA, traveling alone like this," he said.

I asked him where he was going.

"To Dar es Salaam," he said.

On holiday?

"No, I'm a smuggler!" he said, bursting out with a sardonic laugh. Then he said he had lived in Zambia for thirty years. "I'm a citizen, you see. I'm retired: a priest. A missionary priest of the Catholic Church. I'm originally from Yorkshire. York. You know, we founded the United States: New York." He gave me a bright wink and walked away with his tickets, passing as he went this final consolation: "You don't need to worry. She's got you on her list. You'll get on the train."

"I'm sure," I said, and then I called out as he walked away: "Good luck!"

Hearing that, he stopped, turned, walked back, and looked me directly in the eye. "No, it's not luck," he declared most emphatically. "It's the power of the Lord!"

One problem with being a white person in Africa, I began to realize, is that other white people automatically feel you owe them a conversation. There is a certain gravitational force at work: the normal comradeship of any obvious minority, and in Africa, also, the usual curiosity and comradeship of travelers, since many white people in Africa belong to that category. In any case, gravitational force will explain why, not long after I had finally bought a second-class ticket for the train and was waiting to board, another white person appeared suddenly, sidled over, and began talking to me.

His name was Bruce. He was young, perhaps in his early twenties, and he had a small head, carefully trimmed beard, and a soft face. He squinted with contact lenses in his eyes and spoke with an adenoidal whine. He was a tourist, he said. He had been traveling in Africa for ten months and had already had many adventures, which he was eager to talk about. He was just traveling. Just traveling. When he got tired of traveling he would go back home, but for now he wanted to see what it was like to keep traveling. He had planned to do China, but then with the Tiananmen Square crackdown he was forced to make a last-minute change of plans and do Africa instead. "I worked in public relations in Washington," he said, "but then I got tired of the First World." "The First World?" I repeated, only half listening to his already tedious tale, imagining he had just said the name of some large public relations firm he worked for. "You know, the First World. I wanted to come to the Third World." He said his big plan was to take the boat down the Zaire River. "The Zaire River," he repeated. "It used to be called the Congo." "I know," I said.

His recital was cut comparatively short by the boarding of the train. And although we were both destined for the same town, Kasama, and from there to Mpulungu to catch the boat, I was pleased to watch Bruce quickly disappear into the crowd now moving onto the train. The second- and first-class cars were at the rear of the train; and I moved into a chaotic swarm of second- and first-class passengers that was organized with the help of fifteen baby cribs—part of the original Chinese loan, I eventually figured out. The baby cribs were made from wood slats and rolled on wheels, and they were arranged end to end to form two fences. The fences funneled us all into the queue that went out the station doors onto the platform and thence onto the train.

My ticket entitled me to bunk B28, cabin A5, in car 2017. I entered car 2017 and found cabin A5, but once inside the cabin I couldn't locate the bunk numbers. Hidden somewhere. There were a total of six bunks, three on either side, but seven people were already in the cabin when I arrived—two of them already fast asleep in the two lowest bunks. I was the eighth person to squeeze in, and I turned to watch three more people poke their heads and then follow with their bodies in through the door. "This is it," one said to the other, looking around. "No problem," the second one said loudly. The third, a scrawny man dressed in a trench coat, wearing a pull-down white hat on his head, held onto a submachine gun and said nothing. I imagined him to be a soldier on his way back to the barracks or something, but the sight of that lethal metal was disconcerting. And then all three looked at their tickets, and said, loudly enough for the rest of us to hear: "Twenty-six, twenty-seven, and twenty-eight." They began tossing their possessions onto the top bunks on either side.

I recognized the African who had been complaining at the ticket window two hours earlier: the young man with the wide face and narrow eyes, the tan briefcase and gray shoes. I looked at those shoes more closely: Italian-style loafers made of fine gray leather, ventilated and tasseled. "So, are we all in this together?" he said. Then he looked down at the two men in the lower bunks, asleep, and said, pointedly: "Some of us are more comfortable than others!" And then the train began moving.

Eleven people plus one submachine gun swayed softly, tightly, in a cabin for six. When a few more people appeared at the door and tried to crowd into the cabin, I laughed inwardly and began to imagine that the harassed woman at the ticket window had gotten her revenge on all of us. It was getting crowded in there, and pretty soon the man with the submachine gun began arguing with someone else. "Are you telling me I'm a beggar, brother?" Then someone else began complaining that the train had been overticketed: "Ah, these people are corrupt!" And then the conversation turned into an African language. The train clicked and clacked along the rails, it was already dark outside the window, someone began smoking a cigarette—and the conductor appeared at the door, ready to punch tickets. The minute he saw our disgruntled crowd, however, he ducked out again, promising as he went: "We will sort out all these problems."

The scrawny man in the trench coat with the submachine gun began examining everyone's tickets. All our tickets seemed in order, except, it gradually became apparent, he and his two companions were supposed to be in a different cabin. So they gathered together their possessions and left. Now we were only eight in a cabin for six, and our attention turned to the two men still asleep down there in the lower bunks. One was completely mummified in his blanket, head to toe. He wouldn't budge. The other man opened his eyes, and when asked to present his ticket, he impatiently waved a small piece of paper with a signature on it. He and his fellow sleeper were workers for the railroad, he explained, and they had a right to any bed on the train. They were tired. They had worked all day.

A man sitting on the bunk above him leaned down, put his face down near the face of the half-sleeping worker, and spoke in a histrionically reasonable tone. "Why won't you move, brother? We have purchased our tickets. We are in the right. You are in the wrong. We all need to work together, brother. We can't have some people who are special, who are above everyone else. Don't you agree? Everyone has to pull his own weight in this society. It cannot be the other way. Don't you see?" And so on. But the worker just closed his eyes and rolled away.

The man above him continued this line of reasoning, with minor variations, and when he got tired, another one took his place, and then another. This modest altercation gradually expanded into an ambagious perambulation, a palaver, and it became repetitious, persistently so, even musically so, I thought, and it moved from English into some African language or languages I couldn't understand and back into English again. Eventually the young man with the gray Italian loafers and thin briefcase pleaded our cause. "We've got to understand each other," he said to the sleepy worker. "You know, sometimes in society some people have a sense of being above the rest of society. What is the purpose of that? These people think they are beyond the rules of society. They should be members of society, but they stand beyond the rest of us, as if they were a society unto themselves."

At last the worker was fed up. "Don't talk to me like that!" he spat. "I'm a worker!"

"Don't talk to him like that? Ah! These people are all corrupt. What is the point of bothering them?" someone said in disgust.

Coolly, the young man in the gray loafers folded his arms and continued: "So the best way is to seal up yourself and just be cool in yourself. I'll just stand here and wait for the train police."

But the lying-down worker wouldn't give up. He held his scrap of paper out again for everyone to see. "You see this?" he demanded.

"Yes, my dear," said the gray-loafers man, with a sarcastic brightness.

"This gives me the right to be here! I'm a worker, and I need my sleep now. You'll just have to find another place!"

"Yes, my dear. It is too bad that you won't listen to reason, because that means force will have to be used with you."

The door to our compartment was open, and as this discussion continued over the next fifteen minutes, strangers from the corridor leaned inside and joined in. Beers were passed in. Cigarettes were lit and passed around. It was a party—an argument party. At last the second worker, the mummified one, started awake with a jerk. His head poked out of the top of the blanket. He stretched, and his feet stuck out of the bottom of the blanket. His arm snaked out of the blanket as he pointed to the open door. "My friend, can you close the door?"

"There is no need to close the door," someone said. "The air is so much congested in here."

And then the conductor returned. He joined in the altercation, which had become more and more heated. Pretty soon the first worker started generating a righteous fury. He sat up at last and bawled out with great agitation: "I am top management! A conductor has no authority to move me! Don't blame me because you are inefficient!" And the conductor left.

Finally a soldier with a rifle came into the cabin and barked to the two workers: "Hello! I have orders to remove you from this room! Orders are not debatable!" And so after a few more protests they left, and the six of us remaining climbed into the six bunks. I was only too glad to duck my head under a blanket and drift off.

I slept in a top bunk across from the young man with the gray loafers, and in the morning, he introduced himself. His name was Cephas Masuku, he said, and he was getting off the train at Kasama, as I was, and he would be going to Mpulungu, as I planned to. We shook hands in the tripartite style I had observed others use: a quick touch at the fingertips, a grasping slide down the forearm, a clasp of the hands. An animated conversation was going on in Swahili at this time in our cabin, and Cephas said to me: "I like this language. I used to know it better when I was studying in Dar, but I've forgotten many words." What did he study in Dar? I asked. "Dentistry." Was he a dentist now? "Yes."

He climbed out of his bunk, unlocked and opened his briefcase, and removed a black T-shirt, white and pink socks, and a pair of shorts printed with a floating postage stamp design. He replaced those with the clothes he had worn yesterday, and then closed and locked the briefcase and climbed into his new clothes and brushed his teeth. "This train is late," he declared. "We are going to miss the bus to Mpulungu. Perhaps we will get some transport in Kasama. We can hitchhike, but I am worried about the rain. It is raining in the after-noons now."

I don't remember having seen an African wear shorts before that moment. Shorts are an invention of European tourists, I think. The floating postage stamp design seemed utterly tasteless, and his venti-lated and tasseled gray loafers excessive. He was a dandy all right—but he had nerve, too, which I liked, in fact admired, and when the Chi-nese train finally pulled into Kasama, three hours behind schedule, Cephas Masuku and I decided to thumb our way to Mpulungu together.

The train let us off on one side of the town of Kasama, but the logistics of hitchhiking required that we start from a rotary on the other side of town, and so we walked for an hour under the furnace of the sun. It was midday by then, and we became very hot and very tired. We stopped at a small gas station for Cokes. We continued walking. Cephas said that his uncle lived in town. His uncle was a member of Parliament, he said, and had a Land Rover at his disposal. If he were home we could get a ride to Mpulungu with him, but Cephas already knew his uncle wasn't in town. Cephas said he wanted to marry some day and have five daughters. Daughters are cheaper than sons, he reasoned. Sons you have to educate and take care of until they're independent. Daughters you can just marry off. Cephas said he was going to Mpulungu because that's where he grew up. His mother was there, and she was very ill. He had to visit her now. His father was dead, and in Africa, where families are very close, when your father dies his brother becomes your father. Thus Cephas's un-cle, the member of Parliament named Paul Masuku, was now his father.

We came to the rotary and found four dozen Africans already standing and sitting alongside the road there, with babies and baskets and cloth-wrapped bundles, also hoping to catch a ride. Three soldiers with guns also stood at the rotary, and Cephas said that the soldiers were there to make sure all the hitchhiking was legal, a concept I never did understand. But, in fact, ride-giving and hitchhiking here did seem to be business exchanges. An old van would pull up and ten people would disappear inside; a truck would pull up and fifteen people would pile in. But these rides were for comparatively short distances to particular destinations, and Cephas and I waited for one hour, two, then three hours under a fiery sun in burning cinders alongside the road, until at last a black Mercedes with tinted windows drove up right to where we were and deposited a white boy.

My spirits rose when I saw the familiar face, then sank when I remembered who the face belonged to. It was Bruce, the irritating American tourist with the adenoidal whine. He had had lunch in town, he said, and then persuaded someone to drive him out to this spot. He was going to hitchhike to Mpulungu, too.

I told him he could join us if he wished. But he said it would be harder to get a ride with three of us together than if he were hitching by himself, so he walked down the road from us and stood by himself. Sure enough, ten minutes later, a yellow Toyota pickup skidded to a stop in front of Bruce. I watched him chat with the driver for a second and then pick up his bag, walk around to the passenger's side, and open the door. Cephas and I had been standing along the road for most of the afternoon, and I wasn't about to let this opportunity pass by so easily. "Run!" I shouted to Cephas, and I picked up my bag and ran as fast as I could, Cephas following, toward the yellow pickup. "Give us a ride, too!" I called out. The driver, leaning out his window and looking back at us running toward him, said, "I only have room in the back!" "That's absolutely fine!" I said as I tossed my bag into the back of the pickup and climbed in. Cephas hopped in right after, and the truck took off.

We drove north along a one-lane road through hardscrabble red earth and a monotony of woodlands, and here and there fields of maize and round mud huts with thatched roofs, big-bellied children, and sickly dogs. There were big churning white clouds in the sky that looked as if they were rising too rapidly up from the trees at the horizon and following our motion at a supernatural speed. Then it started to rain and soon to pour. Cephas and I had been lying on our backs on top of a wadded green tarp, our packs under our heads, and when it started to rain, we crawled under the tarp. The rain was pounding on the tarp and leaking through and splashing into the bed of the truck, but as soon as I pulled the tarp over my head I fell asleep and began dreaming I was back home in America. When I woke up again, the rain had stopped, but I suddenly felt gloomy, disappointed to have cracked the cocoon of my dream.

The driver of the Toyota wasn't going all the way to Mpulungu, and eventually he turned off the main road onto a dirt track and drove along that track for some time until we arrived at a very small town called Mbala, out past some shacks into a small area of government buildings. *Uh-oh*, I thought to myself. *How are we ever going to hitch from here?* He finally parked the truck in front of a small building, stucco with a tile roof, with a sign out front that said:

GRASS HOPPER INN.

Bruce climbed out of the cab and, without saying a word, disappeared. Cephas and I climbed out of the back of the truck and paused to chat with the driver, a Frenchman, for a minute or two.

The Grass Hopper Inn included a few rooms for rent plus a restaurant and bar out back, and since it was getting late in the day and we were hungry, Cephas and I walked around to the restaurant, hoping to have dinner. Dinner wasn't being served yet, however, and so we settled down at the bar for drinks. Cephas quickly upended a couple of beers. I drained a Coke and a Fanta. There was one white guy at the bar, a fat and sloppy drunk with grizzly chin-stubble and short yellow hair on a square head. The hair looked like someone had recently chewed on it. He turned to me. "Why aren't you having a beer?" he demanded.

"I don't like to drink beer in the afternoon," I said, already peeved by his tone.

"Oh, you're a Yank! That explains it," he said with a slobbering sneer. Then he asked, more friendly now: "How long've you been here?"

"Just got here. How about you?"

"I've been here two days—thirty years, actually," he said. "Where are you going?"

I had silently practiced the pronunciation of Mpulungu all day, on and off, but when I said it now I accidentally tripped and slipped in the extra syllable: "Mapitulungu," I said.

He scowled. "Mapitapitulungu?" he mocked. "Never heard of the place!"

While I became aware of a rage rising in my body, he ordered another beer and began telling his life story. He came to Zambia from Denmark thirty years ago as an engineer, helping to build the Zambian hydroelectric dam. "This country used to be beautiful," he said. "Everything was in pounds and shillings. You could buy a beer for nothing, man. But the people have destroyed it." As for the hydroelectric dam he built, no one knows how to run it now. "That's why there are all these blackouts." As if to emphasize his point, precisely at that moment the lights went out in the bar. Candles were lit, and the

melancholy Dane continued his complaint. "I'm not worried for myself. I've got money. I've got my woman. I've got my little piece of
land, back in the hills. I'll survive. I'm just worried for these people.
What are they going to do?" He gestured with an arm toward the
bartender, who was approaching another customer at the other end of
the bar. "He'll have his pickanins," he declared nastily. "Where will he
get the money for shoes for their feet? For clothes? For their education? All my friends left five years ago. I stayed: 'It can't get worse!'
Hah! Can I buy you a beer?"

Just then the Bruce person walked into the room, and on the
theory that irritating people belong together, I took him by the arm,
gently pushed him up to the bar between me and the Dane, and said
to the Dane: "Buy my friend a beer." It worked! Pretty soon Bruce
was droning away about his adventures in Africa, and as I left the bar
to find a seat somewhere else, I heard him describing his plans to take
a boat down the Zaire River to Kinshasha. "It used to be called the
Congo River," he explained.

In the meantime, Cephas had finished his third beer and disappeared. Now he returned, smiling, and said to me: "You remember I
told you about my uncle, the M.P.? He's here! He'll give us a ride to
Mpulungu." And soon a very distinguished-looking older African,
with white hair and a poised manner, flanked on either side by well-
dressed and important-looking men, entered the room. He was
dressed in a gray, short-sleeved leisure suit, and he carried a walking
stick. Cephas told me that he happened to be, just then, on his way to
Mpulungu for official purposes. I was introduced to Mr. Paul Masuku,
M.P. We shook hands. Then without another word, we left the bar
and walked back to the parking lot. The M.P. and his driver climbed
into the front of a white Land Rover with the insignia of the ruling
party on the side. Cephas and I climbed into the back. And we set off.
I was very pleased by this turn of events.

We drove through tall grass and scattered low trees across a sullen
earth, a land of red dust rising and tired people with flattened feet and
dusted skin, onto a plateau that rose and undulated and at last suddenly descended on a red dirt road into the town of Mpulungu and a
rubble and garbage-strewn market square, fenced on three sides by
three brick and tin-roofed longhouses. We drove past the square,
nearly deserted by this time, and pulled up at a cinderblock building
that declared its name on a sign:

THE BWANANYINA GUEST HOUSE.

Cephas had phoned ahead from the Grass Hopper Inn to find out that the Bwananyina Guest House had no rooms available, but they did always keep one final room open and ready for any government dignitaries who might happen to drop into town at the last minute. It was called the VIP Room.

Cephas's uncle dropped us off in front of the Bwananyina Guest House and drove away. We talked with a pleasant and good-looking woman at the reception desk who sat in front of a sign that said:

SORRY, NO CHEQUES CASHED, NOT EVEN GOOD ONES.

The VIP Room would probably be available, she explained, but we had to wait until 1900 hours, just to make sure no real dignitaries came in at the last moment and needed the room. We waited until 1900 hours. No real dignitaries came. And so we were told that the room was ours. Cephas, however, insisted that they close all the windows and spray the room for mosquitoes before we went in. He explained to me: "We might be hammered. The mosquitoes, they can hammer." So, as we were waiting for the room to be sprayed for mosquitoes, Cephas and I left our packs in the hotel office and went to the hotel restaurant for dinner.

The restaurant was a modest, cinderblock room with a few tables. We sat down and ordered the single meal offered. The meal came. A wonderful bowl of vegetable soup, a plate with a heap of cooked corn-meal—"mealie meal," the national staple—and a big piece of gristle. After dinner, we went back to take our bags into the VIP Room. It was stifling hot in the room, with the windows shut and the mosquito spray still visible in the air as a noxious mist; there were two lumpy beds, and a bathroom with toilet, sink, and shower but no running water to activate them.

Cephas said he was thirsty and that he always had four beers before going to sleep. I was thirsty, too, so we went out to find a bar. Mpulungu is a very small town, and it only took a few minutes of walking down one dirt street then another before we came to the Icalo Bantu Social Club. We entered the bar through a rear gate into a rubble courtyard. The courtyard was dark now—evening had arrived—lit only with a single light bulb suspended over a wooden bench, and many men sat in chairs and on benches in the courtyard, drinking beer. We stood in the courtyard for a minute and then entered the bar proper through a back door. This was a gloomy, cavernous place, two rooms lit by a couple of weak light bulbs supplemented with some candles, with a rough concrete floor and rough wood walls, where perhaps three dozen Africans—men only—sat and stood and drank and talked and listened to loud Zairean music from a tape player. A sign on the wall said:

BAR ARITHMETIC:

1 FIGHT

+ 2 POLICE

+ 1 MAGISTRATE

= 3 YEARS IN JAIL

We bought a couple of beers and took them out into the courtyard to drink, and Cephas told me more about his life. He was one of the very few licensed dentists in all of Zambia, he said, and now at the age of twenty-seven he was a managing director of the national dental and medical supply company. This company until recently had been privately owned, but then it started making too much money. In 1965, the owner made eight million pounds, and so the government said: "There is something wrong here!" It was nationalized. Pretty soon, Cephas became one of the important managers.

I tried to describe a little about my life, and when I mentioned that I taught at an American university, Cephas became quite eager. I could help him get into an MBA program in the United States, he thought. "Then I will be a powerful man when I return, a very powerful man! I am very much ambitious," he declared, "but very lazy." Even now, however, as a manager of the dental and medical supply company, he had been given a company house, a mansion with twenty-four rooms, eight bedrooms, a swimming pool, a servant who cooks and cleans, and a car. Since he doesn't know how to drive, the car comes with a driver. He would have driven down to Mpulungu this time, he said, but something—I forget his explanation—prevented it. He had come down to visit his mother, and he would go see her tomorrow. She was sick and had been having many troubles ever since his father died. Actually, his father had been poisoned.

As Cephas was finishing his eighth beer and I my . . . seventh, I guess—I had lost count by then—we were approached by a thick-necked, big-bellied man wearing a dark business suit, a white shirt, and a black tie. He had a coal black face and heavy eyelids over bulging eyes. His lips curled into a big, friendly smile, revealing a mouthful of twisted white teeth, and his big hands clutched three bottles of Mchinga Lager, two of which he passed to us. "Excuse me," he said to Cephas, "but what is your name? Have I met you before? Are you from around here?"

Cephas said his name.

"Masuku?" the man repeated. "Your name is Masuku? Are you sure?"

Cephas responded: "Of course."

The man turned to me. I introduced myself. He introduced himself. We shook the three-part handshake, ended with a long, lingering handhold as we exchanged a few pleasantries, and then he turned again to Cephas. "You say Masuku? How can that be?"

"It is my name."

"That's not possible. You see, I've lived here all my life, and I know Masuku in this town. But I don't know you. Masuku? It isn't possible."

Cephas responded by naming his brothers and his cousins and then his uncle, Paul Masuku.

"You mean, Paul Masuku, M.P.?" the man said.

"Yes," said Cephas, "he's the brother of my father."

"I would question that, my dear friend, because, you see, I know Paul Masuku, M.P., very well. I am a close friend of his, a very close friend, and I have never heard of you. Are you from around here?"

At this point the conversation turned into the local language, Lungu, and as it did, I began to imagine that it became more heated. Then it turned back into English and continued on the same theme, with minor variations. "Masuku, you say? But how is it that I've never had the pleasure of meeting you before this evening?"

After fifteen minutes of this sort of repetitious exchange, the man turned, teetered slightly, and looked in the direction of a candlelit outhouse at the far end of the courtyard. "Don't go away," he said, "because I must go over there, but I will come back very soon so that we can get to know each other much better." By this time, the smile on his face had frozen and taken on a menacing cast, and I began to wonder how much of his bulk was fat and how much muscle.

He came back and brought a friend over. He introduced the friend and pleasantly explained the problem about Cephas's name, and then they both began questioning Cephas. And whenever the huge guy with bright white teeth twisting in the middle of a menacing face made an emphatic point, he opened his bulging eyes so wide I could see the whites entirely surrounding the irises. He kept smiling and prodding and questioning, pushing his face now close into the face of Cephas.

"My friend, may I ask you this? Would you be kind enough to step over this way so that we can continue our discussion?" he said, indicating a darker part of the courtyard.

"Step over there? What for? We can talk here," Cephas said.

"No, my friend. I must insist. You must talk with me over there, so that we can have our friendly conversation."

And so, eventually, the big man and his companion managed to get Cephas over toward one dark corner of the yard. This was going to be a fight, obviously, and I didn't know what else to do but find the bar manager, a man in a striped shirt who was sitting on a bench in another part of the yard, and ask for his help. "Excuse me, but my friend is in trouble over there."

"What is going on?" the manager in the striped shirt asked. He stood up, walked inside to the bar, and returned with a fresh Mchinga for me. Then we both looked over to where Cephas and the two bullies were collected, with the big one standing directly in front of Cephas, face-to-face, aggressively close now. "What are they fighting about?" the manager asked.

I took a big swig of the Mchinga and felt, suddenly, unsteady. "It seems to have something to do with his name," I said.

"His name? They are fighting about his name, did you say?"

"Yes, I believe so."

The manager turned to me, cocked his head, and affected a sorry smile. "Now, does that make sense to you?"

"It makes no sense," I agreed.

"His name!" the manager repeated in amazement. "Do you know what I think?" I looked over and saw Cephas slowly being forced back, back into the corner. I really didn't care what the manager thought at that point, but now he began pressing toward me: "I think they are nuts. Do you know what 'nuts' means? It means 'crazy.' It means 'insane.' It means someone has a screw loose. Do you understand? A screw loose. What do you think? Why would they argue about his name?"

It continued, this discussion, until finally I left the manager in mid-sentence, walked over to Cephas, and grabbed him by the arm. "Come on, Cephas. I don't feel comfortable here any more," I said, and I pulled him back across the courtyard. He walked backward, unwilling to turn, back across the courtyard to the gate. Bulgy eyes and his pal followed us across the courtyard and the manager came up, too, so finally we stood with our backs to the gate facing those three.

Cephas shook his arm and looked at his wristwatch. "It is time to go," he pronounced. He held his arm with the wristwatch up high, up into the faint bluish glow of a single small street lamp from the other side of the fence, so that he could actually make out the numerals in that faint light. "I am going because it is time to go," he said with some dignity, "and I must help this man get his place now. Good night!"

Thus, we left the Icalu Bantu Social Club in something of a rush and stumbled through a short dark alley, away from the street lamp, and then turned onto the main street of town, which was a wide patch of dirt between fields of elephant grass, completely unlit, pitch black. We walked along in silence for a time, and every once in a while people would suddenly appear out of the blackness, walking toward us, men in ragged clothes, women wrapped in bright prints. The moment they saw my white face, so it seemed to me then, their expressions changed. Their eyes turned into a brief stare, then looked quickly away. We walked for a time wordlessly, and even though Mpulungu is only a three- or four- or five-street town, I didn't remember having walked that way from the guest house, so I was by then not only drunk but completely disoriented as well.

Finally, Cephas said, "There is something I haven't yet explained to you about the people in this town. These people, some of them, are barbarians!"

"Now you tell me!" I said.

"They wanted to hammer us!" he continued. "There is a lot of jealousy in this town about my family, because of who my uncle is, you see? Oh, that made me upset! And then they wanted to know why I was bringing you"—he didn't have to say it: a white person, a tourist, or maybe a spy!—"into the bar. Oh, that bar!"

Just about then I started to have a déjà vu experience. There was something. I was trying to remember what it was. My head buzzed with the effort to remember. There was something coming back to me, yes, a memory, a faint and distressing feeling I had forgotten long ago and only began recalling gradually at this moment as the sensation of sweat appeared on my forehead and a warm wave rose from my stomach to my esophagus and then my throat, producing finally a foul *reflexus vomitus* and a yes-now-I-remember-what-this-feels-like gag and

gape, and I leaned over into the elephant grass and ignominiously
puked my guts out. Then I stood up, wiped my mouth on my sleeve,
and staggered after Cephas, who was still walking up the road, still
complaining: "That bar . . . that bar . . . that bar . . ." he was saying,
trying hard to think of the best possible insult. "That bar," he declared
at last, "is a Third World bar!" Then, having resolved that issue, he
turned to a new one: "I'm so upset now, I think I must have three
more beers before I can sleep."

There was actually a bar in the Bwananyina Guest House, so we
went into that bar. Cephas had his three beers, but I left before he
finished and went back to our room. The VIP Room had a yellow and
green checkerboard tile floor; blue walls; and red, white, and blue
curtains in a design that combined paramecia with yin and yang. The
room was unbearably hot and stuffy, reeking of mosquito spray, and I
passed out and then gradually drifted into a restless half-sleep. In the
middle of the night I woke up, fully awake in that stifling hotbox of a
room. Cephas was out cold by then, snoring. I remembered his concern about being hammered by mosquitoes, but before long it occurred to me that some fresh air would be approximately equivalent
to some risk of malaria: I opened a window. I fell asleep, woke up
again, and closed the window before dawn. But in the morning Cephas was angry. "You opened the window last night. I wish you hadn't
done that. I don't like mosquitoes. They are very bad: You can get
malaria!"

He was genuinely angry. I felt angry right back, but I couldn't
think of any retort more effective than: "Well, I'd rather have malaria
than suffocate to death!" I blurted this out, knowing all the while that
he was probably right and I was probably wrong.

Cephas had to visit his sick mother, so he packed his briefcase and
cleaned himself up. Glumly, we ate breakfast together. After breakfast,
he went to the guest house bar and bought six bottles of Mchinga
Lager to carry with him. We left the guest house, walked along a dirt
road to the end of town, and sat on some stones at the edge of the
road, right across from the New Mwabobeni Bar, Slave Disco & Night
Club. Three of Cephas's cousins who happened to be walking along
the road sighted him and with great delight rushed over to greet him,
and so the five of us sat there at the edge of the road, talking and
waiting for someone to stop and give Cephas a ride to his mother's
place. He opened one of the bottles, explaining, "I like to have two
beers in the morning to wake up."

The sun was rising. It was very quickly getting hot.

Cephas was still irritated with me, it seemed, but as the Mchinga flowed down his throat the quality of his mood rose. An hour later someone stopped and gave him a ride, and we parted company warmly, with his solemn promise to find me at the dock the next morning before the boat left.

I walked to the top of a hill, stood in some tall grass, and looked down toward Lake Tanganyika. A wonderfully cool breeze blew up through the grass and into my face. The sky was gray. Rounded hills around the edges of the lake were dark green, and the surface of the water was gray and opaque, like slate. Then a wind cracked the slate, which settled and then turned alive and writhing.

The lake was long and narrow, almost like a river there, and it curved north and disappeared below the curvature of the earth into its own horizon at the northern end. To the east I could see the forests of Tanzania. To the west I could see the forests of Zaire. And I thought: *chimps there!* Chimpanzees were hiding somewhere inside those wonderful, beautiful, cool forests, I knew, and the scene drew me on like a private memory of paradise.

3

The Liemba

Corrugated Iron *makes excellent boats for travellers; they are stamped by machinery: Burton took one of them to Zanzibar. They were widely advertised ten years ago, but they never came into general use, and I do not know where they can now be procured.*

—Francis Galton, *The Art of Travel*

The *Liemba* docked at dawn. By mid-morning its passengers were clearing customs and then parading up the dirt road into the center of Mpulungu. The great majority of passengers were Africans, but a raggle taggle gaggle of tourists came off the boat, too, white kids with sweaty hair, the girls dressed in loose cotton dresses or dirty blouses and torn jeans, looking grimy, carrying huge backpacks, the guys all in shorts, competing with each other to see who could swagger most convincingly and who had most fully developed the International Peasant look: greasy, ringleted hair, sun-reddened faces, holes in the jeans, earrings in the ears, bandana on one head. Unlike real peasants, though, they all looked full of vitamins, all except one poor wreck: skinny with a sunken chest and belly, a shaved head, a big nose and collapsed cheeks, an open leather vest and a T-shirt that said: "Iron Butterfly—European Tour 1989—London, Paris, Grenoble, Stockholm, Frankfort." These were people who, for all their affectations of simplicity and their nouveau-peasant trimmings, carried loads of expensive

Western trekking gear: bulky hikers' boots, bright red and blue nylon backpacks, sidepacks, frontpacks, fanny packs. Their equipment rolled and jangled as they proceeded in a loose military formation up the street.

Maybe I'd gotten used to being the only foreigner in town, but these people looked like a landing party from outer space or a vanguard of cultural conquistadors, walking up the dirt street of this squalid town. The Africans on either side of the street, barefoot and dressed in rags, for the most part, could only stop and stare. I stared, too, and felt a surge of sympathetic embarrassment for the objects of my attention. They looked so out of place, and yet—was I mistaken?—so certain of themselves, so insular and clannish, so rich! Was I being unfair? Probably. Was I fundamentally any different? Probably not. Nonetheless, the contrast was overwhelming. These were people on vacation and playing at life, stumbling in a herd through a hard place where vacation is meaningless and play ends with childhood.

The tourist invasion stopped at the bank, a simple wooden building with a wood sidewalk out front. Time to change dollars and pounds, deutsche marks and francs, into Zambian kwacha at the bank rate (half the black-market rate). And since I needed to change the remainder of my Zambian kwacha into Tanzanian shillings, I wandered into the bank also and joined the line. I didn't like the tourists because I thought they were arrogant and posturing. But I did warm up to one person in the group, a young woman from New Zealand, modest in appearance and behavior, who told me about a newly opened park in Zaire where tourists could see newly habituated chimps. You could book reservations for this in Goma, she said, fifteen kilometers before Rutshun on the Goma-Rutshun Road. From an intersection, you hiked for five hundred Zairean distance units of some sort to Tongo. Locals would take you to the Tongo Park headquarters, where for twenty-five dollars you would be taken to see chimps. You got up at six in the morning, she said, walked for two and a half hours, watched chimps for two to three hours, and got back in the early afternoon.

Finally, my turn came to exchange money at the window, at which time I discovered the standard pickle of Mpulungu. The standard pickle is this: You are not allowed to take Zambian kwacha out of the country, but neither can you change Zambian kwacha into any other currency at the bank without special permission from the authorities in Lusaka. Thus, to be completely legal, you either have to arrive at the boat perfectly broke or you have to give all your Zambian kwacha away before boarding.

I left the line, and as I did I quietly asked around: Did anyone want to exchange any other kind of money for my Zambian kwacha? Someone gave me some Tanzanian shillings in exchange for about two thousand kwacha.

Soon after that, I began to understand the standard pickle of the *Liemba.* The standard pickle of the *Liemba* is this: That boat is a piece of Tanzania. Legally, you cannot cross a border into or out of Tanzania carrying Tanzanian shillings. On the *Liemba,* however, I would be re- quired to buy all my meals and all my drinks with Tanzanian shillings during the two-day trip up the lake to my destination. Yet no bank or money exchange existed on the *Liemba.* There would be no legal way to acquire Tanzanian shillings at any time during that two-day trip. Legally, in short, I was required to go without food or drink for two days or, at least, to bring my own on board.

The standard pickle of Mpulungu and the standard pickle of the *Liemba* met, were squeezed, and trickled pickle juice at the immigration and customs operation you passed through before boarding the *Liemba.* Contradictory rules meant that many people would be carry- ing illegal money across the border. That meant, in turn, that the customs officers were very eagerly searching everyone for illegal money, no doubt encouraged by the idea that any illegal money they found they might confiscate.

A dozen officers were manning the immigration and customs of- fice. Four of them looked at my passport four separate times, slowly. Three of the four carefully examined the book I had in my hand, riffling through the pages to see if any money had been folded inside. I answered the same questions three times and had my pack searched three times. For no good reason that I can imagine, no one discovered the fat bundle of Tanzanian shillings and Zambian kwacha I had most casually wrapped inside a shirt in my pack. And so I walked up the gangplank onto the *Liemba,* very pleased with life and eager to continue my journey.

As it turned out, only one other white person came on board the boat: that Bruce person, who at the last minute showed up in Mpulungu from somewhere else. I watched him enter and then leave the customs building, and then eagerly climb up the gangplank and move over to where I was standing on the first deck. He was wearing basketball shoes, khaki shorts, and a three-quarter-sleeve T-shirt, green and white, that said "Cosmic Chicken" on the front. He seemed happy to see me. "A napple!" he said. "What I wouldn't give for just one juicy bite of a napple! I haven't had a napple since August! I can go buy all sorts of exotic fruits, mangoes and papayas and pineapples, but it's a napple I really want!"

While I had been waiting to buy my ticket in Mpulungu, I met a Ugandan who was also waiting to buy a ticket for the *Liemba*. He said he was a veterinarian, returning to his home in Uganda after a five-year job in Zimbabwe. His name was Alex, and I first met him sitting back against his car, a blue Peugeot with colander-style screens over the headlights and identification numbers etched into all the windows. He was tall, thin, with a gaunt face and a somewhat scraggly beard, and he wore light blue tennis shoes and a light olive canvas jumpsuit. He spoke perfectly idiomatic English with a British accent. He was obviously well educated, and he had an open yet quiet manner that I appreciated.

I liked Alex, in other words. But now as I stood on the deck of the *Liemba* and waited as the last of the passengers climbed up the gang-plank, I could see him still down there on the dock, next to his blue Peugeot, which was right next to the immigration and customs shack. Several customs police were standing around. All four of the car's doors were wide open. The trunk was open. The hood was up. And I watched Alex drag out every single object and bundle from inside the car and spread them all out for a very thorough examination on the dock. The *Liemba*'s whistle blew, once, twice, three times. The engine started up with a roar and then a pockety pockety pockety, vibrating the whole boat and churning water. It was time to go!

Finally, I watched Alex pack up all his objects and bundles and place them back inside the car. The doors were shut, the hood and trunk closed. The car was driven across a rope sling; cables were attached; a crane on the dock lowered a hook, and the car was lifted up and placed onto the main deck of the *Liemba*. Alex disappeared back into the immigration and customs shack. Fifteen minutes later, he reappeared and staggered up the gangplank at last. The gangplank was removed. The boat clanked into gear, shuddered, and began pull-ing away from the shore.

I could see Alex was glad to be on board, too, and he shook my hand and laughed and told his story. He had arrived in town yesterday and gone early to customs to see about his car. The people at customs said he had to have papers for the car, which he would need to acquire at a government office in Mbala. "No problem," he said, and he drove back to Mbala yesterday and got the papers. He returned to Mpulungu this morning, but when he first tried to go through immigration, he found his passport was out of date. They harassed him about that but decided to let it go until they discovered he was carrying more money than he had declared. That's when they searched his car. Then they took him back into the office and told him to lay out all the money he had, including American dollars. He did. "You are in big trouble," they said, "very big trouble. We are not sure what to do about this trouble. You could be deported or, maybe, placed in jail." They looked at the American dollars, saw a twenty dollar bill, and said: "This will just about enable us to solve your legal problems." They took the twenty dollar bill, and his legal problems were solved.

So now we were on the *Liemba*, officially in Tanzania, and pulling away. There were perhaps two dozen first- and second-class cabins on the boat—the rest was deck class—and someone had already assigned cabins. As we pulled away from shore, the steward gave out cabin keys and informed people of their cabin assignments. There only seemed to be two non-Africans on the boat, as I mentioned before, me and the Bruce person. Much as I hated the Bruce person by then, I suppose it was natural and reasonable for the steward to place us together in the same cabin for two, cabin 1A. *Two white guys: They must be together,* was probably the thought.

There was only one key, and Bruce got it, so he opened the door to the cabin. We went inside, claimed our bunks—I got the upper—and stowed our bags in the small closet. Bruce left. There was actually a small sink in the cabin, with running water, and so I decided right away to wash my dirty socks, including the ones on my feet. There was also a small desk in cabin 1A, and I sat down on the edge of the desk so that I could lazily bend over and unlace my shoes to take off my socks. What I hadn't noticed, however, was that the desk, constructed from cheap plywood with a plastic, imitation-wood veneer, only had legs on one end. The other end was suspended by means of a small bracket screwed into the wall of the cabin. When I sat down on the edge of it, the desk collapsed with a great crash. I picked myself up off the resulting heap. *Great!* I thought. *Now I'll have to pay for this.* But I had a knife, a screwdriver, and some duct tape in my pack. I was able to reset the bracket into the wall and reinforce it with enough tape that, as long as nothing of any consequence was placed on top, the desk appeared almost normal, except that very, very, very slowly it slid down. An evil thought entered my head: *This is fixed well enough to get to Kigoma.* Kigoma was where I got off in two days.

I went out of the cabin and stood on deck right outside the cabin door. It was late in the afternoon, by now, and I looked over a scene of great beauty. Lake Tanganyika was very narrow there, deep, and flanked by high forested hills a deep green receding into a whitish haze and a pale purple into the far distance. The sky was a theater, and clouds over Tanzania burst high and crumbled into gray and white in front of scattered white streaks against blue, while clouds over Zaire had become a soup into which the sun dipped and became a white disk. The water was a deep, beautiful blue, and the *Liemba* cut right through it.

Alex found me standing on the deck. He said the *Liemba* used to be a steamboat, built by the Germans and brought to Africa before World War I. That was about all he knew, and it was only several months later that I pieced together parts of the larger story of Lake Tanganyika and that noble vessel.

The larger story of Lake Tanganyika takes us back to geologic as well as prehistoric times, but, sorry, I don't know a thing about that. There is an African history of the lake too, obviously, but nothing has been passed down in writing. The Arabs, who had been involved in the slave and ivory trade out of Africa for a thousand years, established one of their trading centers on the lake a couple of hundred or so years ago, an outpost called Ujiji. And, then, in the mid-nineteenth century a pair of mismatched Englishmen named Richard Francis Burton and John Hanning Speke arrived on the island of Zanzibar off the east coast of what is now Tanzania with a corrugated iron boat and grand plans to lead an expedition out to an "inland sea" about which they had heard rumors. Burton and Speke, as it turns out, were looking for Lake Tanganyika because they secretly hoped it was the source of the Nile River.

From Zanzibar the two men sailed on June 16, 1857, and landed at the coastal town of Bagamoyo, where they purchased supplementary supplies and hired men. They assembled an extraordinary load of supplies, including that corrugated iron boat from England, altogether enough to require 170 porters. Only able to hire a sixth that number, however, they set off in late June without the boat—with generally reduced provisions carried by three dozen porters and thirty donkeys and mules. The donkeys and mules soon began to die, unfortunately, and the porters to desert, taking supplies with them. Within a couple of weeks both Englishmen had contracted malaria, and for the rest of the trip either Burton or Speke, sometimes both, would be incapacitated by this or that illness and usually carried or dragged along in a hammock.

After five months, the expedition tottered into the Arab slave and ivory trading post of Tabora, five hundred miles inland, for a month's rest and recuperation. Burton and Speke left Taborah in early December, continuing their difficult trek west until, on February 13, 1858, they reached Lake Tanganyika at Ujiji. Burton describes his first sight of the lake in *The Lake Regions of Central Africa*:

> "What is that streak of light?" I inquired of Seedy Bombay [the caravan leader]. "I am of the opinion," quoth Bombay, "that that is *the* water." I gazed in dismay; the remains of my blindness, the veil of trees, and a broad ray of sunshine illuminating but one reach of the Lake, had shrunk its fair proportions. . . . Advancing, however, a few yards, the whole scene suddenly burst upon my view, filling me with admiration, wonder, and delight. . . . Nothing, in sooth, could be more picturesque than this first view of the Tanganyika Lake, as it lay in the lap of the mountains, basking in the gorgeous tropical sunshine.

By this time both men were seriously ill. Speke was nearly blind from a flare-up of chronic ophthalmia; he was quite unable to see the lake. Burton had lost feeling in his hands and feet, and his jaw was so inflamed he couldn't eat solid food. But at least they hadn't started hating each other. Yet.

More about those two later.

Then came the Germans, who managed by 1884 to establish the Protectorate of Tanganyika. Tanganyika soon was incorporated into a larger colonial holding known as German East Africa. But the Germans of East Africa were enclosed, by British colonies to the north and south, by the Belgian Congo on the western side of Lake Tanganyika, and if there was any simple way to extend their power or at least to create a protective buffer it would be on the lake. Thus, by 1914, the Germans had shipped from Europe to Dar es Salaam and from there, via their newly completed railway, to Kigoma, all the pieces for an entire 1,575 ton steel boat. Assembled and launched, this vessel became the *Graf von Goetzen.*

It is possible to imagine the *Graf,* armed to the teeth, helping secure German dominance in that part of Africa, just as it is possible to imagine a Germany of 1914 and 1915 dominating Europe. What actually happened, though, was that the British invaded German East Africa from the northern end of the lake and moved down nearly to Kigoma. By 1916, as an invading force advanced on Kigoma, the Germans removed the *Graf's* steam engine and scuttled the rest in shallow water. After the war, Britain formally took over that part of German East Africa, and in 1924, the British began to salvage the *Graf von Goetzen.* They replaced the ship's steam drive with diesel and finally relaunched her in 1927, reincarnated this time around as the *Liemba.*

The *Liemba* has been chugging up and down Lake Tanganyika ever since, contrary to rumors that Humphrey Bogart and Katherine Hepburn blew her up in 1951.

Bruce found me and Alex standing on the deck. Bruce said a Tanzanian immigration officer on board had harassed him for twenty minutes. Bruce didn't have a Tanzanian visa because he wasn't going to Tanzania. He was going to Burundi. But the immigration officer said he was in Tanzania right now, since he was on the *Liemba.* Bruce had to show all his money to the officer and then pay twenty dollars for a visa stamp.

Alex asked Bruce: "Why are you traveling?"

Bruce said: "Boredom."

Alex wondered: "Did you escape boredom?"

Bruce: "Oh, yes. When you're traveling you have something new to do each and every day. I guess when you miss home enough, or run out of money, that's when you go home."

The three of us had dinner together. On the way back to my cabin from dinner, I passed an open cabin inside of which was the immigration officer. Dressed in an official uniform, he was sitting at a desk and working on a half-full bottle of beer, with three empties next to it. He was drunk, and he grandly waved me into the cabin. A policeman with a rifle sat on a bunk in the room and stared absently at a wall before him. The immigration officer was a small man with small and pinched features, eyes as blank as billiard balls, and he handed me a Tanzanian immigration form with two parts, A and B. He folded the form so that A was on one side and B on the other, and then he muttered something to the effect that I should fill it out carefully.

I took the form back to my cabin and filled it out. It required that I declare how much money I had, and so I did declare all of the money I had, not counting, of course, the two big wads of Zambian kwacha and Tanzanian shillings I had already shoved under my mattress.

I returned to the immigration officer, who was still sitting at his desk in his cabin with four empty beer bottles in front of him and a full one in his hand, and I gave him the form.

"Come in," he ordered. "Sit down." I sat down in a chair next to him. The policeman with the rifle still sat on the bed and stared at a wall.

The officer gave me a very severe and extended look. "You filled out both A and B," he said. He put his beer to his lips and drank deeply. Then he sighed. "I did not tell you to do that. You see, you filled out this and then this. I folded it in half, so that you would not fill out B. I did not hand you the paper open, like this." He showed me the paper open. Then he folded it again. "I folded it and handed it to you closed, like this. Why did you fill out B?"

I protested my ignorance and apologized for my mistake, but he continued. "It is no good. We cannot use this."

There was a stack of blank forms in front of him on the desk. I pointed to the stack. "Why don't I just fill out another one?"

"It is no good. We cannot use another one. You see this number?" There was a printed serial number on top of the form. "This is a computer number!" he said. "We cannot lose these. No, I cannot just give you another. This is printed material. It is very expensive, and we cannot just give them to people. Why did you fill out both A and B? You see, I folded it like this, and I told you! Why did you write on B?" He took another drink of beer.

This went on and on. I was being put through the wringer, obviously, but he was unable to convince me the problem was serious. It was like being confronted by a high school principal—after you had already graduated.

At last, even though, as he said, the official forms were very expensive, for me he would provide another one. We would do it again. He would be kind enough to allow me to fill out another one, but this time it must be done correctly. I must fill out A, but I must not fill out B, and I must also write out exactly how much money I have. Exactly. So I did all he instructed carefully and properly, and I wrote down how much American money I had: $143 in cash and $1,500 in traveler's checks. He read what I wrote. Then he wanted to see my money. I took my cash out, and he counted it three times. Then he handed it back. Next he wanted to see my traveler's checks. So I handed him my checks, thirty checks for $50 each. With great drunken deliberation, he counted through the stack of checks, once, twice, three times, before saying, "This is not right! You do not have the right number. Forty-three. How do you get fifteen hundred dollars from forty-three?"

I pulled the checks out of his hands and counted, very slowly, placing them in three piles of ten each on top of the desk. "There are thirty," I said at last.

He smiled triumphantly. "This is not right, you see! Thirty does not make one thousand five hundred dollars!"

"Look," I said, pulling out my pen and writing on the back of the old immigration form: "Thirty times fifty makes fifteen hundred!" I underlined my arithmetic with a flourish.

"How long do you plan to stay in Tanzania?" he said.

"Two weeks."

"Exactly two weeks?"

"Two weeks."

"Two weeks exactly?"

"Two weeks more or less."

So it went.

Late that evening, Alex and I found the immigration officer sitting in the *Liemba's* bar, drinking. When he saw Alex, he brightened up and said: "Buy me a beer: I made your visa easy." Alex bought him a beer.

There was a half moon out that night, and it cast a white light that snaked and sparkled onto the black surface of the water, while the water churned fiercely and gobbled at the edges of the boat.

Before making this trip to Africa, I had spoken to someone who knew someone who had traveled on the *Liemba*. Word was that the vessel would be crowded, and I was pleased to find that it wasn't crowded at all. We had climbed onto an empty boat in Mpulungu with perhaps only fifty to a hundred passengers altogether. But as we moved up Lake Tanganyika, we began taking on more and more people. At night, the boat turned suddenly toward shore. The horn blasted, and the engine shifted into neutral. A dozen wooden boats, low in the water, overfilled with shouting people and supplies, suddenly appeared from out of the murk and tied up to us, half swamped by the wash of our still-moving craft, and we started taking on passengers and bag after bag after bag of supplies. There were cries and shouts in strange tongues with an abundance of vowels: "Aaaayah

mini pipiepo. Aaaya peeowopoo!" Shouting crowds, people clamber-
ing onto the boat. "Pisaow! Pisawo! Pisah! Pisah! Asina! Getafeda!
Wakke bule! Wakke bule!" Chattering, shouting, babbling, and the
boat became more and more crowded with passengers.

Cabin 1A was at the front end of the row of cabins on one side,
just below the captain's bridge, just behind—all right: nautical termi-
nology here—abaft and aback but neither abeam nor athwart the *Liemba*'s gaping hold, which was deep and filled with bags of cement and
cornmeal and who knows what else. Since our cabin was first in line
of a row of cabins, we had windows on two sides. *What luck!* I thought:
Cross-ventilation. And before going to sleep that night, I made sure that
all four windows were open, two on the side and two facing forward.
I secured the screens, and then I went outside the cabin and hooked
the windows open. They were hinged at the top and lifted up and out,
hooked to an overhang above. I went back into the cabin, undressed,
and turned in, delighted to have cool air rushing through. The boat
rocked slowly now, and it was comforting, and I felt like a baby in a
cradle: tilt to the left, pause, tilt to the right, pause. I fell asleep to the
rocking of the boat, a creaking of wood, a shuffling of sandals along
the corridor outside, a distant rumbling of the engine, the hissing and
rushing of water, and a strange clicking sound that I took to be the
clicking on and off of a steering-assist mechanism, which I imagined
was on the other side of my cabin wall.

I saw *The African Queen* as a movie before I read the book (written by
C. S. Forester, first published in 1935), so it was difficult to read the
book without visualizing a regal Katharine Hepburn (as the missionary spinster Rose Sayer) buttoned to the throat in her Victorian bodice,
turning to Humphrey Bogart (as Charles Allnutt, reprobate mechanic
and jack-of-all-trades) at a crucial moment and declaring: "You're a
liar, Mr. Allnutt, and, what is worse, you're a coward!"

Bogart, who has been drinking gin and sitting with his back to her,
stands, turns, and grins a surly grin: "Ooooh! Coward yasef!" he says.
"Whose boat is this anyway? I asked you on board cause I felt sorry
for ya. . . . I ain't sorry no more, ya crazy, psalm-singin' skinny old
maid!" Hepburn refuses to yield—but her chin quivers with suppressed
emotion.

And it is difficult, too, to avoid seeing anyone other than Bogart in
his terrific portrayal of Allnutt, especially at that classic moment after

he has just dragged himself out of the reeds, covered with leeches, trembling and wincing. Hepburn screams, then frantically removes the leeches by pouring salt on them. And Bogart grimaces with wet lips, almost a slobber of disgust. But then, because honor, Rosie, and the plot demand it of him, he sets his face into that hangdog, secret suffering expression, plunges back into the leech-infested water, puts his shoulder and grip to the rope, and pulls. Someone has to draw the *African Queen* through that swamp.

Or maybe the expression on his face just means Bogart is worried his hairpiece will fall off into the chlorinated water of the four-foot-deep tank where that scene was filmed. (John Huston shot the bulk of the movie, it is true, in Africa, on the Ruki River of present-day Zaire. However, both Hepburn and Bogart, concerned about catching bilharzia, refused to get into real African water, so all of the in-water scenes were filmed in a tank on a studio lot in London.)

The story begins around 1914, somewhere deep inside German East Africa, where two British missionaries, Rose Sayer and her brother Sam, are trying hard to Christianize and perhaps Europeanize the natives. But a European war intrudes. Germans, in Teutonic pursuit of conscripts for their army, march right into the river village where Rose and her brother have established their mission, round up all the villagers, and burn down their grass-roofed houses. The havoc they wreak so upsets the already fragile and unbalanced reverend that he dies, leaving his sister alone.

Charlie Allnutt shows up at the mission just about then, helps Rose bury her brother, and the two leave in his thirty-foot, steam-driven, flat-bottomed, flat-sided, old wreck of a workboat, the *African Queen*. At that point, they have no plans other than to avoid Germans. Allnutt declares they have enough supplies and food—as well as two thousand cigarettes and two cases of gin—to park on the river behind an island somewhere and wait until the war is over. Two months, he figures.

Allnutt and Rose consider the situation further. Escape from their precarious spot on the river would be difficult, at best. Going downriver is impossible anyhow, due to the cataracts and the German fort and the swamps, and even if they did make it out to the lake—Lake Wittelsbach—the Germans had control of it with their thousand-ton steel boat, the *Königin Luise*, otherwise known as the *Louisa*.

"Nothin's gonna cross that lake," Allnutt asserts, "while the *Louisa*'s there!"

Rose wonders: What's the *Louisa?*

"It's a thousand-ton steamer. The Germans brought her overland. She's the boss of the lake because she's got a six-pounder."

What's a six-pounder?

"It's a gun, miss, the biggest gun in Central Africa."

Yes, Allnutt figures the only thing to do is wait right there on the river. Hide out.

Rose's frame of mind, however, has already made the transition from a New Testament tolerance and forbearance to an Old Testament inclination for smiting and smoting. The Germans! She notices that the *African Queen* is carrying some explosives, not to mention two metal tanks that seem to hold compressed gas. Would it be possible to empty those tanks of compressed gas, she wonders naively, and fill them with explosives—like torpedoes?

Impossible, Allnutt declares. And anyway, what would be the point? What would they blow up?

"Why," Rose says, "the *Louisa*, of course."

"*The Louisa?*" Allnutt cries, incredulous. Impossible! The river is unnavigable, first of all.

In the process of navigating the river—three weeks' worth of Nile-like obstacles: deadly rapids and cataracts, anthropophagous crocodiles, swarming mosquitoes, malaria, hostile natives (Germans, in this case, and their minions), and a vast maze of reeds and papyrus swamp—Rose Sayer loses her virginity and Victorian underwear and finds a purpose and passion she never dreamed of, while Charles Allnutt comes up short two cases of gin but discovers courage and love.

Finally, they emerge onto the lake and see the *Louisa*. In both the book and the movie, Charlie and Rosie manage to get the *African Queen* armed like a torpedo with two home-made bombs, head for the *Louisa* at night. They are capsized by a terrific tempest that, incidentally, is better in the book than in the movie. But the book ends as something of a dud. Charlie and Rosie, having survived the wreck of the *African Queen*, are picked up by the Germans, who try them for spying. Then, in part because the German captain is moved by the sight of Rosie Sayer with ripped chemise and large breasts, he turns them over to the English.

The movie ending is more melodramatic, less convincing but more satisfying. Bogart and Hepburn are sentenced to death as spies. Bogart, with a last-minute inspiration, suggests that the captain, about to hang them, should marry them first. Nooses are taken off heads. Nuptial vows are recited. Nooses are slipped back on. At the last possible moment, however, the *Louisa* accidentally plows into the drifting hulk of the still-armed *African Queen* and blows up. Ka-boom!

In the middle of the night, I was awakened by a great bright blue flash and a huge explosion, and the boat shuddering mightily, straining and groaning and rocking violently. There were more flashes and more explosions, a cracking and booming, a rushing of wind and water dropping out of a broken sky. The small curtains to the cabin windows were lifted by the wind, and water was pouring in the windows and washing down the walls, across the desk and across the floor. I jumped out of bed, opened the cabin door, and stepped outside thinking I would close the windows, but a torrent of water immediately soaked me to the bone and took the edge off my purpose. I looked forward and saw only, illuminated by the lights of the *Liemba*, a single white wall of water falling out of the sky. I would have to move around the corner into the full blast of the wind to close those front two windows, and—perhaps as a result of my overwrought imagination—I was afraid to do it. I left the front windows open. I closed the side windows, which at least eliminated the cross-ventilation, and then I stepped back inside the cabin and locked the door. Both Bruce and I had left a good deal of our things scattered on the floor, and since a small river was now coursing across the floor, I placed all those things onto my bunk and his—he slept through all this—and then I climbed back into my bunk, soaked and fully awake, and I thought about the bags of cement in the hold and imagined they made good ballast. A person could die in Lake Tanganyika, I thought. Lake Tanganyika is deep, I remembered, the second deepest lake in the world. Lake Tanganyika was formed by the East African rift, I recalled, which was created by the drifting apart of two major continental plates. I hoped the plates weren't drifting any farther apart just at that moment.

By dawn the storm was gone, and when I got up and stepped outside, we were rolling inside a fog. No shore was visible now, only a gray lapping surface below us and a soft gray wall of mist around us, with the *Liemba* climbing up and down the waves.

Alex and I had breakfast together, and he told me he was worried about the future. His five-year job in Zimbabwe was over, but there was no real work for veterinarians in Uganda. He thought he might start a crocodile farm. It would be inspected by people monitoring trade in endangered species, and he would have to return 5 percent of the mature eggs to the wild. But he believed a crocodile farm could be commercially successful and also good conservation. He said that in Zimbabwe, farmers were taking rhinos on to their own private land to protect them. It was the only way, he said. When he was driving out of Zimbabwe, he said, he saw a lone bull elephant alongside the road. He stopped his car, leaned out the window to photograph the elephant, and as he was looking at the elephant in his camera's viewfinder, he noticed that the elephant was charging. He slammed his car into reverse and backed up five kilometers to get away. He still had to go down the road, but now he was afraid to, so he waited until he saw a large truck coming down the road, and he turned in behind the truck and followed the truck right past the elephant.

After breakfast, Alex and I stood out on the deck. The sun had melted through the fog by then, and the water was green, a pale green, but when I looked at the water down below, folding against the prow of the *Liemba*, I could see how clear and clean it was, transparent as glass, green like green glass with small pools of white bubbles.

Alex said he would set up his crocodile farm near a lake, use fish for crocodile food, and he thought he would only need two to three thousand crocodiles altogether to succeed. . . .

There we were, leaning on the railing of the *Liemba* on a morning that was clearly destined to be the opening act of a beautiful three-act drama, talking, looking out toward the hills far away on shore and then down at the water below. We were perhaps twenty-five feet above the surface of the water, standing on the main deck above a low steerage deck, and I felt a not uncommon desire, a desire rising from a natural curiosity about the aerodynamics of a large vessel in motion combined with a natural human urge to watch the trajectory of something small and light fall into a moving sample of air, and turn and spin and descend far, far down to an interesting surface below. Now, certainly the urge to watch things fall from a high place has motivated thoughtful people throughout history. One recalls the famous case of Galileo Galilei, for example, who, having climbed all the way to the top of the Leaning Tower of Pisa one afternoon in the late sixteenth century, was suddenly overcome by an impulse to toss something over the edge and watch it fall. He happened to have a couple of small weights in his pocket, which he dropped over the top parapet while no one was looking. The rest is history. One recalls the even more famous case of Sir Isaac Newton, who, sitting at the top of his favorite apple tree during the seventeenth century, experienced in one trembling and perhaps giddy moment the deep desire to pluck an apple and let it drop. The inclination was whelming at first, but Newton, in a characteristic flash of intuitive brilliance, paused until it became overwhelming. He plucked the apple. He dropped it. And then Sir Isaac sat there while the branches gently swayed and the morning mists rose, and he began thinking about the glue of the universe. The rest is history. (Later, as scholars now recognize, Sir Isaac circulated the false rumor that he had actually been sitting *under* the tree when the apple fell.) So I was in very good company, intellectually at least, as I leaned over the railing of the *Liemba* that morning and let drop a small but symmetrical globule of spit.

It fell, was caught by the air and pulled into a rapidly descending curve. But as I watched it descend, I happened to see, below, from the open steerage deck, a single pale arm casually draped out across a railing. At the end of that arm was a hand, and in the hand was a cup of coffee. I watched the globule fall down, down, and then land right in the center of the coffee in the cup with a small but certainly visible splash. Then I saw a head appear from below and a face, a pale, scowling face—it was Bruce! He very dramatically poured the contents of his coffee cup into the lake, cleaned the outside edges of the cup with a free hand, and looked up at me once more and scowled once again. It took me a half second to assemble all these perceptions—the small globule falling, the angry face, the pouring of the cup—into a single gestalt, but when I did my first and spontaneous reaction was (I am so embarassed now, recalling this) to laugh with astonishment. I laughed. The scowl deepened. I shouted down, in all sincerity: "I'm sorry, Bruce! It was an accident!"

Later in the morning, the *Liemba* parked a couple of hundred yards out from a small village on the Tanzanian shore. I could see thatched mud houses and, on a bluff over the water, a few block houses with tin roofs. Crowds of people had gathered on the sandy beach. The *Liemba* blasted her horn. The engine was cut, the anchor lowered with a clank-clank-clank of the chain, and soon a dozen boats hove alongside, one a single dugout canoe with two boys paddling, the rest constructed of planks, some flat-bottomed and some keeled, the planks curved belly-out, joined together at a flat bow and stern. They were shaped rather like fish, these boats, fat fish with swollen bellies and flat ends. They were crowded, all of them low and precarious, with a dozen to two dozen people each, perhaps four men at the gunwales pulling on spear-shaped paddles or, in two cases, a tiny outboard at the stern—and the men's bare backs writhing with muscles or covered with ragged shirts or bright printed cotton shirts with tigers and suns, bareheaded men and men wearing Muslim caps with ornate black and white star designs or knitted berets, and the women with hair short or braided in cornrows, wrapped up in cloth, often with a small baby wrapped in at the back, the baby's tiny feet sticking forward. These people in these small and tipsy wooden boats came up to the sides of the *Liemba* shouting, and they tied up two and three abreast, rocking in the waves and wash of the *Liemba*, shouting passionately and unloading boxes, bags, cartons, cans, chickens, everything, passengers too, hawking things for sale, gesturing, tossing or hauling up goods onto the *Liemba* and catching thrown money in return, or gathering out of the water crumpled wads of paper money.

The boats were all tied up toward the stern. At the bow two boys wearing only shorts jumped out of the *Liemba* into the water, pursuing a dead fish, silver and the size of a loaf of bread, that floated on the water. They fought playfully over the dead fish, ducking each other, until one gave up and began a long, slow, inefficient crawl toward the wooden boats, the whitish soles of his feet, in contrast to his dark skin, flashing brightly in the sunlit water like quick and shimmering fish. The second boy swam back to the dead fish, and, holding onto it with his right hand inside the gill, he began swimming back to the wooden boats too, splashing the fish out of the water and over with each right stroke, the soles of his feet flashing and shimmering underwater as he swam. Then a paddler in one of the wooden boats stroked too deeply and fell backward into the water. People laughed as he hauled his soaked self back in.

There was a constant yelling, chattering, and jabbering during all this, until our horn blasted once, and all the people in the wooden boats began disengaging themselves. The anchor was raised with a clank-clank-clank, and we were off again.

Every couple of hours now, the *Liemba* blasted her horn, stopped the engines, and dropped anchor, and then the wooden boats and canoes arrived, and the hollering and whooping and babbling of thirty or fifty people started up again.

As the day progressed, the sky became beautifully clear, with only a few wispy arms of cirrus floating above us, and in the distance a stratum of cumulus became stuck on the mountaintops. The clouds were pulling slowly away, towing beneath them deep pools of shadows onto the green and gullied mountainsides. We added two or three hundred people that day, plus maybe a hundred sacks of maize and two hundred of sugar, and the boat was now filled with people, people everywhere along the decks. I retired to my cabin in the afternoon, read a few pages of *Gulliver's Travels*, and then turned to something less demanding: a reminiscence—or was it a novel in the style of an auto-biography?—written with superb vividness by Frank Conroy, called *Stop Time*. And right outside my windows now, I could listen to the incessant voices of people crowded on the decks and around the edges of the *Liemba*.

We began traveling closer now to the low-forested hills on the Tanzanian shore. In the evening, the sun tossed bright brass rings onto a swelling water. That night, malnourished children slept on the deck outside my cabin door. They had to be awakened every time I opened the door to go in or to go out. And in the morning the *Liemba* shud-dered into a dock at Kigoma. I said goodbye to Alex and wished him good luck with his crocodile farm. I shook Bruce's hand, sincerely apologized for the sixth time, wished him good luck also, and then filtered down the gangplank in the midst of a great crowd and passed through customs at Kigoma.

4

Kigoma Interlude

*A half-drowned man must be put to bed in dry,
heated clothes, hot stones, &c., placed against his feet,
and his head must be raised moderately. Human
warmth is excellent, such as that of two big men made
to lie close up against him, one on each side. All
rough treatment is not only ridiculous but full of
harm; such as the fashion—which still exists in some
places—of hanging up the body by the feet, that the
swallowed water may drain out of the mouth.*

—Francis Galton, *The Art of Travel*

Kigoma seemed a mildly prosperous little town, with a few streets, one or two of them paved, two market squares, a big drainage and sewage gulley, Asian shops in one section along the higher end of the main street, even-planted rows of trees along the main street, and many well-dressed people walking back and forth along the streets. Really, it seemed like a place of rather comfortable prosperity, and yes, the town was situated on a slope just above Tanganyika. In places, you had a beautiful view of the lake.

Kigoma was the stopping-off place to get to Gombe, where chimpanzees and Jane Goodall would be. That's just about all I knew. The *National Geographic* was then funding photography and research for what would be a major feature on the great apes. A photographer had been hired to take many of the photos, and the *National Geo* had already financed some of his travels into Africa, including his trip to

Gombe to photograph the chimps there. I had spoken to this person on the phone before I started my own trip, and he gave me the following information about going from Kigoma to Gombe. First, he said, as soon as I arrived in Kigoma, I should get in touch with a person named Giant. Giant would help me. Second, I should stay at a hotel not far from the train station, a place called the Railway Hotel. Third, I could hire a boat from the Railway Hotel to go up the lake to Gombe. And finally, I should take a little extra food with me to Gombe, some good snacks, because the food there might not be completely satisfying.

"Giant" was actually Jayant, I later discovered, but at the time I wandered through the main streets of Kigoma looking for Giant. I vaguely knew he would be Indian or Pakistani—Asian, as the East Africans say—and so I walked into a few Asian shops and asked for "Giant" until someone realized whom I was talking about and told me Jayant was gone and wouldn't be back for a month.

I wandered down the main street of town until I came to the train station. Then I asked people for directions to the Railway Hotel. I had plenty of assistance finding the right road and the right fork in the road to the Railway Hotel. The Railway Hotel was indeed a beautiful place, but it was designed—or priced, I should say—for people whose expenses are paid by the *National Geographic*. I couldn't afford it. The hotel manager was able to tell me about a boat I could hire to get to Gombe, but it too was priced at *National Geographic* rates: somewhere around eighty-five dollars. He did mention that small boats, so-called water taxis, left from some local village up the coast, and I might be able to ride on one of those boats for the Tanzanian equivalent of about eighty-five cents, but he wasn't able to say much more.

I cashed some traveler's checks and then left the Railway Hotel, not quite knowing what to do next. I began wandering down the road back to Kigoma. I was getting tired by then, and so when I saw a beat-up Volkswagen with a taxi sign on top, vibrating along the road in my direction with great curtains of dust rising on either side, I waved it down. I climbed inside and asked the driver if he knew how I could get a boat to Gombe. He said he did, and it would cost me only the Tanzanian equivalent of about fifteen dollars to get there.

That seemed high, but I agreed to the price and we headed out of town, north through some terrifically rutted mud roads, brick red. Outside of town, we came to a wooden bridge that had a big hole in the middle of it. The driver stopped, and a gang of young boys converged on us and began jabbering to the driver in Swahili. They were asking for money, I understood, and I also understood that the bargaining began with two hundred shillings and ended with fifty shillings, which the driver angrily paid. Once he did, a couple of big wooden planks appeared from out of the bushes, and the boys repaired the bridge. They motioned the driver to move slowly across the bridge, which he did, and once we were across, I turned around and looked out the back window to see the boys pull the planks back off the bridge and carry them back down to the bushes.

The roads got worse, and we began to climb, driving through a burning sunshine onto the grassy hills around the Bay of Kigoma and beyond, until after perhaps twenty minutes of chugging noisily up and up through these impossibly muddy and rutted roads and then bouncing quietly (engine off) down and down, we came to a tree and two mud-brick shacks high on top of a hill at the edge of a steep escarpment overlooking Lake Tanganyika. "This is where you will get the boat," the driver said, and he parked his Volkswagen there, got out, and began talking in Swahili with someone who was sitting inside one of the shacks. Pretty soon he came back to the taxi. "No boats today. Today is Sunday. No boats on Sunday," he said. "What do you want to do? Do you want to stay here?"

Stay here? Where? I looked around and all I saw were those two shacks, that long and rutted mud road, and then in one direction a steep drop-off down to the lake and, in the other direction, barren hills rising and falling until they disappeared in the distance. A strong, steady wind rose up the cliffs and shook the single tree there, as if to emphasize the desolation of the place. "I am going back to Kigoma," the driver said at last. "You can come with me."

"All right," I decided. But as I climbed back into the taxi, he declared his fixed price: another Tanzanian equivalent of fifteen dollars. This was robbery and extortion, I recognized. The driver surely knew there would be no boats on Sunday, and it was no consolation at all to watch the boys with the planks at the broken bridge extort another fifty shillings out of him on our way back to Kigoma. After all, it was my money he gave them.

He left me off in front of the Railway Hotel, where I had started earlier and thirty dollars richer, and I didn't know what to do next. Soon another taxi appeared; I began talking to the driver. Did he know of any cheaper hotels in town? I asked. Yes, of course, he said. He could find me a cheaper hotel. How much would it cost to take me there? I asked. He cited a figure that seemed reasonable, and so I climbed inside this taxi, another bouncing Volkswagen, and the driver took me right back into the center of Kigoma and stopped at a small, single-story hotel on the main drag that had a small, fenced patio out front with white metal chairs and white, umbrellaed, round metal tables. There were only two people sitting on the patio, and I recognized one of them. It was the Bruce person. The other person, a young woman, sat right next to Bruce.

I got out of the taxi, paid the driver, and called out to Bruce. "I thought you were going to Bujumbura!"

"I am," he said. "The boat doesn't leave until tonight."

I went inside the hotel and registered. It seemed like a reasonably clean and perfectly safe place, and a room cost only about seven dollars per night, which included breakfast in the morning. This was my kind of hotel, I thought, and I was, moreover, doubly pleased to be right in the center of town instead of way down a road somewhere. My room was down a corridor, a right turn, a left turn, out a door, across a courtyard. I left my bag in the room, came back out, bought a Coke in the hotel's bar, and carried it out to the patio and up to the table where Bruce and his acquaintance were sitting. I may not have made it clear yet how impervious Bruce could be. He barely glanced at me standing, Coke in hand, before his table. I introduced myself to his acquaintance, who said her name was Polly Boom and that she was waiting for another boat that would go down the lake, and I sat down.

Polly Boom was a New Zealander, it turned out, and she was headed for Zambia. She said she might be interested in exchanging some of her Tanzanian shillings for some of my Zambian kwacha. She would think about it. But meanwhile she sat there on one side of Bruce and I sat on the other side of Bruce, while he talked about his adventures. She was good-looking, I thought, but simultaneously dirty and sweaty and getting raggedy. She had stringy brown hair curling down to her shoulders, a down of blond on her face, and she wore an old blue sleeveless T-shirt and thin and tattered cotton pants printed in a vegetable soup pattern of salmon and yellow and pale blue. Her pantlegs were rolled up to mid-calf, and the left pantleg was torn. She had dark hair on her legs and worn flip-flops on her feet, and she was sprawled out comfortably in her chair, smoking a cigarette and listening to Bruce. At last Bruce had found someone with a willing ear. "I was going to China," he was saying. "Just before I was about to leave. . . ."

And in fact, she listened with an amazing, an astonishing attentiveness. Her eyes seemed to open wide as he told his stories, and he only needed to pause the briefest moments for her to insert eager encouragements: "Oh, yes." "Oh, really?" "That's very interesting!"

Bruce would declare: "The British can fly into Algeria, but they can't go past the land checkpoints. So we lost four days on that one." Pause.

And she would say: "Oh, I didn't know. Really? No kidding."

He would go on: "Very strange stamp on the passport . . . shared taxi . . . about three days, day trip out there and day trip back." Pause.

And she would say: "Interesting place! Oh, yeah, who needs to go through that?"

He: "And then I'll go to the West Bank. You can go way down the Jordan River." Pause.

She: "Yes. Ah, yes. Friendly place. Very interesting place."

He: "I had to pay a three-dollar cover charge to get in there. . . . The next day I went there to drink, and I was kicked out of the bar for not wearing a tie! There were some seedy-looking characters in there wearing polyester ties!"

She: "Yah! No kidding! And so what did you do then?"

I couldn't get a word in edgewise and soon became entirely certain I didn't want to, so I left that table and sat over at another table by myself and started reading a book. But then a rainstorm appeared in the sky, with booming thunder and water cascading off the hotel roof, and I went back to my room and waited out the rain.

Late in the day, I wandered into a small restaurant just down the street and sat at a table with five Europeans who were headed hither and thither, including two German motorcyclists and one friendly French doctor who had a face like a wedge, short hair on his head, and several days of dark growth on his jaw. He had worked in northern Uganda for six months, in the bush, dealing mostly with Sudanese refugees at a small hospital built by an Englishman fifty years ago. "I thought it would be a collaboration," he said, "you know, hand to hand, but it was not. Everyone was—what shall I say?—these people get one monthly salary perhaps every five or six months, and the monthly salary is not very good. In order to survive they must turn to making business. I'm afraid I was not to do very good there, and I feel guilty within myself."

The French doctor had taken a small side trip down to Tanzania, and now he and a couple of others at the table were going to board the

Liemba, right after dinner, to make the journey up to Bujumbura. After dinner I walked with them down to the dock, stood at the gate to the customs shed, and shook their hands. The Bruce person was down there also, of course, about to return to the *Liemba,* and so I had the opportunity to say goodbye to him once again.

He passed through the gate and called back: "Good luck on the monkeys!"

"Chimpanzees!" I corrected him.

He stopped for a second. "Oh, right," he said absently.

"Chimpanzees are apes. They don't have tails. Monkeys have tails," I said.

"Oh, right," he repeated, and he brushed a hand in front of his face, waving away either a pesky insect or a thought, and disappeared into the crowd. That was Bruce: irritating to the finish.

I watched the *Liemba* disconnect from the dock, plow out into deep water, and then disappear off the northern edge of a rumpled and glittering Lake Tanganyika.

Richard Burton and John Speke went the same way, taking two dugout canoes north from Ujiji (itself just south of Kigoma) to the northern end of the lake. There they expected to find a river, the Rusizi, which, if it flowed out of the lake, might represent a flowing start to the Nile. They never made it that far—hostile natives—but the paddlers of their canoes insisted that the Rusizi flowed into the lake.

Burton was devastated. "I felt sick at heart," he was to recall.

The two men directed their two canoes back to Ujiji and departed thence to the central Arab trading post of Tabora. Burton was happy to be at Tabora once again, consolidating his notes, resting, refreshing himself, and recuperating from his latest illness. Burton, I should add, felt among friends. An urbane man and a brilliant linguist, Richard Burton's twenty-seven languages included Arabic.

Speke, however, couldn't speak a word of Arabic and understood even less. John Speke, in fact, was a bit of a dullard, who consoled himself for being so by shooting bullets into animals. He was a good shot.

Some of the Arabs at Tabora had described, due north, a second large lake that Africans called Ukerewe, and Speke soon decided to take a minor expedition north to find the Ukerewe. Burton remained at Tabora. Speke set off with a few porters and guards on July 9, 1858, and by August 3, had arrived at the shores of a body of water that looked big. Very big. With no further evidence, Speke concluded that *this* was the legendary source of the Nile. "I no longer felt any doubt that the lake at my feet gave birth to that interesting river, the source of which has been the subject of so much speculation, and the object of so many explorers," he pomposticated in his journal. He christened the lake Victoria, after his queen, and then, having spent three days in one spot at its shore, turned around and marched back to Tabora to tell Burton the great news.

Burton was appropriately skeptical. Where was the evidence? Speke had done nothing to confirm the size of the lake. He had not examined the dimensions or explored the lake's perimeter. He had found no significant inlet or outlet. He knew almost nothing about this "Lake Victoria," but Speke remained irrationally positive, and open hostility between the two men began.

As Burton was to complain, "Jack changed his manners to me from this date. . . . After a few days it became evident to me that not a word could be uttered upon the subject of the lake, the Nile, and his *trouvaille* generally without offence." As Speke was later to describe the situation, "He used to snub me so unpleasantly when talking about anything that I often kept my own counsel. B. is one of those men who never *can* be wrong, and will never acknowledge an error so that when only two are together talking becomes more of a bore than a pleasure."

The pair, barely civil by this time, left Tabora in late September, heading east now with the company of some 150 porters, guards, and guides. Both men soon collapsed and had to be carried in hammocks; Speke became delirious from pleurisy and pneumonia. After an additional four months, they finally reached the coast, then crossed to Zanzibar on March 4, 1859. From Zanzibar, they sailed north to the British colony of Aden, on the Arabian Sea, planning to recuperate for several days there before sailing on to Britain.

Speke—having promised to utter not a word concerning their various explorations and discoveries until Burton could join him in London—left Aden two weeks early, taking passage on the HMS *Furious*. Upon arriving in London, Speke promptly broke his promise to Burton, so that by the time Burton arrived in London on May 21, Speke had already announced his "discovery" of the source of the Nile to Sir Roderick Murchison, president of the Royal Geographical Society; addressed an enthusiastic meeting of that august assemblage; been given full command of a second expedition to Africa (without Burton, of course) for further exploration of Lake Victoria; and become the darling of the newspapers and London society in general.

Burton, outmanuevered by Speke, ignored by everyone else, published his own account and defense of the expedition, a two-volume, nine-hundred-page opus entitled *The Lake Regions of Central Africa*. At the same time, he began assembling an extended argument that Lake Tanganyika was, after all, really the source of the Nile; he decided that the Rusizi River, at the head of the lake, actually flowed out of rather than, as they too hastily concluded at the time, into Tanganyika.

Finally, after Speke returned from his second expedition, a debate was arranged. The two men were to meet face-to-face at Bath, on September 16, 1864, to present their respective lakes before hundreds of professional geographers and scientists of the British Association for the Advancement of Science. Lake Victoria actually is a source of the Nile. Lake Tanganyika is not. That much was to Speke's advantage. And surely his second expedition, though not perfectly conclusive, had added considerable information to sustain the argument. John Speke was unable to make it, however, having shot himself in the head the day before the debate.

Back at the hotel, I ran into the New Zealander, Polly Boom, who was sitting at a table in the hotel bar and drinking a Fanta, and I asked her if she had thought about exchanging her shillings for my kwacha. She said she would make the exchange. She was staying in the hotel. She had the money in her room and would get it just as soon as she finished her Fanta. I sat down and ordered a pot of tea for myself.

She was a veterinarian, she said. She had started out as a sheep-shearer, but the sheepshearing gangs in New Zealand were all male and very macho, and after a while she got sick of that so she went to veterinary school. Now she was in Africa, traveling about and trying to figure out what to do with her life.

When I mentioned I was in Africa to find chimpanzees, Polly became very excited. "They're brilliant!" she said. She said that she and her mate, another young woman from New Zealand, had just been to Tongo in Zaire to see chimps that had recently been habitu-ated. "As we sort of approached this group of chimps, they were all sort of hooting and panting and that kind of stuff, just all around us, and dense rainforest which I can't even—it was incredible. It was really loud?" she declared, inflecting the declaration into a question. "It was amazing."

I mentioned that I had recently spoken to a young New Zealander in Zambia who had also seen the chimps at Tongo. "That's my mate! I'm meeting up with her in two weeks!"

Polly Boom said she and her mate had come down from Uganda. I said I was planning to go to Uganda and hoping to see some confiscated chimps in the Entebbe Zoo. "We visited that zoo!" she said excitedly. "They had some chimps in there"—on her tongue *there* became *theya*—"and they had some baby chimps that were orphaned, and they had some big chimps. They were in cages. It was horrible. And. But these big ones, there were some other people there and I'm pretty sure they were teasing them. I don't know because I was further over"—this became *feutha ova*—"but they started up this hooting, panting, carrying on in the cage, but it was really stressful? Stress? So you could tell, sort of high-pitched stress? And it was the same sound that I heard in the bush, but without the stress tone to it? It was just something different. It was the same sound, but it was something slightly different. But it was really interesting: That was their natural call."

My understanding of the chimps in Entebbe, I told her, was that they were orphaned by hunters and then someone tried to smuggle them out of Uganda to the United Arab Emirates, but they were seized at the airport. There are also some orphaned chimps in Nairobi, I said, and I was hoping to get up there and find out more about that situation, too.

"Um-huh," she said.

I said I thought they had been smuggled out of Burundi and were bound once again for the Middle East somewhere. Once again, I said, they were confiscated.

"At the airport, yeah," she said.

I continued: There was a lot of smuggling of chimpanzee babies still going on, particularly out of West Africa, and the West African ones usually seem to wind up in the Canary Islands and the Spanish beaches, where they are dressed up in children's clothes and ill-fitting shoes and made to serve as cute photographic props.

"Ah!" she said.

"The funny thing," I continued, "is that I spoke to my brother about this. I told him about it, and he said, 'Well, I don't really see what the problem is.' I liked that response."

She: "Yeah."

Me: "Because I think it is the usual response, and it'll be part of my task as a writer to explain—"

She: "Yeah."

Me: "—why this is all such a cruel and stupid thing to do."

She: "Um-huh."

Before I knew it, I had fallen into quite the same pattern I had observed, and despised, with the Bruce person. I was talking, and Polly Boom was egging me on, eyes wide open, hanging on to every phrase and every clause as if I were absolutely the most interesting person in the world. Her responses were, moreover, I was certain, perfectly sincere—no meretricious flattery here. She could have been a professional audience. And I did start chattering. I must have been lonely. But there was also the stirring effect of all those eager interjections, and as the time passed, the interjections actually seemed to increase in frequency.

Me: "I had an opportunity that I've been kicking myself ever since I passed it up. I was invited to help conduct a gorilla survey—"

She: "Oh!"

Me: "—in the Impenetrable Forest of Uganda—"

She: "Oh! Yes?"

Me: "—surveying mountain gorillas—"

She: Oh! Yes?"

Me: "—and they should be really wild, not habituated at all."

She: "Yes! Yeah! Yeah!"

Me: "I was told I could come—and I didn't go."

She: "Oh, no! Oh, dear!"

Me: "And I've regretted it ever since. I said, 'How long do I have to be there?' 'Oh, maybe three weeks.' And I thought, 'I don't want to spend that much time!' "

She (her voice turning thick with disappointment): "Three weeks is *nothing!!!* Awwwwwwwwwwwh! What a shame! It'd be great! Oh, yeah! I'd love to do something like that. Let's say, like, I went to Gombe last week. I was walking on the beach. I was a bit dreamy anyway! And I said, 'Oh, maybe Jane Goodall's here! Maybe she needs a researcher for a couple of weeks!' Just to sit down and watch gorillas—I mean, chimpanzees!—and take notes. I'd love it! Yes! Oh, yes, I would! Yes! Yes! Yes!"

●　　●　　●

I never wear a watch, and I didn't carry a clock with me on this trip, so when I woke up on Monday morning I had no idea what time it was. I dressed and then padded out to the hotel's restaurant to have breakfast. After breakfast, I thought I'd go out to shop, to buy some interesting food to supplement what the *National Geographic* photographer had said would be monotonous food at Gombe. But the hotel manager stopped me as I was leaving the restaurant. "You are going to Gombe?" he said.

"Yes."

"The boat leaves at nine o'clock. Between nine and ten o'clock."

"What time is it now?"

He looked at his watch. "It's ten minutes to nine."

"My God! I'd better hurry!" So I ran back to my room, packed everything. I did have a couple of mangoes, but obviously there would be no time to buy other food. Oh well. Even if the food at Gombe was monotonous, at least it would be food, I said to myself. I checked out of the hotel, shook the manager's hand, dashed out to the street, and found a Volkswagen taxi.

The taxi took me once again out of Kigoma, onto those red mud roads, across the broken bridge (where we were extorted once again by the same gang of boys holding planks), on and on through steep turns and hills across soft red ruts (the Volkswagen straining and sputtering), until we came to the same place I had been the day before: a couple of mud houses, a tree, and this time several Africans hanging around. I paid the driver and got out of the taxi. "The boat?" I asked. And someone pointed to the edge of the cliff. I walked over there and saw a path descending very steeply down a ravine. A couple of young boys indicated they would show me the way and took off. I followed, my pack heavy and teetering on my back as I bounced and leaped and trotted down the rock-strewn ravine.

The hills on either side were a beautiful green, I could see, and so bright as to be almost luminous. The light! The light before a storm, I thought.

Halfway down this escarpment, we met some people who were walking up. Someone said: "Be hurry! The boat is left in five minutes!" And so we ran even faster.

At last we came down to the beach, and we spun through sand to a small village of mud-brick houses. I turned the corner of a mud-brick house just in time to see the boat, right there in the water, already filled to the brim with about forty Tanzanians. It was already moving away from the beach, but someone poled it back for me. I was motioned on. I tossed my pack aboard, climbed on, and we pushed off–forty Tanzanians, one squawking chicken, and me. Someone was fiddling with an outboard motor. *That motor's going to move this boat?* I asked myself. And just then a great cry or cheer rose from the entire group. I was mystified by this event until I felt a sudden rain pouring down and watched how, within a few seconds, a ratty old green tarp was pulled by everyone in the boat over our heads. Suddenly it was pouring.

The motor was started, and we chugged out into the lake. The rain pounded on the tarp, pouring through some big holes in the tarp and dripping through smaller holes, while we all huddled underneath. Then the rain stopped, and it cleared up. We pulled the tarp off and exposed ourselves to sunlight and the vision of brilliant green hills along the lake, with cultivated red patches in the green, cultivated plots cut on land so steep you wondered how the cultivator maintained his or her balance.

Out on the lake, I watched the progress of another storm, a huge storm, a moving gray column beneath a broad gray cloud. When this storm hit, half an hour later, we pulled up the tarp again, and suddenly it was a torrent, and the water was whipped and pitted around us. We entered a whitish tube of weather, and the boat was lifting and falling on high waves. The tarp was held over us with the collective exertion of perhaps twenty heads and thirty uplifted hands, which meant that the top surface of the tarp was very uneven. A number of small lakes began to form up there. There were several holes in the tarp, as I mentioned, and as the tarp slowly shifted to and fro, a small lake above would discover a hole and quickly drain through that hole. When the man standing next to me suffered a lake draining into the top of his head, the effect really was comical. People laughed. I tried to stifle my laughter and half succeeded. But another small lake had been forming over my head, and when a hole in the tarp migrated above my head and then suddenly became a drainage conduit, people burst out laughing.

The storm became worse. Pretty soon we were surrounded by electricity, crackling and booming and flashing, and the waves became higher. I had recently heard this true story: A couple of months earlier one of these local boats had sunk and two people had drowned. A vision of beautiful children drowning settled behind my eyelids, and the man next to me started chanting softly to himself in a local tongue.

A woman nearby started singing what I knew was a serious prayer. Thoughts of mortality entered my own head, very seriously now, and my brain struggled to find an effective prayer. "Our Father who art in heaven, hallowed be Thy Name." Then I started feeling sick. My stomach turned into a tight knot—coffee, eggs, rolls, fruit, whatever else I had had for breakfast—and I became convinced that the knot was about to rip apart. I already knew the Swahili word for "white person": *mzungu.* I began to imagine there was a very pithy expression for "white person who pukes." And the boat was going up and down and up and down.

I could see outside the tarp, but what I saw was not comforting—big waves and a dreamy whiteness all around, torn and torn again by violent flashes of bluish light. I stared at my feet and focused my mind on the important task of not throwing up all over my neighbors.

Eventually, after the passage of much time, I looked up and saw forming out of the whiteness the outlines of something solid and steady: trees and brush and rocks and then a pebble beach. The boat swung around and crunched stern first right into the pebble beach. Someone touched me on the back, and someone else said: "Gombe!"

And so I got up, climbed through the people across the bottom of the boat, pack in hand, stepped out into the rain onto a small platform at the stern of the boat, gave my payment to the boatman, hoisted my heavy pack onto my back, and promptly slipped back and fell three feet from my perch at the top of the stern to a plank near the bottom of it. I caught myself there, all my own weight and the added weight of my pack, with the big toe of my right foot, stressing and thereby fracturing a very important phalanx. It hurt!

I stepped back onto the platform of the stern, hopped off the boat into a few inches of water, and then walked up onto the pebble beach. The boat was poled away, and the boatman started up the motor.

This was Gombe? I looked around and saw a beach, brush, and some high trees. I heard the boatman shout, and I turned to see him pointing to the right. I looked to the right and saw a trail going away from the beach.

The boat disappeared into the weather on the lake, and I hobbled up the trail through the rain. My toe was broken, but my stomach felt better.

5

Photographing Gombe

*To see Things deep under Water, such as
dead seals, use a long box or tube with
a piece of glass at the lower end. . . .*

–Francis Galton, *The Art of Travel*

When Jane Goodall first traveled by boat to Gombe, in 1960, she "retained the strange feeling" (as she recalls in her remarkable book *In the Shadow of Man*) "that I was living in a dream world."

I know exactly what she means. Gombe had simply appeared, magically. The boat had simply disappeared. I was alone inside that misty rain, moving away from the sound of water slipping, slapping onto pebbles, moving into a yawning trail toward a hanging garden of trees, a green and foggy Babylon, a familiar unfamiliar territory I knew through the dim and remote eye of films and pictures and books before I knew through my own eyes. But it was like touching fire after imagining phlogiston for too long. If my little camera hadn't broken in Zambia, I would have dropped my pack and started taking pictures right there in the rain.

Gombe was beautiful and, yes, dreamlike . . . but now I rose out of the weather, vexed and stretching, to deal with waking reality. My toe was broken. My plans were incomplete, imperfectly formed. I had spoken with Jane on the telephone a month earlier, and she had hoped she would be at Gombe just when I arrived. It was important that we meet and discuss our project, and also it would be important to see some chimpanzees and learn something about the chimpanzees of

65

Gombe. Jane had told me that if she wasn't there when I arrived, I should locate someone named Qoli, who would be expecting me. She would write to Qoli. With luck the mail would reach him in time. Qoli would take care of everything.

I hobbled up the trail and arrived at some tin-roofed stone buildings. No one was there, however, and I walked on, past two baboons sitting in a windowsill, until I came to an open door and looked inside to see a person seated at a desk. This person wore a khaki uniform. He had regular, fine features, and he said his name was Qoli. Qoli! I was glad to find him.

I said I was looking for Jane Goodall. She was in Dar es Salaam, he said.

I said I was supposed to meet her. She had just written a letter, he said, and he understood she would be here in about a week or so. He took out the letter and read it over: "She does not mention your name." He looked at the date of the letter: November.

"Oh. I spoke to her in late December," I said. "Well, anyway, I was going to meet her here," I repeated, not knowing what else to say.

Qoli was unimpressed. He pulled out his list of rates for tourists at Gombe. Tanzanians and other Africans can stay for reasonable African rates, but non-African tourists are charged reasonable non-African rates. Fair enough! Converted into dollars, the non-African rates became fifty dollars a day for Americans, another ten dollars a day to use the "hostel," and more to hire a guide. Had I brought food? There was no food at Gombe, he added, but I would be able to purchase soft drinks and crackers.

I was soaking wet, and my pack was soaked as well, but deep inside the pack and tucked inside a couple of other packs I found my traveler's checks, still dry, and with those I paid for five days at Gombe. Someone escorted me down to the hostel—a cabin with a tin roof, wire-mesh sides, and five cells with five beds—and I changed into dry clothes and hung everything that was wet on a clothesline in the main half of the cabin. There were no other tourists in the park, so I had my choice of beds. A pleasant adolescent showed up soon after, pointed out the matches, kerosene lantern, and filtered drinking water, and stated the prices for soft drinks and crackers. I bought both, placed my two mangoes on a wooden table in the main half of the cabin, and then sat down in a wooden chair to collect myself for a few minutes.

I examined my toe. It hurt. It was swollen. It was red. It reminded me of a fat vegetable. But I found some dry socks, very carefully placed a sock and shoe on that foot, and soon found I could walk reasonably well as long as I remembered not to place any weight on the toe. I was hungry, and I ate both mangoes right then so I wouldn't have to think about them further.

It stopped raining, and a troop of baboons, very big baboons, I thought, congregated outside the cabin. Soon my guide showed up and asked me if I was ready. His name was Halid Kuwe, he said. He had a strong chin, high cheekbones, and small eyes set widely in his face. A small, neat mustache marked his upper lip, and he wore the park uniform: olive drab with black, ankle-high boots, and a brown and green beret trimmed with a tiny black leather queue at the back.

Halid and I walked out through the baboons. He led me into the forest along a red-earth trail that turned and turned and led upward until it opened onto a clearing where sat a couple of tin-walled sheds with tin roofs covered over in thatch. One of the cabins was a provisioning station, I learned, and the other was an observation cabin. The chimpanzees were given just enough bananas from the provisioning station that it had become, in essence, a very good fruit tree. I could see a couple of Tanzanians inside the other cabin; they were part of the permanent chimpanzee observation team, waiting for chimps to come for bananas dropped out of a small slot from the other cabin.

No chimps came, however, and so after a long while, Halid and I left and walked along a trail back into the forest. Vaguely, I recalled Jane Goodall's description of her first walk into the Gombe forest: ". . . the sort of African forest of which I had always dreamed. . . . giant buttressed trees festooned with lianas . . . brilliant red or white flowers that gleamed through the dark foliage."

Pretty soon we had located three red colobus monkeys, sixty or seventy feet up in the trees and making great leaps from branch to branch and tree to tree, their long tails bent foward, all four limbs reaching forward to catch themselves—leaving, as they cast off, one waving tree in their wake, then diving in a long, leaping dive fifteen or even twenty feet into a second tree that swayed deeply when they landed. These monkeys had black and tan bodies, a red cap on their heads, and a long, thick black tail. There were over a hundred red colobus in that group, Halid said, and I began to see more of them. They would hop up into higher branches and then dive out into other trees and lower branches. The trees became wild with their leaping, and the monkeys made squeaks and chirps.

I heard a choked bark behind me, to one side, and then an answering choked bark to the other side. Baboons, Halid said. "They tell each other that there is a predator," he said. "But they are not very agile."

We walked into a shallow streambed (following, again, Jane Goodall's trail of words: "We moved along beside a fast-flowing shallow stream") into a part of the forest with many palms, where many small ferns grew out of the sides of trees, and I could still see some of the colobus monkeys far, far above us. The trees had thick, meandering trunks. A breeze blew, and water fell out of the trees.

Eventually we came to a canyon and gorge and a stunningly beautiful waterfall in the midst of forest. "This is just a waterfall," Halid said. Water shot out of a split rock sixty feet above us, spraying into a high pool and then spilling down a smooth, curved chute and breaking into space, plummeting and splintering white in a long freefall before shattering onto a bulb of rock, falling from there into a shallow, stone-strewn pool, and then filtering away through a bed of brown- and cream-colored rocks with blood-red speckles and a big mossy boulder.

The flowing water of the stream swelled and gurgled, and it lifted and dropped small stones with a clacking noise. The plummeting water of the falls created a rushing of cool air that brushed and waved the moss and ferns growing along the side of the gorge.

We walked farther and came out into a trail along the side of a steep hill. Halid said something I didn't understand, and I looked up to see a chimpanzee coming along the trail toward us, walking on all fours, his back rising as he walked, swaying as he walked, but moving fast and very quietly. Halid and I both jumped off the trail onto the steep upper side, so quickly that I nearly lost my balance and fell back down onto the chimpanzee, who by then was walking on the trail right below me—and who, as he walked along, without even a preliminary pause or look, with merely a quick rise of the torso and a sudden single skip of the feet, whipped his very long left arm out and smacked me on the left buttock—swack!—then continued along the trail as if nothing unusual had happened.

We turned and followed him along the trail. "That is Frodo," Halid whispered. "Second born of Fifi." (Fifi was the daughter of "ancient" Flo, a prolific mother with, as Goodall has written, recalling the old female as she appeared in the early days at Gombe, "deformed, bulbous nose and ragged ears." Fifi had been an infant in 1960, two years old and still riding everywhere on her mother's back.)

Now Flo's grandson climbed a small tree, and we stood on the trail and watched him. Since we were on the side of a steep hill, Lake Tanganyika and the far mountains of Zaire were visible beyond the tree, and the lake was gray and striated with silver. Halid said this was a mzigaziga tree, and the chimpanzee sitting in it ate hanging clusters of berries that were red and black. His ears were big, and his eyes were dark, deep in the shadow of his face. "This time chimps can find much food," Halid whispered. "So they stay separate. They can stay elsewhere they like."

Pretty soon we heard, in the distance, a series of cries, hoots, and then screams—a-huh, a-huh, a-hooo, a-hoooo, a-hooooo! a-hoooo! wraaaaaaaaahh! wraaaaaaahh! wraaaaaaahhh!—rising fast in an orgasmic burst of sound. But Frodo, ignoring the message, continued eating right there in the tree.

He let go of a branch, which flipped up, and the branch he sat on swayed slightly with his shifting weight.

Frodo had a long thin lower jaw and lip, and he sat there now with a contented pursing of the lips. He casually looked our way. In the distance, the regular hoots and screams seemed to turn into violent barks and screams, as if there were a fight: braakwraaaaagh wraaaaaaagh wraaaaaagh braaak! He turned to face us directly, and then turned away and crawled deeper into the tree until he was sitting in the center of it, reaching out and picking berries with both hands. He would reach up with one hand, pull a branch down, and pluck a berry cluster from the branch with the other hand.

He climbed down the tree, headfirst in a calm and four-legged fashion, and then walked quietly through the underbrush and out onto the trail before us. He walked slowly along the trail, with an exaggerated spring and sway. So quietly! And we followed.

Pretty soon Frodo left the trail again, and he walked through some brush down into a creekbed with still the same swaying and deliberate pace, came out the other side of the creekbed, and then reached up and climbed onto and along a lateral branch and from there onto a vertical tree trunk—still moving at the same pace—up twenty feet, same pace, same rhythm, up into a dense, wet cluster of leaves and branches and vines at the end of a broken tree. He became a mildly swaying spot of black inside a shadow beneath leaves, in that cluster, and Halid said he was eating ngwiza fruits. "He is taking dinner now," Halid said. "He does not want to lose even one minute because the time is going!"

I couldn't see him at all any longer, but I heard him climbing higher into the cluster, a rustling through the leaves. Several minutes later, he left the cluster and crossed back over the creek by walking across a vine and then flipping down to the ground.

Flo's grandson walked on the trail again until he came to a fork in the trail with two tines, one turning higher, the other lower. He paused at the fork and sat quietly down on a root across the trail, as if thinking. He looked back at us, and then, quiet as a shadow, he moved quickly into the higher tine.

It was getting late in the day, and so Halid and I took the lower tine and began walking back to camp. On the way, we saw the footprints of a bushbuck, and then we heard a crash and saw the buck appear, big, with pointed horns and a tan body. He hid behind a screen of trees of vines and leaves, but I could see him back there, craning his neck way back and then craning his neck way forward.

At last we returned to camp, and Halid went home to his family for supper. I ate some crackers, and then, feeling lonely inside the shadowy, empty hostel, walked down to the beach. The water in Lake Tanganyika was absolutely clear. A wave curled over, and I could look right inside the wave before the curl was finished—it was like looking through a lens—and see, perfectly, sand and pebbles on the bottom and even occasionally small fish.

Late at night fishermen came out on the lake. Their calling and whooping and shouting woke me up, and I looked out to see their night lanterns, white lights floating on the water. And then I fell back asleep to the breathing of the water, the splash and hiss of surf.

Next day, Halid and I went out again. While we were walking along a trail, we heard a deep grunt-exhalation. "Bush pig!" Halid said, and then a very big animal of some sort crashed away. I looked into the forest and then saw him turn, seeming to look in our direction. He had a very big head and a snout long and heavy, like a fireplace log, and he was flicking a longish tail. He stood stock-still. Now I saw others, three of them, oscillating nervously at a distance back there in the brush. "Sometimes they are dangerous, and they don't see by their eyes, so they can come up to here. Is not good," Halid said. Then I began to see baboons. They were all over, I soon recognized, on the ground and in the trees, and they seemed to be looking at the bush pigs.

The male baboons were huge, twice as big as the females, and they looked as nasty as junkyard dogs. They would yawn, displaying a mouthful of two-inch fangs, and they would flick their eyelids up and down. Their fur was a dark tan or olive, but their eyelids were pure white. When the lids flicked down, the white flashed very brightly, a semaphore of warning. But they were so big and looked so much like dogs, with long doggy snouts and dog bodies, I was surprised to see them sitting in trees.

By my third day at Gombe, I was getting hungry. I took a long, hungry stroll down the beach and came across two white guys—*mzungus* was the word I had begun to think with—walking into the brush and trees right behind the beach. At first I thought they were British, for no very good reason, but after preliminary greetings I realized they were American.

The first mzungu was tall, and I suspected he was a clone of the actor Elliott Gould. He had a long face, a long jaw, and a dense black beard with touches of gray. He wore a black Indiana Jones hat with a gray, pleated band. He said he had been one of Jane Goodall's students, years ago, and that this was his first time back to Gombe. He shook my hand vigorously and declared his name to be Hank Kline.

The second mzungu was short. He had a lean, sunken face, thin beard, and regular features. He was going bald on top, but wavy brown hair flowed out around the sides and back of his head, almost down to his shoulders. He wore khaki shorts and a khaki shirt with epaulets. His legs were muscular, and a fancy camera with a very big lens was strung around his neck. When he heard my name, he cried out: "Dale Peterson! Author of *The Deluge and the Ark*!" He pumped my hand up and down and said his name was Gerry Ellis.

"Ah, yes! Dale Peterson!" Hank said, right after Gerry repeated my name. "I thought you sounded familiar. Jane said you might be here!"

They had spoken with Jane Goodall recently, in Dar es Salaam. She would be coming to Gombe in a week. Hank was a zoologist, he said, employed by the Seattle Zoo, and he was writing a series of four books about the four great ape species: chimps, bonobos, gorillas, and orangutans. Gerry said he was taking photos for the book series; he also hoped to get a good photograph for the cover of Jane's soon-to-be-published book, *Through a Window*. Gerry said he was a professional wildlife photographer. Hank said that Gerry didn't actually have any talent at wildlife photography, but he worked hard.

They had just arrived, two or three hours earlier, and had discovered two chimps near the beach. The chimps were gone now, and Hank and Gerry were about to cook dinner.

What was I doing for dinner?

The two Americans were staying at Jane's cabin, a screen-windowed, tin-roofed, stone-and-wood edifice with a nice front porch situated several yards up from the pebble beach and discreetly tucked inside a thick grove of trees and brush. Gerry cooked dinner, some kind of soup supplemented with small dead fish, while Hank told jokes. Hank must have possessed a brilliant mind at one time, but he played football in college, and as a consequence much of that mind had been turned into a world repository of jokes. The jokes soon turned all three of us into goofy Boy Scouts, and we laughed ourselves breathless and ate dinner and tested Hank's memory by naming subjects. For any subject, he knew a joke. Animal? He knew an animal joke. Vegetable? He knew a vegetable joke. Mineral? He knew a mineral joke.

There were extra beds in Jane's house. Hank and Gerry told me to take my pick.

After breakfast the next morning, the three of us walked up to the provisioning station. Hank chatted in Swahili with the researchers who were already up there, while Gerry adjusted his camera on top of a battered tripod. No chimps showed up. We waited for an hour, two hours. "This is the problem with chimps," Hank said. "They're not like gorillas. They don't necessarily travel in groups, and they don't leave a trail. It's very difficult to see them. And when the food supply is not concentrated, it's actually a disadvantage for them to travel in large groups."

We decided to go looking for them. Gerry took apart his camera and had begun folding up his tripod when a chimpanzee walked out of the woods and began moving through the clearing toward the three of us. Gerry stretched out his tripod again, and then began setting up the camera. "It's Frodo!" Hank said. "I recognize him! He looks just like his mother, Fifi!"

Frodo came out on all fours and circled once around the three of us. He went up to Hank and whacked him with an arm and a leg at once. Hank ignored this. "To me Fifi was one of the most attractive chimps around," he said. "I can see the resemblance."

Frodo walked up to the banana window at the provisioning station, stood up on his hind legs, and soon had acquired an armful of bananas. Two baboons had lately appeared in the clearing, too, and one of the baboons slunk up behind Frodo. Frodo spun and warned him away with a free hand, then climbed a nearby tree, where he sat and ate his bananas. Hank said, "Funny, when these chimps eat a banana, they peel it, and they eat the banana first. Then they chew on the skin for a long time. They don't swallow it. They chew it in their lip. They chew and chew and chew it, make what Jane calls a 'wudge.' Then they spit it out. Well, looks like I'm wrong. He ate the skin."

Frodo ate the skin, and then he climbed down the tree and walked away on all fours and disappeared back into the forest.

Almost as soon as Frodo had disappeared, another adult male chimp appeared. His name was Wilkie, Hank said. "He was one of my subjects as well: cute little kid. He had a very distinctive white beard as a baby." Wilkie ambled into our clearing with a long, swaying, spidery walk. He acquired an armful of bananas at the provisioning station, and then he climbed with them up into another tree and disappeared inside a cluster of vines and branches that swayed with his weight.

Wilkie left and entered a trail into the forest. Gerry took apart his camera and folded up his tripod, and the three of us, Hank leading the way, followed at a quick pace. Wilkie moved very quickly, and he climbed right to the top of a steep hill and then climbed into the top of a tree. We reached the top of the hill out of breath and exhausted.

Gerry set up his tripod, screwed the camera on top, and aimed it at Wilkie.

Up in the tree, Wilkie began hooting—slow at first, a noisy inhale and a hooting exhale, lips and mouth pursed into a trumpet, increasing in rapidity and pitch and volume, crescendoing at last into a series of great screams. And soon, as if in answer, we heard a series of hoots and screams from a far ridge. Indeed, Wilkie climbed down the tree then and began walking quickly back down the hill. Hank scrambled after, and Gerry—quickly breaking down his camera and tripod—followed, actually running down the hill until he stumbled and fell and cut his leg.

We lost Wilkie during all this, but later in a lower area we saw a young female walking through the forest and followed her. She walked quickly and took a steep, switchbacked trail up another hill. We followed, panting, but she disappeared, reappeared, and disappeared again, and then we became lost and stuck in a terrific tangle of brush. But eventually we discovered, through sheer luck, a vast tree with four chimpanzees sitting in it. They must have been fifty or sixty feet above us, sitting on branches. They looked to me only like obscure dark bunches up there, except I could make out an arm here and a face there, looking down.

My count of four soon became six. They were high above us, walking across the branches in this great tree now, as I saw through my binoculars, climbing up into clusters of leaves, two of them actually lying down on a large branch, one grooming the other. Then began a series of clucks and grunts, followed by hoots increasing in tempo and pitch, turning into wild brays and suddenly exploding into a terrible din of hooting and screaming and screaming and screaming.

Gerry disappeared. Hank and I looked around, and Hank called out: "Gerry? Gerry, you up in the tree?"

"Almost." A boot fell out of the tree and landed in a clump of vegetation. Another boot fell. I looked up to see Gerry, twenty-five feet up in the tree now, barefoot, a camera accessories pack on his back and a big camera in his hand, climbing out on a rising limb. The chimps were still high above him, and as Hank and I stretched our necks looking up, they leaned over and looked down at Gerry.

"You're being watched," Hank called out with a timbre of warning in his voice. "I don't think they like it."

But Gerry was way up there already, barefoot and climbing higher. This was a huge tree with no lateral branches for the first twenty-five feet, only a big trunk overgrown with a mat of vines and lianas.

"How'd you climb up there?" I called out. "In the vines?"

"Yeah," Gerry called down. "Just went hand over hand upside down in the vines."

I sat down beneath one of the spreading limbs of this tree, looking at two chimps sitting above me, sitting on a branch of that limb, face-to-face, knees up, grooming each other. Their lips were pursed in concentration as they slowly plucked away at each other. Sunlight streamed down through a maze of leaves and branches.

Gerry, camera in hand and pack on back, began shinnying up a vertical trunk until he was about thirty-five feet above us, still below the chimps.

Hank said to me: "I told you he works hard."

Now Gerry was crawling out onto a limb. I saw one chimp sitting on a branch in another part of the tree, his legs dangling, watching

Gerry's progress. Gerry called down: "Hey! It's nice up here! Our ancestors were stupid to leave the trees!"

He was climbing higher. Hank called up: "Just be careful, Gerry! If one of them comes towards you, hold on tight!"

I saw another chimp in an adjacent tree, lying on his back on a branch high above us, knees spread casually out, frog style, arms out and hands forming a pillow behind his head. With one hand, he held onto the branch beneath his head.

"Uh-oh!" Gerry said, and I looked up to see a big chimp walking down a branch toward him.

"Watch out, Gere!" Hank called up. "If he gets too close, gesture like you're going to strike out with the back of your hand." I heard a splashing of leaves and then saw the same chimp moving away from Gerry, climbing into a clump of leaves and branches.

Gerry, barefoot, continued up, forty-five feet up now and moving into an area of the tree where chimps were lounging in the branches.

"Gerry, be careful!"

But Gerry had his camera out, clicking away. "This is so beautiful!" he called down. "With the fruit in his hand!" Now he was perhaps fifty feet above us.

Hank called up: "Gerry, you know the best thing about Alzheimer's? The best thing about it? The very best thing? . . . You get to hide your own Easter eggs!"

Gerry: "I've got them all around me now!" Then, suddenly, he said: "Damn!"

"What's wrong, Gerry?"

No response.

"Gerry? What's wrong?"

"My balls!"

"I told you you should wear underwear! Underwear would help!" Hank called up. Then, to me: "That's the secret of his success. He never wears underwear."

"Oh, my God! Wide-angle lens! Absolutely gorgeous stuff! Oh, there's a baby up here! A little, tiny baby!"

Jane Goodall is not an ordinary person. She can survive on an egg and a glass of juice for most of a day. She goes without sleep. She has stamina, not to mention determination. And she has patience. She can sit. Even as a three-year-old child, so she has written in her first book, she spent five hours sitting still in a henhouse, waiting to see a hen lay an egg. Jane once told me she felt like a spider: quietly waiting with infinite patience for things to start vibrating in her web.

But what, in my opinion, the young woman really brought to Gombe in 1960 was a capacity to see chimpanzees fully as individuals. Whereas many other animal scientists at the time were determined to study animals as members of a species, to describe them with the neutral pronoun "it," and may have preferred identifying individuals with numbers, Jane casually and perhaps naively broke the rules. She was, she has written, "always interested in the differences in individuals." She referred to male chimpanzees as "he" and females as "she." And she gave them names, common and ordinary names, often based upon her own private and sometimes comical associations. Mr. McGregor, a dour old male with bald head and a scoldy style, who sometimes would threaten her with "an upward and backward jerk of his head and a shaking of branches," had reminded her of the gardener in Beatrix Potter's *Peter Rabbit*. The chimp Goliath was so named because he possessed an imposing, "splendid physique and the springy movements of an athlete." David Graybeard was "David" because she found him so often in the company of Goliath, and "Graybeard" because he had a silver beard. The chimp Olly, an old female with a "fluff of hair on the back of her head," reminded Jane of her aunt, Olwen. Having named them, she proceeded to watch them—for two years, four years, ten years—and to write about them.

Hugo van Lawick showed up at Gombe the year after Jane did: a photographer sent out by *National Geographic* to place some of Jane's discoveries on film. In the process of Hugo's photographing Gombe, as Jane writes in *In the Shadow of Man*, they fell in love, got married, and had a son—nicknamed Grub—whom they raised on the shores of Lake Tanganyika.

Jane and Hugo were divorced well after the publication of their collaborative effort, and so the book remains a haunting memory of a serene young couple, their charming infant, and a community of chimps all alive in the shadow and sunlight of Gombe, the best of times. One or two of Hugo's photographs from *Shadow* have a staged quality—I'm thinking here of the photo showing Jane standing between two trees, framed as if in a doorway, looking expectantly up as if watching a great drama. "I would follow the chimpanzees through the forest," is how the caption describes it. And some of the pictures seem merely documentary—a young chimp swinging along an overhead branch, face obscured by the angle of the camera. "Young chimpanzees are very agile."

Yet many of Hugo's photographs are dramatic, storytellers. Some are classics—young Jane Goodall walks behind two wild apes on a trail curving slightly to their left, all three intent on their varied purposes, all three leaning slightly to the right, marking an unconscious synchronicity of motion and mood (or maybe the camera is crooked). A few are astonishing, glimpses into a secret universe, unveilings—as in "Figan performs a rain dance." Had anyone ever seen a chimpanzee performing a rain dance before this book? Had anyone even heard of a chimpanzee rain dance?

Gerry got his photographs. Hank and I spent a week helping him, carrying his tripod, handing up various lenses and so on, wandering through the forest and discovering chimps. We followed them when they didn't care, photographed them as they let us. When they did care, the chimpanzees would just disappear. They would lean over until they were shaped like bowling balls, and then roll right into a thicket. We would be left seeing only a vibration in leaves and twigs, and hearing a rustling noise that receded into nothingness. We would crash into the same thickets and try to plow through and find ourselves lost in a sea of vines.

At the end of each day, we tossed off our sweaty clothes and went swimming in the lake. Late one afternoon, I swam off by myself, following the shoreline south for a hundred yards or so. It was raining a little, and the falling drops made small mushrooms on the water, rising and subsiding on the surface. When I swam back to where Hank and Gerry had been, they weren't there. I met up with them later at Jane's house and found them in a state of great excitement.

Hank told me what had happened. "We were swimming in the lake when I noticed some hairy arms along the edge of the beach. I said, 'What the hell is that?' Gerry said, 'Chimpanzees!' He goes running back to Jane's house and comes out with his fanny pack around his belly and nothing else on but his camera. At first we saw two chimps, but pretty soon we realized there were six altogether. There were five males, including Wilkie and Prof, and I believe also Pax and Gimbol, and another young male. And then a female that had joined them, and the female had a bit of a white streak between her nostrils and her mouth. But she seemed to be rather skittish and was hanging back. I was thinking it was rather unusual to see them on the beach, and they were walking along, stopping to examine things occasionally. We went along, way up the beach, and then we came to one of the fishermen's huts on the beach, where the fishermen spend their day while they're drying their fish. The five males entered one of these huts with the grass sides on it, and they sat around the stones for the fire and started licking the stones. It was as if they were cavemen or prehistoric humans, or as if they were saying, 'Hey, I've got an idea. Let's pretend that we're cavemen. Right, look at this. They should get some good pictures.' The sixth chimp never actually came into the hut. She stayed in the distance. My feeling was that she was actually afraid of us, not that she didn't want to participate. Oh, I had gotten Gere his shorts earlier, so he would have something to cover his tush. Meanwhile, the chimps stayed in that hut for a little while, and then they moved on to another. Actually, this hut did not have the grass sides, but just basically the wooden framework. Gerry actually went inside the hut with the chimps, which surprised me because I felt they might feel caged at that point. They might be a little tense. But they weren't at all. They continued to lick the rocks, lick a post that was holding up the structure, and spread the ashes in the fire ring gingerly with their fingers and then licking up some of the ashes. After a while, the chimps moved out the backside of the hut, continued to walk for a ways even further up the beach, and then gradually disappeared in the brush and walked up the cliff behind the beach and disappeared in the forest."

It was getting dark, and we built a fire in a rough grill fashioned from the bottom of a steel drum and cooked dinner on the porch of Jane's cabin. Hank and I began wondering about the likelihood of more rain. We worked on safe meteorological predictions.

Hank: "I have a very strong feeling that we could have some rain, some time in the next few days possibly."

Me: "I think it's quite certain that it either will or won't rain, quite possibly in the next few days."

Hank: "There's a hundred percent chance that it might rain someday."

Me: "I agree. In fact, you could say that the probability is very high that some sort of weather will occur, at least sooner or later."

The weather on Lake Tanganyika was grand and unpredictable. One night we watched huge thunderstorms over Zaire, up and down over a calm lake. Another evening, a brief electrical storm came through quickly and left, but the lake turned into a crashing surf that woke me up many times during the night. One day a breathless calm took over the air and trapped us inside a closed bottle of heat. Insects came out.

One night I lay on the beach and (while Gerry aimed his camera directly upward and somehow propped the shutter open for I don't know how long) looked up at the stars. I thought how reasonable it had been for the Chaldeans to invent astrology, to create those myth-ological figures and their various forces. Chimpanzees have good vi-sion, so I was sure they could see the stars, too, and I wondered if they had any feeling about them. But then, I thought, perhaps they never see the stars, because they build their nests and turn in the minute it gets dark. But do they sleep through the night? Don't they wake up? Chimpanzees don't have any of the defenses against night that we have—fire or artificial light. It must be a dangerous time. It gets very dark in the forest, and it must be dangerous even to move. So one would have a tendency to sleep. And in a nighttime storm, when the thunder and lightning move in and start crashing in the air and whip-ping trees back and forth, it must be very unnerving to be rolled up in a nest in the trees.

Hank had to catch a flight out of Nairobi on a certain date, so he left one afternoon and took a boat back to Kigoma, leaving me his Indiana Jones hat, a generous replacement for a less dramatic hat I had lost.

Gerry and I remained and settled into a routine. Gerry must have been a hyperactive child. He was full of nervous energy and constant good spirits, even when good spirits weren't called for, and in the morning he would move around and make all sorts of noises—whis-tling, singing, squeaking air through his lips, and so on. "Would you please stop making so many noises?" I said.

When he wasn't taking photos, Gerry kept a journal. It was a bound accounts book with graph paper that he wrote in with an ex-pensive fountain pen. He would sit down at the beach late in the day, when the water rolled in and rattled the pebbles, and write. He wrote quickly, effortlessly, it seemed, and his handwriting was beautiful, al-most calligraphic. The fluidity of his writing unnerved me a little. "I tell you," I said, "it makes me very anxious when you start writing in that thing." "It's just thoughts," he said. "Just random thoughts."

But we had some things in common. We could both recite the same passage from Goethe. We had both done some traveling in the tropics, looking for wild animals. Gerry, in fact, seemed to have been everywhere as a photographer, and he would certainly qualify as a professional traveler, so I was interested in his theories about the activity. I told him my theories, which are very simple and have to do with baggage.

We were sitting on the porch of Jane's cabin one evening, waiting for a kettle of water to boil for our after-supper tea. "For me, the biggest lesson I ever learned about traveling," I began, "or at least have learned so far, is something that I constantly remind myself about, and that is to travel light. I feel that if I can place everything in one pack and carry that pack on my back, there are not too many problems I'm going to have. If the bus breaks down, I can walk. The second big lesson is one I learned when I made my first long trip in Brazil. I like to do things spontaneously, and so before that trip I would always just toss things in a bag. But in Brazil, I learned that if I didn't have my pack absolutely organized, I got very disturbed after a while because I couldn't find anything. Everything became all mixed up. So the way I do it now is I start with my main pack, and then inside of it I have several smaller bags, each with a particular function. I have my repair bag—a pair of pliers, duct tape, some wire, a screwdriver, and so on, along with things for bodily repairs, such as medicines and Band-Aids, and so on. I have a bag for my regular street clothes, one extra shirt and one extra pair of pants. I have another bag for underwear, and another one for dirty underwear—that way I can keep from getting exhausted by confusion, for example not knowing which is dirty and which is clean. That can be very disturbing after a while. And the dirty underwear bag is red, so when it starts bulging it becomes like a red flag, and I pay attention! I have a camera and film bag—cheap camera, a little one. It's broken. And, oh yes, also a journalism bag: my note-books and pens. I also keep a consolation bag that has mostly books in it, something good to read when I'm feeling blue and need consola-tion, plus Alka Seltzer, which I use as a soft drink when I need a consoling drink."

Gerry's wisdom focused on the idea that there were mental barri-ers to traveling. "The first is the laundry barrier. That hits you at three weeks, when it's time to do your first laundry. You notice, like a lot of these safaris, they're only designed for twenty-one or twenty-two days or something. Just about three weeks."

"The laundry barrier!"

"Yeah! It is! And then the second one is the food barrier, and that's about three months. That's when you really start missing all those ridiculous foods—for me it's Italian food. I start really dreaming about a nice *big* plate of fettucini with basil and garlic! And then the last one is the one-year barrier. And that's just, it usually hits people around a holiday or something. Christmas is a big one. But I think it doesn't have to do so much with the holiday itself. It has more to do with family and friends, the sense of nobody-here-understands-what-I'm-going-through kind of idea. It's funny: If you can make it past those barriers, I think especially the last one, you're home free. You can be nomadic the rest of your life."

"Being nomadic has never sounded good to me," I said, thinking that Gerry must belong to the cockroach-at-the-nosehairs school of travel.

"I absolutely love traveling," Gerry replied. "I feel like I could go on forever. It wouldn't bother me too much, you know, just to get to the next airport, have a new shipment of film be there, send off the old film to be processed, and just keep going. And I think the reason is I really do think of it as one giant backyard, this whole place, the whole planet. And so I don't carry a lot of baggage around—I mean mental baggage."

This desultory conversation continued, with lapses into silence and sips of tea and sudden shifts in subject, such as: "Unbelievable the difference between last night and tonight in terms of the noise," I said. "You know the waves were crashing last night, and now they're just kind of gently . . ."

"I am so amazed by that lake," he said.

"Right, and it's so nice to be able to get on those ridges, and you can look down: There it is!"

"It's like an inland sea, I mean the way it can change its moods—like the pummeling of the shore last night. I don't think I've ever been in place in which every single night or every single day had its own personality, like this does. I mean three nights ago it was lightning storms over Zaire, you know, incredible lightning storms, and then yesterday it was those winds whipping through and then the waves pounding."

"I don't remember that there were winds last night," I said. "I don't really know what made those waves. Maybe Jane will be able to clear up this mystery."

It was pitch dark by then. Our fire was burning low. The one candle still alive was just about sputtering to a finish when three children appeared on the porch. They had beautiful, perfect faces, and Gerry amused them by juggling onions. Then he pulled out his camera and took pictures.

People are easy but chimps are very hard to photograph, I've learned. One begins with all the usual technical problems: depth of field and F-stops, focus and aperture, zooms and booms, speeds and grains, all those fancy concepts and accoutrements intended to pilfer an image that pauses only at the speed of light. Then there is the matter of contrast, or lack thereof. Chimps are shadowy creatures to begin with. They live in a shadowy forest, and when they move, it's usually a shift from lighter to darker shadow. Their eyes, indeed their faces and whole bodies, can become black holes sucking every possible photon out of the space between subject and object. There are the dangers, the discomforts, and the damages. The physical aspects: carrying that fragile box and equipment and tripod up a hill then down a hill then up a hill. And the climate. Plus, chimps don't usually pose. They do their most interesting things behind a tree or with their backs turned. Indeed, if chimps aren't actually habituated to a photographer's presence, they will actively flee. They see that strange ape carrying all those bags and that bazooka with a bottle in the middle. Who wouldn't flee?

Photographers bang their knees, that I know.

To my mind, the very best of Hugo's photographs are the (mostly black and white) portraits of chimps: peeved Rodolph, serious Mike, cogitating Worzle, venerable Flo, Melissa holding and adoring Goblin, and a calm and self-assured David Graybeard. Some of these have a secret and stolen feel to them, snatched and dappled memories of light. The portraits show the chimps best as Jane writes about them—trapped yet enduring the days of their lives, real-life characters in an endless gothic romance or a soap opera.

The day before Jane was due, I took off from chimpanzee watching and photographic assisting. It was time to deal with reality: to clean her house, read a book, and coddle my broken big toe, which by then had turned chartreuse, maroon, purple, black, and a plethora of other exciting colors.

She arrived in mid-afternoon of the next day, driven up from Kigoma in an aluminum boat with an outboard motor. I saw her in the boat, her hair drawn back in the ponytail you see in every photograph ever taken of her, and she smiled and waved. Then the boat turned and crunched softly into the beach, where several members of the Gombe staff were standing. She stepped out of the boat and greeted everyone with a warm hug. Some very heavy suitcases followed, as did Ken Pack, a British veterinarian who had come along to look at some of the Gombe baboons, who were ill. Ken was carrying a blowpipe, darts, angel dust, and an antibiotic.

Jane said she hadn't slept for two days.

We went for a late afternoon swim in the lake. Jane, wearing an orange-and-black one-piece suit, dove into the water and disappeared. Ten seconds later she popped out. "Supah!" she said.

She and I talked about our hypothetical project, squatting on two tiny stools in her tiny kitchen, while Gerry and Ken hauled the grill down from her porch to the beach and began building a fire for dinner. We talked until it became very gloomy in the kitchen. It was still light outside, though, and we went down to the beach where Gerry and Ken were working on the dinner. Pretty soon dinner was ready, and we ate it and watched the sun set over the mountains of Zaire. The mountains of Zaire looked like three lines of mountains, receding one behind the other. The closest line of mountains was a dark bluish gray, and the two receding ranges were progressively obscure, a whitish gray, an ashen gray. The lowering sun poured molten silver into the water, and the silver rolled over pewter.

Then it was dark, with bright stars overhead. Jane pulled out a bottle of Scotch, and we all four drank Scotch and water and told stories. Jane said that Louis Leakey had chosen to send her to this spot, Gombe, because he had heard there were chimpanzees at the shore, and all his discoveries of early hominids had been along ancient shorelines, so he thought Gombe might be a most interesting site. As it turned out, being along a shoreline was irrelevant, she said. "But wasn't I lucky? Of all the possible places I might have been in Africa studying chimps, to come here to this paradise!"

6

The Road to Bujumbura

*Before going to a rich but imperfectly civilised country,
travellers sometimes buy jewels and bury them in their
flesh. They make a gash, put the jewels in, and allow
the flesh to grow over them as it would over a bullet.
The operation is more sure to succeed if the jewels are
put into a silver tube with rounded ends, for silver
does not irritate. If the jewels are buried without the
tube, they must have no sharp edges. The best place
for burying them is in the left arm, at the spot chosen
for vaccination. A traveller who was thus provided
would always have a small capital to fall back upon,
though robbed of everything he wore.*

–Francis Galton, *The Art of Travel*

I stood on the beach. I had my pack on my back. I had my Indiana
Jones hat on my head. Mose, the bookkeeper at Gombe, said he would
wave down the taxi for me. But there was only one taxi a day, and it
was late. I took off my pack and sat on the beach. Butterflies came and
began probing the sweat on the straps on my pack. A long time after
noon, we saw the taxi moving out on the lake, and Mose waved both
his arms up and down, up and down, and the taxi turned in and came
to shore.

I tossed my pack in and climbed aboard. There were about eighty
people in this wooden boat, and it was powered by a beat-up red,

white, and blue Kawasaki outboard motor that strained and shuddered and slowly pushed us forward in the emerald water. For about a minute it pushed us, and then it choked out, so the boatman and the motorman began meddling with it. Reluctantly, after a few minutes, it started again.

This boat included a corrugated tin roof mounted on four posts to protect from the elements eighty Africans, dozens of sacks of cornmeal, one bound chicken, and me. We moved north on the lake, along rugged hills and a rocky shoreline. At the northern boundary of Gombe, the forests disappeared and were replaced by open hills, bright green with the season's new grass and interrupted with rocks, trees, scrub, red gashes of erosion, and mud houses with tin or thatched roofs. Along the shore, women carried buckets and baskets on their heads, and in one place four naked boys fished, standing on a submerged rock just off the shore. They looked as if they were standing on water.

The boat regularly spun around to land, stern first, at any collection of houses on shore, and where we crunched into the shore, crowds appeared. People sometimes stared at me, I thought, and young boys called out: "Mzungu! Mzungu! Mzungu!" Then the boat would leave again, the motor cranked into life with a spin or two of the rope, with a churning of water behind us, and three or four or five or six boys, naked, perched on the stern or floating in the water and hanging on with their fingers, would ride the boat back out into the lake until they were shouted at or pushed away by the motorman. So they would leap or fall off and swim back to shore. They swam with all sorts of homespun styles, including doggy-paddle and what I called the "flap-crawl": flapping their arms into the water in a dramatic but ineffective imitation of a racing crawl.

The hills were shaped like lying-down farm animals, with smooth, rolling summits, steep ridges, and bony protrusions, a hide of green grass stubbled with brush, a few trees scarred with cultivation and burns. Houses were cut into the slopes and made of the same red mud they stood on.

Most of the people on the boat seemed to be locals. They spoke Swahili and local languages, I concluded, and in general they dressed in a manner I had come to expect, the women wrapped in beautiful African prints, the men less glorious in often-tattered Western clothes. But at least one man who stepped on the boat was attired very well:

blue and green striped sports shirt, well-pressed brown slacks, blue shoes, and white socks. He was a tall man with a jutting chin, and I remember him particularly because he addressed me in English. "Hello, how are you?" he said as he stepped on board from one of the small stops along the way. "Where are you going?" No one else on the boat spoke English, as far as I could tell, and since he was headed toward Bujumbura, as he told me, I imagined he might describe at some point exactly how one got there.

We came to the end of Tanzania. Everyone climbed out of the boat and walked up a path to the customs and immigration building. A fat officer there said something to me again and again that I only gradually understood. "I like your hat!" he was saying with a Tanzanian accent. "I like your hat! Where did you get it from?"

"Oh, you like my hat," I said.

He stamped my visa, and from there I walked a long way, following not far behind three African men, one of whom was very big and wore a white crocheted skullcap and carried a briefcase, another of whom was the jutting-chin man in good clothes who spoke English. He carried a plastic bag in one hand and a briefcase in the other. It was later in the afternoon by then, pleasing and peaceful, with the smells of rained-on grass and the sounds of birds calling out to each other, and the trail took me for a couple of miles through high elephant grass. People strolling along this trail, coming from the other direction, were country people, I thought, almost all of them very pleasant to see and nod to: a few giggling girls, some tired-looking women balancing old hoes on their heads, people riding bicycles through the dirt and ringing dingaling bells, a boy riding a girl on the handlebars of his bicycle and laughing. People would call out casual greetings to me, in English, but pretty soon the greetings changed to French. "Bonsoir, monsieur!" I liked that. "Bonsoir!" I called back, and I began to think that my three years of high school French with Miss Reba Masterson had been worthwhile after all.

The path took me across the remains of a collapsed bridge and then up a slight rise to an official-looking wooden barrier. Here was the border. On the other side of the barrier, the trail turned into a mud road, and parked on the road was a Toyota pickup truck with some people standing nearby.

The three men in front of me walked past the barrier. I walked past it. And suddenly we were rushed by several young men who shouted: "Shillingi! Shillingi! Shillingi!" The men in front of me started pulling money out of their pockets.

They were changing Burundi francs for Tanzanian shillings, it became apparent, and I pulled out all the Tanzanian shillings I had and acquired some Burundi francs. I also pulled out a ten-dollar bill, hoping to change that, but the money changer I was dealing with offered a thousand Burundi francs for it, which seemed not very much and also an excessively round number. I asked the well-dressed man with the chin if that was a fair exchange, and he stepped up and began negotiating for me, in Swahili, eventually seeing to it that I got sixteen hundred francs for my ten dollars.

By then, a number of other people had crossed the border, and they were changing money, too. The apparent owner of the Toyota pickup, meanwhile, had a bucketful of water and was washing caked red mud from the vehicle's wheels. After enough of a crowd had accumulated, he emptied the bucket, threw it into the back of the truck, and then told us all to get into the back. I climbed in along with everyone else. (There was actually a big steel cage surrounding the back of the truck, the purpose of which was to support as many passengers as possible—standing, sitting, leaning, and hanging on.) Since I was one of the first people into the truck, I took a reasonable seat on top of the wheel well. Next to me on the wheel well sat the only woman in the entire group, full-bodied and full of energy, a fast talker and a wit. Her wit, however, was wielded in Swahili, so I could only judge the sharpness of it from the laughter of everyone else piling into the truck.

She had all the men in stitches with some animated talk that seemed to concern her handbag, and later on, after the truck started moving, the conversation moved on to me, I thought. I noticed many covert glances, heard the word *mzungu* pronounced frequently, and noted the laughter. The chin man who spoke English pointed to a space of six inches on the wheel well, separating me from the woman, and so I moved closer, thinking that he was suggesting we conserve space in this crowded situation. But when I moved closer, everyone laughed uproariously, and the bearded man said: "My friend, they are saying she should be with you!"

I laughed.

The Toyota was bouncing along a very rutted and difficult mud road, and my steel seat quickly became uncomfortable. We were moving fast, too, through a couple of small villages and past some houses, past women carrying bundles of sticks on their heads, past a woman, a child wrapped to her back, bending over and washing her feet in a small stream. We moved fast, and I saw a white chicken scrambling toward the road, heard a thump, saw a rising bundle of white and then a burst and flutter of feathers, and then I turned my head and looked back to see the chicken still running.

This was the life! I was enjoying myself immensely right then, relaxing with a wonderful warm air blowing across my face, feeling an easy comradeship with my fellow travelers, watching those chicken feathers fly away behind us into the distance. Meanwhile, shouting above the noise of the bouncing vehicle, the man with the chin introduced himself as Bunda. I introduced myself as Dale. We shook hands. He said, "Bunda is my last name. My first name is Paul." I proceeded to call him Paul and then explained the arrangement of my names. He persisted on calling me Mr. Dale. In profile, his face had a goatish look.

The truck stopped in a very beautiful place on a grassy knoll with a view of the mountains on one side and Lake Tanganyika on the other, right in front of a school. It was getting to be late in the day now, the air was becoming cooler, the shadows longer, and insects were chirping. The school was built of stucco with a tin roof, one long building with five entrances, and at each entrance stood three columns of marching-in-place schoolchildren, a couple of dozen children per column, all marching in place and singing a wistful song in some African language. The columns began moving then, the children marching around and whipping their arms in cadence, until they were all aligned and facing a flag on a flagpole at the front of the school. The children saluted the flag, sang another song, and the flag was lowered. Meanwhile, a lout in uniform had walked up to our truck and was spot-checking luggage and looking at identity papers and passports. He looked blankly at mine for a long time, ruffled through it idly, ostentatiously compared the photograph in the passport to my face, and then at last waved us on.

We were soon stopped again, however, this time by a self-assured young man, dressed in blue with a blue nylon jacket and a dark blue beret. The skin of his handsome face was chocolate, smooth and fine, and he had a carefully trimmed mustache about the size of an eyebrow. Paul said quietly to me: "It's the police. The immigration police." The man examined all documents and passports very carefully. He wanted to look into the woman's handbag, but she protested vigorously in Swahili. I imagine she was saying, "But these are just female things! I'd be so embarrassed!" Whatever she said, it worked. He gave up. Everyone was looking tense, but at last it appeared that all was in order. I thought we were ready to proceed again, when suddenly the officer in blue walked up to the cab of the truck and made one of the two passengers sitting there next to the driver get out and come into the back of the truck. This man joined us in the back, producing as he did a face of exaggerated high drama, and the officer took a seat in front.

The truck started up again, and we began tearing along that rutted road once more. But I could see inside the cab of the truck, through the back window, and I noticed that the remaining passenger—the heavy man with the crocheted white skullcap and briefcase who had walked in front of me out of Tanzania—was showing his identity papers once again to the officer, and after that he was passing money over to the officer.

We came to a small town, and the truck stopped. "Mr. Dale," Paul said, "we will get a bus here." Indeed, I saw a Toyota van parked there, apparently waiting for us.

We all piled out of the truck, haggled briefly over the price of the journey—I paid two hundred francs—and began climbing into the Toyota van. But the handsome young officer in blue stopped us. He began talking to me in French, but it was an Africanized French I didn't understand (which is not to say I would have understood it in French French). He climbed into the van with us and continued talking to me. The Toyota started up, and some of the passengers began arguing with the officer—I heard something like the word "tourist" spoken several times. Finally, Paul said to me in English: "Mr. Dale, perhaps if you give him five hundred francs as a tip, he will help you make a fast immigration."

I gave five hundred francs to the officer. But the officer spoke to the driver of the van, and the van made a U-turn in the street. The woman with us said something with what I recognized to be disgust, and the van door slid open and everyone got out—everyone except the driver, the officer, Paul, and me. "Mr. Dale," Paul explained, "we must go to the immigration office. It is a little ways down the road."

The van drove to a quiet and deserted area outside of town, a few mud houses and an official-looking stucco building—a few doors and windows cut into the sides of a long, rectangular cube. It was dark now, and that building was completely deserted. The officer opened a door and a window, gave me a white paper form to fill out, handed me a flashlight, and took my passport. I started filling out the form. "Mr. Dale," Paul said, "I told him that you are a tourist from the United States and that you are very tired. He is a good man. I am helping you this way." He may have been a good man, but this procedure took a very long time. We discussed the details of my form three times. He ambled through my passport three times. And then, slowly, slowly, slowly, as if double-checking, triple-checking the impulse, he rose the official stamp into the air and finally plunged it down on my visa.

We got back into the van, drove back into town, and found the other passengers, who had been waiting at a crossroads in town. The officer in blue got out of the van, these people climbed in, and we turned onto a paved road and took off, for about twenty feet, until we came to a roadblock that consisted of a piece of twine with some red and white tags tied on it stretched across the road. Some semiofficial-looking men sat in wood chairs alongside the road, and they got up from their chairs, sauntered over to the van, and began checking our papers and passports, and then checking luggage. Eventually, they lowered the twine roadblock, and we proceeded.

"What were they looking for?" I asked Paul.

"They are checking to find smuggled goods."

We drove on, Paul sitting in a seat behind me, the woman who had sat next to me in the truck sitting beside me now, and after a few moments, Paul leaned forward and said, "Mr. Dale, you can help me. I need a car for my business. You could help me buy a car in the United States, yes? How much would a car cost? You write to me, and I write to you, and we will arrange it." I agreed that buying a car in the U.S. was possible, but I suggested that shipping it from there to Tanzania might be expensive.

Soon, Paul leaned over again and said, "Mr. Dale, you are a professor? You can help me. You can help my wife come to the United States. My wife is a school manager in Dar es Salaam. She will study and get her M.A. at an American university. Yes?" I agreed to correspond on the subject.

I asked him what his business was, and he said, "If you work for the government in Tanzania, you might only earn two hundred shillings a month, which is not enough to support a wife and children."

That wasn't quite an answer to my question, of course, and so a few minutes later I repeated it. "But what do you do for a living?"

There was a pause, and then: "I'm a smuggler. I smuggle money, shillings from Tanzania, francs from Burundi, and American dollars. I can make about fifteen percent in exchanging shillings into francs and back again, and I make ten percent on American dollars. This is my money," he said, holding up a plastic bag that all along I had thought was a lunch bag.

We passed through long stretches of very dark and crickety countryside, were stopped twice more by officers, now with flashlights, wishing to examine our papers and the contents of the van. We stopped at a stream and the sound of bullfrogs to pick up, after a long haggle about price, two men with several large plastic jerry cans. The bullfrogs were having an argument. "Do it! Do it! Do it!" some of them said, hoarsely, but others kept insisting: "Don't do it! Don't do it! Don't do it!" We passed through towns and stretches of mud-brick hovels, and then we stopped at a place where Paul got out. He shook my hand. "Mr. Dale," he said, "I will meet you tomorrow morning early at the Novotel in Bujumbura. We can exchange money." I never saw him again.

We came into another town. The mud-brick huts gave way to wooden shacks, and then the van pulled up at a ramshackle place, a rough bar and a very crowded restaurant, and everyone got out except for me and the woman sitting next to me. We had a long wait here. Many people were walking back and forth on this road, and when they came close to the van, several of them did a double take upon seeing my face—not many mzungus in this part of Burundi—and some made casual wisecracks through our window to the woman sitting next to me. She wisecracked right back. She was very nice, actually, and during the long wait she managed several words of English and French, so that we had a minor, if rough, conversation. "The driver takes whiskey!" she said with a disgusted pout.

An hour later, the driver came out, staggering, with breath that smelled flammable. He started up the van and tore out of that little town at top speed, careening down the road, the woman now snuggled comfortably against me, half asleep, all the way to Bujumbura.

7

Peace in the Hills

*Fevers of all kinds, diarrhoea, and rheumatism,
are the plagues that most afflict travellers; ophthalmia
often threatens them. Change of air, from the
flat country up into the hills, as soon as the
first violence of the illness is past, works wonders
in hastening and perfecting a cure.*

–Francis Galton, *The Art of Travel*

I didn't know a thing about Bujumbura, except for the name of the person I was supposed to meet and the name of the hotel where Hank and Gerry had stayed recently. The hotel was the Novotel, a link in a European-owned chain, and it was vastly overpriced, but at least I could delay reckoning with a credit card and bathe in warm water.

I stayed at the hotel, and late the next morning I went looking for Mimi Brian. Mimi was employed by the American embassy in some capacity having to do with logistics and supplies. When I met her she wore a white cotton skirt, a forest green blouse with white buttons, dangling earrings, and tortoiseshell glasses with a matching hair band. She had blue eyes and honey brown hair in a pageboy cut, and her skin looked as if it would freckle in the sun. She was a Southerner with a mild Southern accent.

The old American ambassador to Burundi was just then being replaced by a new American ambassador, and so I sat in Mimi's office for a long time while she discussed on the telephone what the new ambassador needed. I hope this is not classified information.

"Check the doorbell of the ambassador," Mimi said. "Make sure it's all in working order. She'll need all of that ready by tomorrow." Some talk occurred on the other end of the line. Then: "She wants a dog? What kind of dog? A fully made dog?" More talk on the other end. Then: "She wants a medicine cabinet. We haven't found anything yet—it's kind of a rare item. We're working on the drapes. She wants glass on one of the tables in her office, and I'm waiting for her to tell me which one." And so on. This conversation ended with an extended closure: "You dawg! You dawg! I'm mean! I'm bad! Okay! D'Accord! Okay! Ciao! Okay! Bye!"

I liked Mimi. She was forthright, mature, dramatic, and obviously competent. But she had work to do, and so I waited in her office for a long time, while this and that phone call was made and as people stepped into the office with requests and statements. One of her assistants poked his head in the door and announced: "I have a special appointment with the Minister of Impossible Affairs today at four-thirty."

In spare moments, she explained some things about the chimpanzee situation in Burundi. "It's a small country," she said, "so crowded that you can see the environmental destruction." The government of Burundi, she said, was in the process of creating an environmentally sound policy. With some help from the Jane Goodall Institute, the Burundi government was also planning to establish a chimpanzee sanctuary, perhaps an area of one hundred fifty to two hundred hectares, for the rehabilitation of confiscated chimps. There were perhaps twenty captive chimps just in the Bujumbura area alone. She was aware of eight. I should see André Niokende, she said, who was an excellent person and the director of the organization overseeing everything related to conservation and the environment. I should also go into southern Burundi and find Charlotte, who was sitting on top of a hill and looking for chimps.

Mimi told me that a European diplomat in Bujumbura once had a chimp, four or five years old, who used to wander around the town, sometimes disappearing for a day or two. One time he disappeared for several days, and when he returned, the diplomat's children, apparently to teach the chimp a lesson, placed him inside a steel shipping container and locked the door. This was Africa, under an African sun, in normally very hot temperatures. No air, no water. "Apparently they were surprised three days later when they found the chimp dead," Mimi said.

On her lunch break, Mimi took me out to see a couple of the captive chimps in town. We went into a part of town Mimi called "the Asian quarters," down an alley, and came to a large, cinder-block automotive garage. A sign said:

ATELIER DE CONSTRUCTION MÉTALLIQUE.

We walked through high steel gates into an open lot filled with old cars and car parts, and next to that, a repair shop. There were sounds of hammering, an air compressor running, a spray gun hissing. The owner of the shop greeted us. He was small and slight, a pleasant man with black curly hair. His name was Raju, and he said he was the owner of Whiskey—Whiskey the chimp.

He took us over to one end of the shop, where there was a small, open, cinderblock-and-concrete cell that used to be a toilet, and inside was Whiskey, attached with a heavy chain and a thick steel collar to a steel post in the center of the cell. When we approached, the ape was curled up in the corner of his cell, very quiet, facing away from us. He may have been asleep. "Whiskey!" Mimi called softly. "Whiskey!"

Whiskey turned and looked at us, sadly, I thought. He stood up and lethargically moved our way, dragging his chain along the floor. Mimi offered him a banana, which he took without enthusiasm. He ate most of it and threw what was left back at us. He turned away from us then, and placed his hands on the post in the middle of the cell. With one foot on the floor, he stretched back the other leg and foot behind him, like a ballerina at the practice bar, reaching back with his leg and looking over his shoulder at us, waiting for a second banana. Mimi held one out. The chimp grabbed it with his foot, turned around and ate it, once again throwing a final scrap back at us.

Mimi had a few snapshots of Whiskey, which she showed to Raju. "C'est joli," he said. He said that he sometimes dressed Whiskey in clothes and took him out for rides at night in his car and told people Whiskey was his bride.

Mimi and I went to another place in the Asian quarters, a small electronics and electrical supply shop called Maison Zarine, where a friendly woman at the sales counter smiled, greeted us, and gave us permission to pass through into the house and out to the courtyard. We went out into a small, paved courtyard, where there were two African gray parrots in cages and also three small concrete and steel-barred cells. Two of the cells contained dogs, three dogs altogether, who were barking constantly. The third cell contained JoJo, a young female chimpanzee with a brownish-cream, slightly freckled face, and a very full lower lip. She reached through the bars, very quietly, took my hand, drew it to her face, and kissed it. With her other hand, she reached out and took Mimi's hand. Both Mimi and I reached through the bars with our free hands and stroked JoJo's hairy arms. She seemed desperate for stroking.

Her entire cage was about the size of a small closet. "These people definitely want to get rid of her," Mimi said. "The man tells me, 'We're Muslim. My wife doesn't like these animals.' They've had her about four years. Bought her. I can't imagine her being normal with all the dogs barking all the time."

We stroked JoJo's arms for some time. She was absolutely quiet.

I found a hotel that cost about a tenth what the Novotel cost, and in the morning of the next day, I took a taxi out of town to the offices of the INECN, the National Institute for the Environment and Conservation in Nature, and met the director, André Niokende, who was very helpful. We had a long discussion, in French, over coffee and bread and eggs and milk. Just a few years ago, he said, hardly anyone even knew that there were wild chimpanzees in Burundi. Now it is recognized that perhaps three hundred chimpanzees are surviving in some of the remaining forested areas, and the government is hoping to protect them with parks and reserves. Yes, the government would soon be confiscating all the illegally held "pet" chimps. And yes, he said, I should go south to find this woman Charlotte, who was living in the southern hills and trying to see chimpanzees. She was living in a rural village out there, and in fact someone from the INECN was driving south in a couple of hours. I could get a ride with him. His name was André as well.

The second André drove me south, back toward Tanzania, for two or three hours through hills and hills and hills all deforested: only a stubble of trees remaining, and grass and collapsing gashes of red soil, and then cultivation everywhere else. There were very few cars on this road, but many pedestrians were plying the edges: women carrying on their heads hoes, sticks, bags, and pails and basins of water; a man pushing a wooden wheelbarrow full of bananas; one hundred barefoot schoolchildren running in a pack.

André drove me to a government office in the southern town of Rumonge, and eventually we found an American Peace Corps worker from Ohio, who said his name was Matt and that he had just come from a hospital in Nairobi, where he had been treated for meningitis. Matt had bright blond hair and an American candor and enthusiasm that I enjoyed. Matt and I drank some soft drinks at one of the local stores, and as we sat there, three other American Peace Corps workers showed up. They had an American candor and enthusiasm, too. Two of them were named Rose and Rob, and I don't remember the third person's name.

But all four of them managed to get hold of a four-wheel-drive truck, and under that grinding power we proceeded up a series of ruts and rocks and gulleys and gulches and gaps and gashes supposedly representing a road, way out into the back country and way up into the hills—hills with people and houses and cultivation—up to a quiet village at the top of a high hill, a hill almost fully deforested but still beautiful. The truck stopped, and I looked across a tremendous panorama of great rounded hills, in spots dark green with trees, but mostly lighter green with grass and cultivated plants, with patches of red where the soil was cracked open. In the far distance I could see a gray blur of rain, white wisps and pockets of smoke here and there, and the hills receding northward into a haze that made them paler and paler and paler. Looking over to the west, I saw other hills declining toward Lake Tanganyika, and I observed on the lake a smooth gleam of light, ruffles of wind, and some smeared patches of rain.

We were stopped in front of Charlotte's house, a small brick construction with a tin roof, wood-framed windows, and a door. Charlotte wasn't home. The neighbors, living in similar brick houses, said she was out looking for chimps. But the door was open, so we went inside and waited.

A couple of hours later, Charlotte appeared. She was young, and she had a very pretty face. She had a full head of rich, dark hair that reminded me of Hester Prynne's hair, the one time she unfurled it in *The Scarlet Letter*. Charlotte spoke with a polished British accent, and as I soon discovered, she was a natural dramatist. She told stories in great and dramatic detail, sweeping her hands to establish conceptual constructions in the air, snapping her fingers, tossing her waterfall of hair, flashing feelings in her eyes. The six of us visited casually in her tiny living room, drinking tea, while some of the neighbors and their children walked in and out and visited also, and I said that I was looking for chimpanzees. Charlotte said that an Israeli tourist had showed up the day before, and it was very irritating to have mzungus show up and expect to be entertained just because she was there.

The four Peace Corps workers left after a while, and Charlotte showed me around the place and told me I could sleep in her living room. I might have to share it with the Israeli, if he came back. He was out somewhere. She showed me where the bathroom was: a hole in the ground in her backyard, surrounded by a low mud hut for privacy. She made some more tea and then excused herself and said she had work to do. This house had four rooms, and Charlotte sat at a table in one of the other rooms and began typing on a portable typewriter. I sat down in her living room and began reading a book.

It was very quiet after the four Peace Corps people left, except for a mild whistling of wind through the walls and the sound of neighborhood children chattering, laughing, playing, plus a baby crying in the distance and a battery-run radio somewhere playing African music. Oh yes, and I could hear Charlotte's slow pecking on the typewriter in the other room, a clucking of chickens somewhere, and the occasional mewing of two kittens who walked in and out of the house and then climbed into my lap, at which time their mewing changed to purring.

But it was peaceful. There was no electricity in the village, no motors, no cars, no televisions, just a wind moving across and many soft noises, becoming softer as the sunlight became softer and the shadows grew longer. Charlotte's house was built of real bricks, not pressed-mud bricks but kiln-fired red bricks, mortised with clay. Sunlight shone through a thousand holes in the walls, where the mortise wasn't perfectly finished, and a pleasant breeze winnowed through those thousand holes, so that the inside of the house seemed fresh and sweet-smelling.

This house was smaller than most Americans' garages, and internal brick walls divided it into four even smaller rooms. The floor was packed dirt, but grass mats had been tossed over the floor in most places. The front door, which opened into the living room, was well made, dowel-joined, the door frame nailed optimistically into the brick, but the lintel was so low I banged my head several times while passing through. The lintel of the back door was low, too, and I banged my head on that as well.

After a while, Charlotte finished pecking on the typewriter, came out into the living room, and we talked. "Actually, it's so exciting when you think it was only March last year when Jane Goodall first came to Burundi," she said. "So much has happened since then, and already in Bujumbura et cetera there's a growing awareness of chimpanzees. I mean people in the taxi: 'Oh, you're the person who is studying the chimpanzees. When can we go and visit the chimpanzees?' I mean most people didn't even know there were chimpanzees, even the people that lived here, you know, in Bujumbura. It was an absolute revelation that there were chimpanzees in Burundi."

She wondered what had happened to the Israeli tourist. "I have a terrible feeling he may well turn up some time tonight–I don't mean–I told him quite frankly. I blame the Peace Corps more, because somebody at the Peace Corps said, 'Well, if you're looking for something to do, there's this funny English girl that's tracking chimpanzees in Rumonge. Lives in a little local house. Why don't you go up and see her?' For me, people who come here, they are doing something. I said, 'Well, would you like to go and track the chimpanzees?' He said, 'Uh, all right.' At least if he had said, 'Yes! Chimps! Walk to the ends of the earth for them!' I would have been more sympathetic. He just kind of arrived and expected me to amuse and entertain him. It was not what I was prepared to do."

At dusk, a herd of goats paused in the rough road out front, and I saw the Israeli walking through the goats. He had curly, sandy hair, a narrow face, brown beard, and a grim expression. He shook my hand limply, said his name, and then, after I told him my name, said, "I will not remember your name. It isn't important." He came into the living room, sat in a dark corner, and began grinding his teeth.

Charlotte was busy preparing a pot of dinner on a wood fire out back. While she did that and while the Israeli sat in his corner, I began to observe a high-pitched squeaking noise emitted from the top of one of the walls. I first thought the noise came from bats, but then I saw mice up there. As evening moved in, the mice came alive with squeaks and double-squeaks. Then rain began pattering on the tin roof, and soon it was raining hard outside and fast becoming gloomy inside. A couple of candles were lit. Charlotte served up supper–vegetable stew over rice–and after supper we drank whiskey and talked.

The Israeli said he was an accountant from Tel Aviv. He said he had taken the boat down the Zaire River to Kinshasha. He saw baby chimps for sale on the boat. He shared his cabin with three Zaireans. He had the top bunk. When the boat first started up, he was asleep, but he soon woke up because the bed was shaking wildly. He looked down and saw the couple in the bunk below. "They were"–he paused, searching for the right word–"fucking."

After they were finished, the Israeli looked down again and said, "Excuse me." The man on the bottom bunk looked up and said, "No problem! This is my wife. You can have her next."

Charlotte said she was very happy in this village. "I often had people drop in here when I first arrived: the mzungu's place," she said. "It was just bizarre at first. They used to come in just to watch me. And now, I'm no longer 'mzungu.' I'm Charlotte. They say, 'Have you seen the chimpanzees today?' This village is actually a wonderful place. I feel like it's my home. I tell you, the children here are beautiful. And tough! You ask one to fetch you a bucket of water. None of this, 'Aw, do I have to?' The sort of thing you get from English or American kids, who are lazy and spoiled. Their faces light up. They run off to do your errand. And I am amazed at the things they can carry! They are strong!"

Charlotte told the story of two chimpanzees in northern Burundi. "There was a French director of a tea plantation," she began, "who bought two chimpanzees. Jolie Coeur was a four- or five-year-old male, and the other was a very little one called Cleopatra, who was only about two years old. She was bought afterwards. When I first met the Frenchman, he was very interested in the sanctuary, very sympathetic to our cause, and this kind of thing. But I got the impression that it was a kind of academic interest more than anything else. Now, as he had these chimps, more and more, I think, their behavior began to fascinate him, as it does to virtually all their owners, I believe–they can't believe how intelligent they are, and how similar these chimpanzees are to ourselves. And Jolie Coeur virtually adopted Cleo, as if he was her mother. He would chew up food and give it to her in his lower lip. He used to hold her at night. Anybody ever tried to take Cleo away from him, and she started whimpering or anything, he would go berserk and attack them, and retrieve Cleo. And then about two weeks ago, I'm not sure quite how it happened, but a dog or something–or maybe it was Cleo–upset a beehive, and these African bees swarmed on the two chimps. Cleo started to get stung by the bees, so Jolie Coeur just pulled her to his breast and bent double over her, and completely shielded her with his body, and he took, I think, over two hundred and fifty bee stings before he finally died. Cleo is still alive because of that, and I think the Frenchman, that was really the moment when he suddenly realized he was dealing with incredibly sentient creatures, who have really the same kind of emotional–are capable of the same kind of emotional attachment as us. That this chimpanzee had basically allowed himself to be stung to death to save a little infant that wasn't even a relative of his or anything, but he just adopted. And now, of course, Cleo is in serious trouble, because she's lost a second mother. For the first three or four days after Jolie Coeur was killed by the bees, she didn't eat. She wouldn't do anything. And now she's eating again, but she just attaches herself. She just clings to anyone that comes near. I went to see her, and I was sitting on the ground near her, and she flew into my arms, and just put her arms around me and held me like a wrench. She wouldn't let go. And if we tried to take her away, she would start screaming and screaming."

Charlotte was quiet for a long time. The Israeli and I were quiet. Then Charlotte said, "Yes, poor Jolie Coeur. Well, I knew them both very well, those chimps. I went up to see them several times. And I was so happy because of all the chimps here in captivity in Burundi, they were the only two together. All the others are isolated. So I always used to feel quite happy about those: 'Well, they're all right. They've got each other.' "

It became late. The candles sputtered and sizzled to a close. The Israeli had a sleeping bag, which he rolled out onto a mat. Charlotte found a blanket, some pieces of cardboard and some pieces of foam for me, and we all turned in for the night. I listened to the squeaking mice and the drizzle on the tin roof. I fought off the kittens the first half of the night. The second half, I fought a chill in the air that passed right through the brick walls and penetrated my blanket.

The Israeli left right after breakfast the next day.

Charlotte employed five local men to help her track the chimpanzees. She was conducting her own research project, and simultaneously, the Burundi government hoped, habituating the chimps to human observers for the future benefit of tourism.

The first full day I was there she sent me out with one of the trackers, a short man with powerful legs. These hills looked steep, but they became steeper when you walked them and steeper yet when you walked with a fast walker. I have forgotten the name of the tracker who took me out that day, and he spoke no European languages except for a few words of French. "Ici Carrera!" he said, as we stood on a steep hillside in a maize and manioc plot, looking down into a forested ravine known as Carrera, listening to the sound of rushing water. "Ici l'habitude de chimpanzees beaucoup—avec la mabango." Mabango was a fruit.

We walked along ledges above the ravine and then descended on some of the slickest paths I've ever fallen on. The soil was clayey. The paths were hard-packed and lubricated by a film of fine green moss.

Charlotte told me that evening that the first word she learned in Kirundi, the local language, was *haranyiyera,* which means "slippery." The paths were haranyiyera. But down inside the ravines, we entered restful forests with hidden birds calling and chirping. There was a gurgling of water down there, dense ground cover, and many ferns and wildflowers. One of the flowers was called *itondoh,* and it looked very sexy. It had a split vase made of four or five petals, two of them large, pink on the outside and yellowed ivory inside, and down in the center of the vase was a soft ivory stamen. Below the stamen, way down into the secret heart of the vase, there were tiny red veins. We came to a guava tree, climbed it, and ate guavas. We crossed three or four streams, gurgling with a rust-colored water, and we stopped at one stream where the water slipped behind a mossy tree and disappeared through a dark tunnel, and we drank there and rested. We neither saw nor heard chimpanzees that day.

The next day, Charlotte and I went out together with two trackers. We were on top of one of the hills, walking through some high, rough scrub and scattered trees and even patches of forest, along the top of the hill but away from the trail, when Charlotte became tired of the walking stick she was using. She decided to put the stick on the trail, so we could find it on our way back. "I'll be right back," she said. "You keep on walking. I'll catch up. I'm just going to leave this on the trail."

I kept walking through the scrub, accompanied by the two trackers. Pretty soon we entered an area of scrub where a troop of baboons was hiding out. I could see their four-legged dark shapes galloping through the brush, acting nervous. I heard a cough-bark, and I looked into the brush to see a bobbing head, then a dark shape jumping nervously back and forth, back and forth, and then other bobbing heads looking out of the brush, coughing, hiding. Soon there were ten baboon heads looking out, and then a nervous approaching and retreating that went on for some time, but gradually the whole troop receded, yet still pausing, pawing the ground, hopping in place, bobbing and weaving. One baboon climbed a tree to get a better look at us, then jumped down. Another did the same. And then they were gone.

We must have watched the baboons for twenty minutes, even more, but Charlotte hadn't shown up yet, so we stood there and waited another twenty minutes. No Charlotte. Then we walked back to where she had left us and gone off. No Charlotte. One of the trackers ran up to find the spot on the trail where Charlotte had gone to leave her stick. He returned ten minutes later, his face solemn and troubled. No Charlotte. I tried to recall exactly what she had said: "I'll be right back. I'll catch up. Just going to leave this on the trail." The trackers were starting to get concerned now, I could see. They were saying a few words to me in French, then talking quickly to each other with many words in Kirundi. We fanned out, the three of us, and began plowing systematically through the high grass and the brush and the trees and vines all across the top of this hill. It was a big hill. There were many thick places in the vegetation. No Charlotte. As I saw how very worried the trackers were becoming, I started to imagine all the bad things that could have happened. As we continued over the next half hour to stumble and search through the rough brush for signs, any signs at all, of Charlotte, it occurred to me that she might be dying and we could save her but only if we found her in time. I began feeling gloomy.

We ran into Charlotte an hour later, much farther down the trail. She hadn't seen us, as we paused to look at the baboons, and had walked on past knowing we would be right along in any case. She teased us for being worried.

We didn't find any chimpanzees that day. Charlotte said she had no idea where they were. Their food was dispersed now, she said, but she didn't believe they would run out of food. "The chimps eat all sorts of things, including probably crops. They'll eat the pith of banana trees," she said. "Most bananas here are for beer, not sweet bananas." They also eat oil palm nuts, manioc leaves, and even perhaps goats. "They're opportunistic. If meat presents itself, they'll eat it. But there are also baboons in the area, and lots and lots of vervets, who eat crops as well. The vervets are terrible. They eat maize and rice; the chimpanzees don't. But they just all get bunched together as 'those animals that eat crops.'"

Actually, I never saw chimpanzees while I stayed with Charlotte in the little brick house in the village on the hill, but I did come to appreciate the house and the peace of that village. I loved the place, in fact, and I think I felt more at home there than anywhere else I visited in Africa. To tell the truth, I was quite taken with Charlotte, whom I regarded as unreasonably beautiful. But my pleasures moved well beyond Charlotte. The village itself was a very pleasing place, and I like to imagine that here I came close to understanding and appreciating the best side of African village life.

It was so peaceful. Only a history book (or a crystal ball) could keep one from overromanticizing that village, those hills, that country. Burundi, so the book tells me, was settled originally by the Twa Pygmies, displaced around 1000 A.D. by the Hutu agriculturalists. The tall, martial Tutsi arrived from the north during the sixteenth and seventeenth centuries and over time subjugated the Hutu with an African version of the feudal system. The Germans arrived in the second half of the nineteenth century to be displaced during World War I by the Belgians who, as colonial rulers, consolidated and exploited the existing feudal system by granting the Tutsi considerable political power over the Hutu. In the 1950s, an independence movement led by a Tutsi, Prince Rwagasore, emphasized tribal cooperation—but Rwagasore was assassinated. Independence in 1962 brought nominally democractic institutions, but not enough to keep Tutsis from dominating government institutions at every level. An attempted coup by disgruntled Hutu military officers led to a Tutsi purge of Hutus from the military and government. A Hutu rebellion in 1972 ended the lives of over a thousand Tutsis; Tutsis responded with a genocidal reign of terror, killing some two hundred thousand Hutus outright and driving an additional one hundred thousand across the borders. In 1988, another series of conflicts and massacres brought about the deaths of thousands of Burundians in the north. . . . That's what the history book says. (And the crystal ball might have told me that I would be passing through this same land in February of 1994 on my way to Rwanda and Zaire, three months after the assassination of Burundi's first Hutu president led to riots, massacres, one or two hundred thousand Tutsis dead—and seven weeks before the double assassination of Burundi's replacement president along with next-door Rwanda's president began another gruesome wave of blood, this time in Rwanda, where perhaps half a million men, women, and children, Tutsis mainly, were murdered.)

We had several visitors: a drunk man who showed up one night, walked in the door, sat down in a chair, and started sounding angry about something abstract; one of the neighboring women; children from the neighborhood.

One afternoon while Charlotte was working in her study, a man appeared at her window, speaking English, asking for a job. She was the only actual employer in the village, I believe. "Jambo, madame," he said. I was sitting in the living room. I didn't see the man, and I reproduce the conversation here only in its abridged version. "I came here in order to find a job," the man said. "If possible, all right. If not possible. I am here to find an answer that is good, yes or no. Is there a job or no? I am in civil engineering. I can build a house like this one. I can build a house from the bottom all the way to the up."

"I'm sorry," Charlotte said, putting him off with the direct approach, "but I have no jobs to offer right now."

"So," the man said, refusing to be put off, "you will have a job soon, in the future, but soon."

"At the moment," Charlotte said, "I'm not thinking about the future."

"So it will be a temporary job. It will not be permanent," he said.

"Yes, but I don't have any available right now. There is no job."

"About it to concern the forest. If there is a chance, I am all ready to enter."

"That's very good of you, but I already have enough jobs for the forest."

"Yes, but there is a chance soon. I am ready."

"I already have enough jobs for the forest."

"But, I'm sorry: I stay here in the bush. To get a job it is difficult. So I tell you if there is a place to enter I will be grateful."

"I'm sorry, but if you can come back in several months."

"So, it will be better for you if you have someone who can speak English."

"Perhaps so, but you see it is not possible right now."

"I will come and speak to you tomorrow."

"I'm very sorry, but there are no jobs available right now."

"I will come and speak to you tomorrow, and then we will see if you have something to offer, yes or no."

"Not tomorrow. Come back in six months."

"In one week I will return, and you will tell me, yes or no."

"I already have five guards, and they all work. I cannot afford to hire another man."

"So, you will give me a job when I return again."

"I cannot promise anything, but perhaps you could try again."

"I will be glad if you think about my problem, because to stay here without a job is very difficult."

"I can understand that, but I cannot do anything about it."

"Yes, I will show you that I do very much work."

"I'm sure you can. Unfortunately, there is nothing available right now."

"I live at Mambe village. Just beyond this village."

"I will be leaving soon and then will not return again for six months. Perhaps then you could stop back."

"So, you know many people who has job for me. I see all these people come to your house. You can tell them about me."

"I can try for you, but I make no promises."

"Okay, but I demand it. If it is possible, just contact with me."

"I can ask, but I can make no promise, eh?"

"All right, but I can make much good work. That is, to arrange it, to arrange it, is to answer."

"Okay, but my answer to you is there is no job at the moment."

"We shall meet again soon."

"Yes, perhaps we will meet again."

"We shall meet again soon, if God will like."

I was impressed. This must have been what Billy Graham was like, in the old days when he was a supersalesman for Fuller Brush. Was the man desperate or merely persistent? I could not figure it out, although I now suspect he was both.

Another time, a bright new car with two big Belgians inside appeared in front of the house. I didn't quite believe the car had actually made the trip up that road. I still don't quite believe it. It may have drifted down more directly from the moon. The Belgians, dressed in their brightest clothes and white tennis shoes, climbed out of the car and said hello to Charlotte. They knew her from some connection in Bujumbura. They both wore sunglasses, and the husband chain-smoked and was overweight. The wife was aggressively fat and assertively plain. They stood out in the middle of a quiet African village on top of a breeze-blown hill with a wonderful view, pushed their sunglasses up into their hair, and held up their machines. The wife held up a video camera and waved it back and forth at Lake Tanganyika. Then she turned and waved it back and forth at a couple of villagers and some goats who happened to be nearby. Then she turned and waved it back and forth at Charlotte's house. The husband had a camera with a blunt lens and some kind of magical, automatic-focusing device driven by a little whining motor. He held the camera over his face like a long-eyed mask and pointed it at his wife, who by then had put down her video camera and was sitting in the doorway of Charlotte's house. The motor whined, the lens moved out like a robot's inadequate erection, and then the camera gulped and swallowed an image of the fat wife.

After they had finished sucking images into their image machines, the couple pulled their sunglasses back down over their eyes, said goodbye to Charlotte, climbed back inside their motion machine, closed the doors and windows, turned on the air-conditioning, and tried to make a U-turn. In the process of turning around on the road, however, the car's tail pipe buried itself into a small hill of mud, and so the engine coughed and choked to death on its own exhaust.

They fixed their car at last and left, bouncing back down the road, but it took some time before the waves from their visit turned into ripples. Charlotte said, "It's just so peaceful here. It's so peaceful! I sit at my neighbor's house. You know, they bring me food, just a present of food. They'll just come around and bring it. I'll go and sit over at the other next-door neighbor's house some evening. You know, it's so tranquil. And then occasionally, this kind of roar of a motor! And a car appears and mzungus come with cameras and things. I just think, 'Oh, goodness, that world!' "

Madness in the City

I had agreed to meet the photographer Gerry Ellis at a certain time on a certain day in the lobby of the Novotel in Bujumbura, and I did. We both wanted to go to Nairobi, and so we bought tickets, boarded a plane, and made the hop to Nairobi.

As a matter of principle, or autonomic predilection, I prefer rural to urban. Rural is quiet, urban noisy. When you do hear sounds in the country, they're soft, plangent sounds, like rain falling or leaves rustling, not the jagged shriek and squeal of metal on metal, city sounds that usually mean your soul and body are being transported without your mind and against your will, perforated and processed inside an assembly line of urban machinery. When a person smiles in the country, you relax. When a person smiles in the city, you crank up your defenses: *What does he want from me?*

Nairobi has the additional problem of a British colonial history, which means that the taxis are old-fashioned and the traffic runs backward, a confusing and dangerous situation. And as I sat with Gerry in the plushly cushioned backseat of a taxi, moving from Jomo Kenyatta International Airport into the city, I recalled the slightly insane hero of that French book about an upset stomach, *Nausea*, who discovers, while sitting on a plush red seat of the Saint-Elémir streetcar, things starting to detach themselves from words. Meaning drifts out the window, and the world turns unattractive. His seat grows into a thousand little red paws floating in the air, for instance, and then it turns into a dead donkey, bloated, with a huge belly. The author had been messing with mescaline when he wrote *Nausea*, and I've often suspected that his mysterious disease was as much chemistry as philosophy. But aren't chemistry and philosophy the same thing? I observed the backseat of the taxi creep and swell with a terrible organic enthusiasm.

I had been to Nairobi twice before, and the place was not unfamiliar. But Gerry, out of sheer exuberance, began acting like a tour guide. The taxi drove past Nairobi Park, where it seemed to me a couple of giraffes were placing their necks against the barren savanna skyline. "Nairobi Park," Gerry pointed out.

"Yes, I know," I said, stifling an unreasonable irritation that rose much too quickly.

Just about then, there was a tremendous commotion behind us on the road, a wailing of sirens and a honking of horns, and I looked out the cab's rear window and saw a road full of motorcycled police about to run us over. We pulled over quickly and then watched the motorcycles roar past, followed by some overstimulated police cars and a couple of black limousines with dark fish-tank windows. Our taxi driver said: "Moi." It was Kenya's president, Daniel Arap Moi, on his way from Alpha to Beta.

In the city, we drove past the New Stanley Hotel. "That's the New Stanley Hotel," Gerry said. "Used to be quite the place around the turn of the century."

"I know, Gerry."

"It's too expensive now."

"Obviously."

Gerry had been to Nairobi many times, and he certainly knew much more about the city than I did, including the name and location of a decent hotel, the Boulevard. Gerry said he liked this hotel because Africans stay there, which was true. It was comparatively inexpensive yet somewhat luxurious. The hot water lasted a full tub. True, all the bathrooms opened (via a two-inch vent high at the top of a frosted window above the bathtub) onto the main hall, giving one a precarious sense of privacy, but really, the place seemed fine. Our room looked out onto the hotel swimming pool, inhabited by French and Italian beauties dressed in string bikinis or less and working hard on their malignant melanoma, and beyond the fenced pool area was the street.

The street was the problem. It was very noisy at night, I thought, although Gerry was the sort of person who slept right through the rumbling of trucks and the braying of horns, and then he was the sort of person who whistled brightly in the morning when he got up. Gerry was the sort of person who took stairs two at a time, after breakfast, and also the sort of person who moved like a sprinter when you went out in the city to conduct the day's business.

"Slow down, Gerry," I said. "My toe's still broken."

"Sorry!"

He slowed down, moderately, for about one minute. Then he forgot and had to be reminded again. "Gerry, let's reduce the pace for a while."

"What? Oh, sure."

Gerry was also the sort of person who, after dinner in the evening, made abrupt decisions for two. We walked into the hotel bar and cocktail lounge, for example, and immediately my eyes settled on a couple of easy chairs in the corner. "Let's sit there," I said. "Let's not," he said, and then without waiting for even a minor degree of concurrence he marched right up to the bar where there were some unoccupied stools.

This was getting to be like two male chimpanzees! This was a dominance contest. I didn't want to sit on a stool. "No!" I said, with absolute and total and irrevocable and utter finality. "I don't want to sit here! Let's find another place!"

Gerry shrugged. "Okay."

My main business in Nairobi was to get a visa to Uganda as well as a ticket, but I also had some chimpanzee business to conduct. Someone had given me the name and phone number of a person in Nairobi who supposedly was taking care of three recently confiscated baby chimps. The person's name was Mike Garner, and I telephoned him while waiting for my Ugandan visa and arranged to meet him and see

the confiscated chimps, which by then were two instead of three because one had died. "Righteo, sir," he said before hanging up the
phone.

Mike Garner breeds racehorses and organizes safaris, and I took
a taxi out to his place in the Nairobi suburb known as Karen (after
Karen Blixen). Mike, short and trim, wore a rancher's outfit of Levi's,
cotton shirt, and brown vest, and his face was a Celtic production of
very fair skin and sun furrows. "The traffic in them is unreal," he said,
referring to smuggled baby chimpanzees. "Dr. Richard Leakey, a mate
of mine from school, says this is the sixteenth or seventeenth shipment
to come in the country. It's a hell of a problem."

We were standing in Mike Garner's backyard, and at that point
two baby chimpanzees appeared. They were both wearing diapers,
and they were both carried in by their surrogate nursemaids, two
Kenyan women, who had the chimps wrapped in cloth to their backs,
like human babies. The caretakers unwrapped the two chimps, and
they jumped to the ground. One of the chimps walked very vigorously
over to me and looked up into my eyes. He took my hand, sniffed it,
kissed it with delicate lips, placed my hand on top of his head, then
took the hand off and kissed it a second time. That was BooBoo, Mike
said, and after kissing my hand, BooBoo ran away and began climbing
and jumping on some patio furniture. The second chimp—Mike said
his name was Grumpy—had during this time climbed up a steel pole
supporting a patio awning. He began swinging by one arm from a steel
crosspiece.

"All three chimps arrived late last year," Mike said. "They weighed
about one kilo each. Very weak, dehydrated, and malnourished. The
female was very sick. She rallied for a couple of days around Christmas, but pneumonia hammered her in the end. They're amazingly
different in character. The other guy, you can see, we call him Grumpy.
He's a very, very quiet guy. We call this one BooBoo because he's
always in trouble."

The three chimps appeared at the Nairobi airport in a basket covered over with a burlap sack, going around and around on the baggage
carousel. A local woman recognized that there were chimps inside the
basket and made "a hell of a row," as Mike put it. So they were confiscated. As it turned out, the chimps had been sent as luggage from
Bujumbura, bound for Cairo. For the pet trade? For a laboratory
somewhere? The young Egyptian who was arrested as the courier

claimed he had paid two thousand dollars each for them in Bujum-bura. The Egyptian was finally tried in Nairobi and convicted of cruelty to animals but was only fined twelve hundred Kenyan shillings–roughly sixty dollars–the maximum under Kenyan game laws, because chimps are not an indigenous species.

Gerry's business in Nairobi lasted only a couple of days. He was trying to arrange some sort of Kenyan operation having to do with future photography in Masai Mara or somewhere. Lions? I don't recall exactly. But after he left, first I was relieved not to be walking at a near run down the street during the day and not to be fighting over bar stools in the evening, but then I was not relieved at all. My room was twice as expensive. The prostitutes in the bar were three times more assertive. Nairobi was tedious and hot.

I began taking all my meals at the same fish-and-chips place. Reli-able grease. Anomie and abulia began creeping into my skull, and my moods began sloughing erinaceous exfoliations. This was a tropical fatigue, perhaps, or perhaps it was the ineluctable avoidance of the still part of one's own mind, which–who knows?–may not be still at all but a raving lunatic.

Meanwhile, as I could read in the newspapers, one of President Moi's top ministers, Dr. Robert Ouka, had been murdered mysteri-ously not so long after he started critizing President Moi's government. The government was speculating that Dr. Ouka had himself forcibly removed from his house at three in the morning, shot himself in the head, and finally set himself on fire as an ambitious act of suicide. One day the newspaper said: OUKA'S WIFE URGES PATIENCE. The next day the newspaper said: SCOTLAND YARD LEAPS IN. The third day it con-cluded: OUKA WAS MURDERED!

There were big protest marches in town, milling crowds of stu-dents and others blocking traffic and waving leafy branches, carrying signs that said STOP THE MADNESS and WHO KILLED DR. OUKA? and WHERE IS CAIN? The crowds raged and chanted, stomped and shook their branches and signs with a barely suppressed fury.

Nairobi: I was glad to get out of there.

9

Yahoo in Uganda

Our own senses do not make us aware of what it is
disagreeable enough to acknowledge, that the whole
species of man yields a powerful and wide-spreading
emanation, that is utterly disgusting and repulsive to
every animal in its wild state. It requires some experi-
ence to realize this fact: a man must frequently have
watched the heads of a herd of far distant animals,
tossed up in alarm the moment that they catch his
wind; he must have observed the tracks of animals—
how, when they crossed his path of the preceding
day, the beast that made the tracks has stopped,
scrutinised, and shunned it—before he can believe
what a Yahoo he is among the brute creation.

–Francis Galton, *The Art of Travel*

Customs and immigration into Uganda were surprisingly easy. Some-how I had expected Idi Amin to meet me at the airport and make life difficult. He didn't, and I found the customs and immigrations officers friendly, efficient, and altogether agreeable. I was happy to be in Uganda.

In the airport bank, I changed dollars into Ugandan shillings, and, as I stepped out of the bank, I was accosted by a taxi driver. Was I going into Kampala? I said I was either going to Kampala or to the Entebbe Zoo. I wasn't sure which. He didn't know where the Entebbe Zoo was, but he would take me into Kampala for several thousand

Ugandan shillings—the equivalent of, according to arithmetic spun quickly in my head, roughly sixty dollars. That seemed like a lot of money. A second Ugandan entered our discussion at this point, and I turned to him and asked if that was a fair price for the trip to Kampala. Was Kampala my final destination? he wanted to know. It was either Kampala or the Entebbe Zoo, or both, I said. Who was I looking for at the Entebbe Zoo? this second person asked. I pulled out of my pocket a scrap of paper and read the name on it. "Tim Holmes," I said. Oh, he knew Tim Holmes, and he would take me right there if I could just wait a few minutes.

This second person was a lanky helicopter pilot for the Ugandan Air Force, and as we drove out to Entebbe, he asked me how Nairobi had been. I mentioned the demonstrations. "Things haven't yet reached bottom in Kenya," he said. "Some time they will. Moi is amassing all that wealth."

Within several minutes, I had been deposited in a yard of the bungalow of Tim Holmes. Tim was a Brit who looked to be in his early thirties. He was sinewy, with an angular face and curly, sandy hair and a beard. He wore faded blue jeans, dirty white tennis shoes, and a red T-shirt with a picture of a proboscis monkey on it and the line: "Our future is your future. Help protect the primates." He had worked at the Jersey Wildlife Trust for a time, he said, but one day felt an urge for adventure, so he and his wife, Rosie, purchased a World War II ambulance and drove the overland route to Uganda. (Driving overland is one of the things people do in Africa. The underland route is too difficult for all but the most intrepid.) They crossed over from Europe, went through the Sahara to Nigeria, Cameroon, the Central African Republic, et cetera, into Uganda, where the ambulance was now surrounded by high grass in their yard. Rosie found a job teaching at a local international school, and Tim found employment at the Entebbe Zoo.

Tim was telling me these things as we sat on the front porch of his bungalow. The front door was open a crack, and two tiny faces were peeking out. Actually, it was one face at a time—two chimps were pushing each other out of the way to get a peek. But soon these two chimps came out onto the porch. Tim told me their names were Pan and Dora. Their eyes were big and bright, and they looked my way with an inquisitive gaze, but they were so busy holding on to each other that they could only concentrate for short periods on anything else. They walked on four, sometimes five, sometimes six legs and arms, and the remaining arms and legs they used for clutching each other. In other words, they walked out across the front porch in a waltzing embrace. Their faces looked human, tiny and big-eyed.

"Why are they named Pan and Dora?"

"Pan as in *Pan troglodytes*," Tim said. "Also, they came in a little pathetic box: Pandora's box. There's the box, actually, and as you can see, it's tiny. I reckon they'd been there for more than forty-eight hours with no food or water." On Tim's porch was a small wooden box with some holes drilled in the sides. Tim found a tape measure, and we measured the box: eight and a half inches high, and thirteen by fourteen and a half on the sides. Both chimps had been squeezed inside the box and then exported from the Entebbe Airport without export papers to Dubai. They were either to be sold as pets or for laboratory research. But since the box was not accompanied by proper papers, the two little chimps were stopped in Dubai and then sent right back to Entebbe and confiscated. "Pan, physically, he wasn't too bad when we opened the box," Tim said. "But Dora—extreme diarrhea, bad worms, and she was vomiting a lot. But now she's in really good shape. In fact they're both in very good shape. Basically, they're spending their days just in the garden. And there are certain plant species they actually recognize and they eat. Obviously we give them food, but it's nice that they're actually eating leaves."

"They seem very close," I said.

"Yes, and the problem there is they obviously have been taken from their mothers. Chimps—well, I'm sure you know—should be with their mothers until they're three years old. These guys have been wrenched away from that. And they rely on each other. Well, most of the time. And Dora, you can pick her up, you can play with her, and she's very inquisitive. Climbs the trees. But Pan, his main interest is food. And if you try and pick him up or if he's by himself, he really panics, makes lots of noise and dashes back to Dora, and they cling to each other. Having said that, she's also dependent on him, because if she's separated from him she gets a bit panicky and rushes back to him. But it's nice that they have got each other and they know they're chimpanzees. Although I play with them a lot, because I think they need the stimulation, but they do know they're chimpanzees. But psychologically Pan is, he's really, really—if anyone comes he's the one who sort of makes a lot of noise and runs away. He obviously went through a really bad time when he was caught."

"No idea where they came from?"

"No idea at all. It could have been Uganda, but it could have been eastern Zaire, because apparently the way it works is, there's someone in Zaire and someone in Uganda, and between them they get a license to export from Zaire. It comes to Uganda and then disappears through Entebbe, a main gateway out."

"For chimps?"

"Yes."

By this time, Pan and Dora had walked their embracing, spidery walk off the porch and out into the garden. We followed them out there. They started eating flowers. They had large, liquid brown eyes, a soft white down around their chins. They were very cute. Pan was the scared one, I could see, and Dora the bold one. I held my hand out, and gently with her tiny hand Dora took mine. So gentle! She placed my forefinger between her lips, softly, gently . . . and then bit my finger hard. I jerked my finger away. "She bit my finger!"

"Yes, she bites fingers sometimes," Tim said. "I should have told you."

I looked at her teeth: all incisors. I looked at a small trench of incisor dents in my finger. No break in the skin, though, no blood.

Tim and I ate lunch and then went out to look at the zoo. It was situated on a beautiful piece of land right on the edge of Lake Victoria. But there were problems. There was no meat in the zoo, because someone had neglected to pay the meat supplier for several months. So they had had to shoot a zoo waterbuck to feed the zoo lion. Now there were four waterbucks left.

A huge crocodile lay in a small circular cement pool, empty of water except for one small green puddle. His scales looked dry and gray, like stones. He blinked his eyes open, and then he closed them again. The zoo water had been turned off, Tim said. He didn't know why.

The zoo included some spectacular shoebill storks that someone had attempted to smuggle out to a Dutch address, an importer in West Apeldoorn. Actually, someone had tried to export five shoebill storks, highly endangered, a couple of months previously. By the time the storks had been confiscated and sent to the zoo, two weeks previously, however, there were four. Just last week, Tim said, someone stole the youngest shoebill stork, so now there were only three. A crowned crane had been confiscated in Kampala a couple of weeks earlier and given to the zoo. A gray-cheeked mangabey was brought in—dead on arrival. Also, seven gray parrots had been confiscated, bound for

Kenya. Three giant rats. The next day their mother came in, but her back was broken, so she died and was fed to the python. A terrapin. An oribi. One DeBrazza's monkey. All these animals had been brought into the zoo during the past two weeks, Tim said.

Someone had written a letter to the school where Tim's wife, Rosie, taught, offering a chimpanzee for sale. The person wrote that he needed a thousand dollars for educational purposes and would sell a baby chimpanzee for that amount or even less. Rosie met him and arranged for the illegal transaction to take place. Tim invited the police and a representative of the game department to attend the meeting, and they all moved in for the confiscation only to find that the "chimpanzee" offered for sale was actually a DeBrazza's monkey.

That's how the DeBrazza's monkey was acquired. But the zoo already had a number of confiscated chimps. When Tim arrived, a couple of months before, there were seven confiscated chimps in the zoo. Another chimp came in: eight. Pan and Dora were brought in in December. When they were big enough, they would go to the zoo. That makes ten. Other chimps were going to be confiscated here and there in the country. A Frenchman in Kampala had a chimp that drank beer and watched television. Meanwhile, someone had decided to open a biomedical research laboratory in Uganda, and official permission was given to capture six chimps for the lab. The idea was eventually scrapped, but not until at least one chimp had been caught and was being held at the site for the planned laboratory. Tim went to see the chimp, who was named Saturday, perhaps because he had been caught on a Saturday. "So this chimp was a wild-caught one?" Tim said he asked the person in charge.

"Yes, I caught it myself."

"Well, how did you do that? What did you do, shoot the mother and various relatives?"

"Oh, no no. I set a very clever little trap that just caught that chimpanzee."

Saturday was eventually taken to the Entebbe Zoo, but then, unaware of the social situation at the zoo, he approached the wrong testy male and had his arm badly broken. Delayed veterinary care led to a worsening of the wound, and Saturday was finally put out of his misery.

•   •   •

Tim thought that a taxi from Entebbe to Kampala might actually cost the equivalent of sixty dollars, more or less, but that a bus would cost about sixty cents.

I took a bus.

The bus, which was a crowded VW van, discharged all passengers into a large field, an open bus terminal and parking lot, somewhere in Kampala. It was late afternoon by then, a hot and dusty time, and the driver of the van pointed to one corner of the field where he said I could catch a bus to the western side of Uganda at six o'clock the next morning. He pointed in another direction and said: "Hotel."

A sign out front said it was the Lion Hotel, and the woman at the desk was very friendly and helpful. I paid about twenty dollars for the night and found myself with the key to a decent room on the second floor.

Kampala includes a prosperous downtown of concrete edifices, but this hotel was elsewhere. My window opened onto a view of the less-developed section of the city: a half-grown pioneer town of dust and rust over a chaotic sea of corrugated tin roofs. I listened to a heavy rumbling of traffic, horn honkings, a regular tap tap tap of someone hammering, the ripping and whining of a handheld power saw some-where, birdcalls, cries and laughter of children, the shuffling of feet, the murmuring of voices. In the distance, I saw a heavy black plume of billowing smoke, and closer, all around, I saw whitish ignes fatui of hovering smoke. I saw a disorder of low buildings and treetops—trees with no evidence of city planning to them, as if the city was sitting on a recently overrun forest or as if the trees had planted the city, rather than vice versa, as is the case in American cities. I heard a joyful African music rising from the streets, and I watched crowds emerging from the late afternoon dust.

I visited some shops down the street and bought a few supplies and then ate dinner in the hotel restaurant. After dinner I returned to my room, killed mosquitoes, and settled down to a piece of escapist fiction by a best-selling British writer of horse mysteries. But my con-centration was weak and my transom open. I heard a knock and a door turn open just down the hallway, and then I eavesdropped—would it be transomdropped?—on a man and a woman talking intently with East Asian accents.

She: "Take two in the morning, one at night."
He: "I'll take two now."

She: "No, you'll die. You want to die: Take two."

He: "I'll take one."

I returned to the book, but the plot was so tedious, the pace so slow—on the back cover, someone famous was quoted: "break-neck roller-coaster ride of a plot." Well, maybe. But the dialogue was absolutely wooden—on the back cover, someone else famous said: "remarkable ear for the way real-life people really talk." And I found the characters one-dimensional walking stereotypes, utterly lifeless and predictable—"peopled with an entire cast of originals, absolutely believable." I put the book away with disgust—how much had I paid for it in Nairobi?—and turned to *Gulliver's Travels*. I had been reading bits and pieces since Zambia. By now I had reached part 4: "A Voyage to the Country of the Houyhnhnms."

It was still completely dark outside when I ate my early breakfast in the hotel restaurant, right beneath a handsome portrait of Uganda's president. I checked out of the hotel, hoisted my pack on my back, and stepped outside. Little traffic. Few people. Cool air. Very dark. I walked down toward the bus field and, on my way there, stepped from a murky sidewalk into inky space. This was an open sewer trench, and I saw the abyss open beneath me and smelled the stench just as I stepped into midair—and just in time to kick off with my other foot and turn my moderate step into a small leap.

I came to the bus field, a dark region containing three buses that were dimly lighted inside, with dim headlamps poking short light tubes outside into the smoking darkness. The bus motors rumbled, black diesel smoke spilled and swirled out of black shadows, and the shapes and shadows of people moved into the dim yellow tubes of the bus headlamps and then disappeared back into deep shadows and darkness.

I really didn't know much about where I was going, except that I needed to get to the western town of Fort Portal, so I asked a man in a uniform which bus was going to Fort Portal. "Ooteeahs," he said.

I asked some other people which was the Fort Portal bus. "Ooteeahs," they said.

The way this was said indicated to me that the Fort Portal bus was not there, in that dark field. I found a taxi out on the street, and I said to the driver: "Ooteeahs."

Ah, yes, he could take me to Ooteeahs for about sixteen hundred Ugandan shillings. It wouldn't be far, he said. So I entered the taxi. The taxi drove down the street a block, turned a corner, and pulled up at a large, enclosed bus lot with a sign that was revealed in a thin film of light: "U.T.S."

I recognized that the taxi driver was cheating me. We had driven hardly more than a block, certainly not enough to charge what would be several dollars worth of shillings. I told him he was a cheat, and we haggled over the price until it became six hundred shillings. I didn't actually have six hundred shillings at hand, though, so I dug into a large wallet inside a secondary pack inside my main pack and came out with a big new stack of bills, many thousand Ugandan shillings that I had gotten from the bank at the Entebbe Airport. I peeled off six hundred shillings, rolled up the rest, and hastily plunged that great wad into my left front pocket.

The U.T.S. terminal was big. It was open to the stars above but walled, like a stockade. It was very dark inside the stockade, dimly lit in places, and there were several rumbling buses and milling groups of people. A man in a blue uniform told me the Fort Portal bus would be there at seven thirty. But there was an actual terminal building, too, and so I entered the building and talked to a man inside a ticket cage. He didn't know anything about the Fort Portal bus, but he said I should go to Enquiries. Enquiries was in the one brightly lit part of this building, and the man there was shouting garbled announcements in an incomprehensible language through a disintegrating public address system. He paused for a moment, and I asked him about the Fort Portal bus. He said, "Over there," and pointed out into the darkness to an area where I could see three buses, all their engines running, their headlamps dimly lit, their insides glowing yellow, surrounded by crowds of people and with shadows of people entering and moving into the yellow glowing insides.

"Which bus goes to Fort Portal?" I asked a man at the edge of this crowd, and he pointed to one, rumbling deeply inside its own aura of dirty light and swirling smoke. It was being boarded, and it seemed to me now very big, looming and almost mythical, like a departing continental train or an oceanic ship, surrounded by a stationary crowd of well-wishers and bon-voyagers, pressed against by a flowing crowd of travelers burdened and eager for the door. A man crouched on top of this huge steel vehicle and dropped luggage onto the top rack; a man halfway up a steel ladder on the side of the vehicle was heaving luggage up. Bags, bicycles, wheelbarrows, sacks of meal were being heaved up and dropped on top, while people surged into the door of the bus. I moved into the crowd and found myself pressed and pushed forward, shoved into the door, and popped right inside the bus. As I was propelled forward toward the front of the bus, I felt the slightest pressure, a tug and release at my left hip—a pressure, as I began slowly reflecting on it, so finely different from the pushing and crowding and touching that constituted my passage onto the bus, a passage through a tunnel of hands and arms and elbows and knees and legs—so finely different, I say, that only after a long moment's thought did I begin to wonder back at that one experience and begin to remember that the release felt like a loss of bulk, a release of the wad of bills from my left front pocket, a theft! My pocket had been picked, I began to realize, as I settled into a seat right next to a Ugandan woman holding a straw basket in her lap.

I immediately thought to rush back, find the thief, grab my money out of his hands, his pocket, wherever it would be by now. But of course he would be long gone, and I would probably lose my seat. The bus was already so crowded people could barely move. So I just sat there, felt the incident's disturbance fade, and began comforting myself with the following analysis: I once worked on a Chrysler assembly line in Belvidere, Illinois. I could earn in four hours' work on the assembly line what I had just lost, but it was probably worth four weeks' wages to the poor bastard who just stole it. The value of my money had just expanded fortyfold. *On the other hand,* a small voice said inside my head, *stealing is bad. Stealing is mean.* A second voice countered: *It's no meaner than the crazed divisions of the world, the absurd spinning of fortune's wheel.* The first voice replied: *Stealing from tourists discourages tourism. Pickpocketing rewards mindless hand-eye coordination and punishes honest labor.* The second voice shot back: *So does Nintendo.* The analysis degenerated from there.

There was a tremendous crowding onto this bus until all the seats were filled and the aisle was packed with luggage, with baskets and bags piled waist high, and then more people came in and assumed positions of repose on top of the baskets and bags in the aisle. The woman sitting next to me was becoming concerned about something inside her straw basket. She was pulling out clothes, some food, two green rubber boots, and finally she pulled out a woven grass nest with eggs inside, broken and dripping. She showed me the broken and dripping eggs. Her English was very heavily accented, hard for me to understand, but we exchanged a few pleasantries. When I told her my pocket had just been picked, she said, "Ah, that is bad! There are many thieves in this place!"

As a white light of dawn drew open the city, the bus turned and circled and at last left Kampala.

A sign at the very front of the bus informed everyone that Labn Singh Harnam Singh, Ltd., of Nairobi, Kenya, had built it. The bus was built by Asians, I concluded, and then I began to think it was built *for* Asians, since my legs didn't fit, nor did the legs of any of the Africans on the bus. Or perhaps this was the Asians' revenge for terrible persecution during the Amin era in Uganda. The seats were placed just about two inches too close together, so that it was impossible to sit with your legs forward. No matter how well you sat and how conscientiously you pressed your trim buttocks into the cushion behind you, your legs and knees could not be pointed directly forward. We were all forced to sit twisted and angled and still, nonetheless, crushed into the steel back of the seat before us. I opened up my *Gulliver*, turned to page 234, and tried to beam myself up into the Country of the Houyhnhnms.

The main highway west out of Kampala was a two-lane tarmac affair that within a few miles became a rutted dirt track that the bus, amazingly, navigated. Every hour or so, the bus pulled into a huddle of mud houses or a row of connected shops, stucco with tin roofs, and dropped off and picked up passengers. Simultaneously, people converged on the bus and tried to sell things: chickens, baskets full of fried and baked treats, drinks, bananas, pieces of pineapple. If the stop was on level ground, the engine of the bus would be left running. If the stop was on a hill, the driver would turn off the engine and perhaps even get off himself and buy a soft drink or a pastry. Then, when it was time to go, the driver would allow the bus to roll backward down the hill and jump-start the engine. The conductor would rap out *ready-aye-ready* on the door, the engine was wracked into gear, and we were off.

I read my book. *Gulliver's Travels* is a children's book, of course. Lemuel Gulliver travels to these fantastic and delightful imaginary places. Grown-ups, if they want to appreciate it, have to read the notes—*Gulliver's Travels* is also a satire of English and European politics and life, and the notes will help you figure that out. It works, as all satire does, I expect, by holding the mirror up to human pretension, purpose, and politics. *Gulliver's Travels* was at least partly a looking glass of eighteenth-century British politics—the book was first published anonymously in 1726—so the original subject we now see reflected is partly faded from most people's perceptions. You need the notes, as I said. Notes will tell you that, for instance, the pompous and miniscule Emperor of Lilliput, "Delight and Terror of the Universe," strongly resembles King George I. The tiny, treacherous Lord High Treasurer Flimnap is Walpole. And the "King's cushion" saving Flimnap's life when he falls while trying to dance on a tightrope, must be the Duchess of Kendal, who used her influence as unofficial bed warmer for George I to engineer Walpole's return to government office in 1721.

By and large, A represents B in *Gulliver's Travels*.

Book 4 doesn't work that way, however. Here, Gulliver wanders into a land ruled by talking, rational horses who call themselves Houyhnhnms—the name is supposed to sound like the neighing or whinnying of a horse. And while the horses are running the country, who do you suppose is being kept in the barn and, when a Houyhnhnm requires transportation, hitched to the buggy? The Yahoos. Yahoos look quite like people—in a disconcerting fashion, since they are naked, filthy, disgusting, and when not domesticated in the stables can be found wild in the trees.

Gulliver's antipathy increases considerably when these creatures, obviously shocked at the sight of him, approach. They recognize—he doesn't—that Gulliver is a Yahoo, too, or at least looks like one. But Gulliver with utter revulsion strikes one with the flat side of his sword. "When the Beast felt the Smart, he drew back, and roared so loud, that a Herd of at least forty came flocking about me from the next Field, howling and making odious Faces." Finally, the Yahoos climb into the trees and shit on Gulliver. By pressing close to the trunk of one tree he is able to escape the bulk of this battery, although in the end he has been "almost stifled with the Filth."

What do the Yahoos represent, in book 4? Are they really humans: an overrated species that would look most at home squatting in the trees and tossing excrement bombs? Perhaps. But if so, what do the Houyhnhnms represent? Humans only as we imagine ourselves—*animal rationale*—rational animal? Perhaps. If so, is that an ideal? Should humans be Houyhnhnms? I think not. The Houyhnhnms are clean, quiet, rational, and productive . . . in a horsey fashion. But their cleanliness and complete rationality make them emotionless. They have no feelings, no resonance. They're boring. They could be robots or equoids. Additionally, they rule the land and each other with a chilling efficiency. They're superrational, irrationally rational. They're cold. They would make the trains run on time, if they had trains. Anyway, that's what I like about book 4: It defies simplistic analysis.

But why does Gulliver find the Yahoos so utterly disgusting? "I never beheld in all my Travels so disagreeable an Animal, or one against which I naturally conceived so strong an Antipathy." Why? The answer seems as obvious as Freud: They remind him too much of himself. Maybe the Yahoos were like . . . Neanderthals?

I remembered an article I had read a few months earlier in *Discover* magazine, written by Jared Diamond, a physiologist at the UCLA Medical School. According to Diamond, humans and Neanderthals lived side by side in western Europe as recently as thirty-two thousand years ago. The Neanderthals looked somewhat like people but still different enough that any modern *Homo sapiens* would be alarmed to see one dressed in a business suit and walking down the street. They had long faces and low foreheads, heavily ridged brows, deeply set eyes, a protruding nose and upper jaw, a chinless lower jaw. Their bodies were very powerfully built, at the shoulders, in the arms and legs, in the hands. Although they stood slightly shorter than modern humans, Neanderthals weighed about 20 percent more, and their skulls could have held 10 percent more brain tissue. Neanderthals were relatively successful: a short time ago, a mere thirty-two thousand years, they were living in communities as far west as western Europe and Great Britain, north into northern Germany, as far east as Uzbekistan near the Afghan border.

Anatomically modern people appeared much earlier than thirty-two thousand years ago in Africa and the Near East, and modern people moved into Europe while Neanderthals still thrived there. The Neanderthals were distinctly bigger and considerably stronger than the modern humans, so why are humans now around and Neanderthals not? Diamond made a best guess, based on the evidence. Humans were physically weaker, but by then had developed their most powerful quality: language. With the ability to speak to each other– "Hey, sneak over there while his back is turned. I've got you covered from here"– humans had the capacity to overcome the Neanderthals.

I hope I'm not oversimplifying Diamond's impressive argument here. It was a case of genocide, or maybe species-o-cide, comparable, he wrote, to the current and ongoing human extermination of gorillas in Central Africa.

It was a long trip on that bouncing bus, and it had begun raining long before we passed through a flowing green-plant-and-red-earth land into tea plantation country and out to the Mountains of the Moon and the town of Fort Portal in a late afternoon drizzle. Fort Portal seemed bleak and very small indeed for such a solid dot on the map. I saw no other buses, no cars, no taxis. I saw no hotels, and none of the people hanging around the small bus stop had ever heard of my next destination, which was, according to my tattered little sheet of instructions, Kanyawara.

I wandered around town. It would be dark in another hour, and the drizzle felt like it was about to turn into rain. But soon three young boys ran up, eager to help for the simple pleasure of helping a stranger, it seemed. They hadn't heard of Kanyawara, either, but they ran off and eventually ran back and began pulling me up the street to a butcher's shop and a man with a green car parked out front.

The man with the green car was friendly. His name was George, and he said he knew where Kanyawara was. That was in the Kibale Forest, where the research station was located. Was I going to do research? Was I a scientist? He said he was a taxi driver and his car was a taxi. He said he wasn't sure his car would make it all the way to Kanyawara on those roads, which were very muddy right now, but he was willing to try. He thought eight thousand shillings would be a fair price. I would have had much more than that had my pocket not been picked in Kampala, but now I could only patch together about six thousand shillings. We agreed on that as the price.

So I put my pack in the back of George's car and sat in front with George, whom I already liked and trusted. We drove out of town and passed onto a mud road that soon degenerated into deep puddles and slippery ruts. George told me that he had been educated in a mission school and that he worked as a driver and mechanic for the scientist Tom Butynski, who once ran a project at Kanyawara. Now he was trying to survive as a taxi driver, as I could see. George wanted to know why I was going out there, and I told him. He said there are many cases of AIDS in Uganda, and he wondered about AIDS in

America. I said that so far most AIDS cases in America seemed to be transmitted by dirty needles and homosexual contacts, although the pattern was apparently changing. All AIDS in Africa, he said, was transmitted heterosexually. "There is no homosexuality in Africa," he declared, reintroducing an idea I had already heard from other Africans. I mentioned that I had seen at least one very feminine-styled man, wearing chartreuse fingernail polish, in Tanzania. "Ah, yes, the Tanzanians are different. When they came into this country during the war, many people were very shocked by their practices." I said that, so far, and with the exception of one anonymous pickpocket in Kampala, I had found Ugandans to be supremely friendly and helpful to a fault. Why was that? "Our history in the past was very bad. We want people to forget. We want to erase it."

The roads became worse, and eventually our set of ruts disappeared into a shallow lake. George stopped the car. Before we had much time to consider what to do next, I saw in front of us a white shape plowing slowly through the lake and raising on either side dirty wings of water. It was a Land Rover, I soon realized, and as it emerged from the lake and wallowed out onto the mud, I saw that the driver was a mzungu. The Land Rover came up to us and stopped, and then I saw a painted sign on the door of the vehicle that said: "KIBALE FOREST PROJECT." The driver opened his window and asked if we needed help. He said he had just left Kanyawara and was going to return there after completing a small errand in town.

George's car could make it no farther, so I said goodbye to him and transferred myself and my pack into the Land Rover, which was driven by someone whose first name I've forgotten but whose last name was Einstein. "Any relation to Albert?" I inquired. He was Albert's grandson, a very agreeable young man working on some kind of village development project in the area, and within an hour he had completed his errand and we had floated, plowed, and slithered through enough mud to arrive (after dark) at a couple of small houses inside the Kibale Forest. A mzungu with a long, clean-shaven face and a bottle of beer in his hand walked down from one of the houses, bent sideways to look in past our muddy windshield, and declared: "My God, it's Dale Peterson!"

This was an Englishman emoting like an American, and his name was Richard Wrangham. He shook my hand with warm enthusiasm and offered me a hot meal and a cold beer, both of which I accepted gladly. They were having a party, celebrating a month of excellent chimp observations, Richard told me, and he introduced me to the crowd sitting on the front porch of this stucco, tin-roofed house: two Ugandan women, including a charmingly bashful teenager named Grace, about a half dozen Ugandan men including two slender young men named BJ and Peter, and one bearded mzungu named Kevin.

I quickly ate my hot meal, gulped my beer, and then joined the party, which was just about then turning into a wild dancing party. We danced to tapes of American rock and then Afro-pop, and since there were only two women among eight or nine men, we generally danced in a communal mass. But Grace the bashful teenager remained the center of attention, as a dancer, and after we had exhausted all the tapes of African and American music, someone hauled out the drums, and Grace draped a folded cloth around her hips and demonstrated a traditional African dance.

I enjoyed this completely. I felt in great spirits, happy to be there and to be taken care of.

The next morning, Kevin and I walked into the forest and, after some time, found a chimpanzee sitting in some branches of a tree. The chimp was a greenish shadowy clump inside green. This shadowy clump was high up, perhaps thirty-five feet, and as we stood and watched, it shifted and changed shape. We moved around on the ground to get a better look and finally arrived at a position where I could see the chimp more fully.

Kevin, after looking through binoculars, declared him to be a male. I looked through binoculars and saw this chimp sitting on a branch that swayed up and down with his weight. One leg was stretched out, and with the foot of that leg he held onto a second branch, slightly higher up. His right arm was stretched out and up, and with his right hand he grasped a branch above him. He scratched under that arm with his left hand, and the action of scratching caused his left elbow to jab back and forth.

We heard coughing. It sounded rough, hoarse, like a smoker's cough, and I recognized that the coughing came from another chimp, high in the trees somewhere. "When it rains a lot, they cough," Kevin said. We found the location of the cougher, and soon after that I began to realize that several chimps were sitting up there. We listened to their sounds, and gradually we began to sight them, or at least moving pieces of them, an arm, a hand.

We listened to a crashing sound in the lower leaves and vegetation, a sound of falling grenades, and Kevin said the chimps were defecating. We saw a couple of chimps very high up. Kevin waded through the vegetation to a place where we had heard the sounds. I came over to see what he was doing. "We collect the dung to see what's in it," he said. "So now we can find out what they've been eating this last day and a half that we haven't seen them."

Kevin had reddish hair, and he wore green knee-high boots and olive pants that had expandable pockets. He pulled some plastic bags out of one of those pockets and then stooped over, looking for the dung. I stooped over, looking also. But we couldn't find anything. "This is terrible," Kevin muttered after a while. "It should be here." We listened to the whunk whunk whunk whunk whunk whunk of a hornbill casting off and wingbeating the air, and then we heard more grenades falling through the vegetation just several yards away. But we stayed in the lower vegetation right there, still stooped over and looking. After we had searched the ground for some time, Kevin said, "Incredible, isn't it, how shit can get away from you."

About a minute later, I heard a crash overhead, followed by a light splattering of water off wet leaves and then a heavier splattering into my hair, my shoulders, my shirt, even my hands. I smelled a rich, barnyard smell, and then I looked at splats of yellow brown on my hands and felt an interesting grit in my hair.

"Maybe they have diarrhea," I said. "That would explain why it's disappearing."

But Kevin had in the meantime walked over to a different cluster of vegetation. "Ah, found it!" he exclaimed, having tracked down his turd at last. I came over to see. It looked rather like a small baked potato, yellowish and slightly squashed.

Kevin carefully placed the potato in one of his plastic bags, and then labeled the bag. Then he had me place the labeled bag inside a small maroon pack on his back. "There must be more right around here," he said. He stooped over to continue looking, and I stooped over, too. We heard more falling grenades and some small rainstorms, too, and all of a sudden a small rainstorm cascaded onto my back and my head. "Hey!" Kevin said. "You're being urinated upon." I stood back and looked up to sight the source, but all I could see above me were swaying leaves and branches and little moving speckles of sky. Just then another rainstorm splashed down and into my face. *Yahoo!* I thought.

We continued moving around in that area and soon had sighted a total of nine chimps. We found one mother chimp and her very young juvenile in a nest. The nest looked like a giant bird's nest, and the mother must have been lolling back in it. Most of the time all I could see was the back of her head and one hand casually stretched out and plucking leaves slowly, a relaxed fiddling. Her infant clambered around in the branches and leaves at the edge of this nest.

Kevin said these chimps were habituated to human observers, but only mildly so. They were still easily disturbed. "Don't point," he said. "It bothers them."

Not far from where we stood there was a gigantic fig tree, arching very high up with a vast networked dome of limbs and branches. We observed an estrous female gradually moving through the trees toward and then into the lower reaches of that fig tree. Her name was Jolly, Kevin said, and I saw that her bottom was swollen into a big pink doughnut. This pink signal of sexual availability would help explain why at least two adult males with erections had been hanging around the general area. They, too, along with some other chimps, were slowly gravitating toward the fig tree. One of the erections was "slimy," as Kevin expressed it, and he said he thought perhaps that chimp had already mated with Jolly. The second male moved into a tree near the fig tree and then sat by himself with a big erection between his legs and a rather forlorn expression on his face. He sat with knees up, arms on his knees and crossed at the wrists, and chin resting on his wrists.

Then we saw a shadow, some moving arms and legs, and a third adult male appeared up in the leaves. Kevin said that chimp's name was Johnny. "He's coming this way. He might be interested in Jolly."

Johnny moved through the trees until he was sitting almost directly above us, sometimes looking down at us but more often, it seemed, looking in the direction of Jolly. Johnny had a big erection, too.

It was a quiet drama, a game of meaningful looks and subtle gestures—shattered by the high and noisy entrance of a fourth male, a very large one, who suddenly appeared from somewhere in the highest reaches of the fig tree. He climbed across outer branches on all fours until, reaching a broad main branch, he stood upright on his hind legs. The hair on his shoulders, neck, and back bristled, so that he appeared absurdly big and bulked up, like a weight lifter, and the chimp swaggered down that limb on his two legs, steadying himself as he walked by reaching with his hands into some upper branches. Then he exploded into a burst of hoots and brays, faster and louder, climaxing finally into a chilling series of screams. At about forty feet above the ground, this ape jumped onto another main limb and then leaped into a tree where a young female bystander had been situated. She screamed and moved into another spot in another tree. Other chimps chimed in, screaming, grunting, moaning, while the big chimp moved into an area of branches where hopeful Johnny was sitting with his hopeful erection. The two males did nothing—no fight or physical contact—but poor Johnny turned aside while the carrot between his legs turned into a mushroom. The big guy then climbed back toward estrous Jolly, and they mated.

The big male was named Stockey, Kevin told me. Perhaps half an hour later, another huge male appeared on the scene. This was a large body walking four-legged with a sure pace across a high, swaying branch bridge into the dome of the giant fig tree. His name was Stout, and after extended preliminaries he also mated with Jolly. They were very high in the fig tree, then, perhaps seventy feet above the ground, and their liaison was quick and vigorous.

Soon after Stout and Jolly mated, a British ornithologist appeared from out of nowhere, wandered beneath the fig tree, and introduced himself as Miles. "I'm watching birds," he said modestly.

His two companions showed up behind him, and all three of them had boyish faces, floppy canvas hats, and binoculars strung around their necks. Kevin said, "You just missed all the sex. There's been a lot of it in the last hour."

"Yes," one of them replied quietly, "we thought we'd wait until it was over."

Another day Kevin and I, along with BJ—his full name was Joseph Basigara—and Peter Tuhairwe, followed four or five wandering chimpanzees through the forest. BJ was actually the best chimp tracker and observer of all, and he possessed a good-humored charm and verve. He had curly eyelashes and a few hairs on his chin, and he wore a red baseball cap. Peter wore a blue baseball cap.

BJ said: "I was almost bitten by a dog this morning. You know, I was visiting someone's house this morning, and I sneezed. A dog came running, and he was very serious. If you run, the dog thinks you are a bad-doer. I walked very slowly. The dog was standing still with his hind legs, and whenever he barked he jumped with his front legs." BJ demonstrated a dog jumping with only his front legs. He said: "Bark. Bark. Bark. Bark."

Peter said that he thought all Americans were rich. They all have cars. Kevin and I came out on opposite sides of this particular discussion. Kevin argued that, in spite of superficial appearances, some Americans are rich and some aren't. I said I thought just about all Americans are rich—from an African perspective.

The chimps decided to disappear, and we hacked our way after them into some thorny thicket until we came to a trail. The trail turned into a tunnel, green and interrupted with mossy logs. Then it started to rain, and we hacked into brush again and somehow entered a swamp. We found elephant footprints in the mud, and then we discovered a meandering rivulet, muddy and opaque, that was blocking our further progress. The rivulet was just wide enough to discourage a casual leap, and when we plumbed its depth with a stick, we found it to be more than waist deep.

Kevin swung across, using an upper branch. BJ and Peter risked leaps and just made it. I pushed a clump of saplings over to create a sagging, temporary bridge, and gingerly hopped across. *Life must be easier when you have long fingers and strong thumbs on your feet,* I thought. By this time, the chimps were absolutely gone, and I don't think Kevin or either of the Ugandans knew quite where we were, except inside a swamp. We wandered and pushed and hacked our way deeper until we became stuck inside a very dense thicket of brush and vines and thorns and wallows and fishbowl-sized elephant footprints. We sat down to rest and eat some lunch. "This is what I imagined Africa would be like," Kevin said as he and I ate a couple of boiled eggs.

I thought about that. For me this was less Africa, more just a stinky, muddy hole somewhere, anywhere in the world, with a lot of pesky bugs.

After another hour, we squeezed our way out of the swamp and found a trail, which we followed. We came across a large piece of chimp dung on the trail. All four of us carefully examined it. It seemed to have whole figs in it.

"That's strange," Kevin said. "Why should a chimp swallow a fig whole?" We wrapped the dung and put it inside Kevin's pack.

Later that day, we heard a sound of chopping. We walked very, very quietly along the trail, moving closer to the sound. After a few minutes, the chopping stopped, and then I saw something moving very fast and the color blue flickering away behind tree trunks and vines. It was a poacher, Kevin said. Peter said: "They are trying to get out honey."

There was a small billowing column of smoke, and, after chasing the poacher's vibrations and then returning, out of breath, to the smoke, we found a small fire at the base of a tree. There was a half-chopped hole in the side of the tree, and a few bees languidly turned figure eights around the hole. "African bees," Kevin said. "Stay away: They can be pretty aggressive."

The poacher had been after honey in the hive. I said to Kevin that I didn't see what was so harmful about that. "They may seem innocuous," Kevin said, "but they're not. People who go into this forest to get honey, or anything else, come to view the whole place as an open resource. These are the people who become most familiar with the forest. Someone wants a chimp, they'll be the ones to get it."

Both Richard and Kevin were anthropologists, and I was glad to be in Africa among experts. I especially wanted to talk to a real anthropologist about the Neanderthals. I wanted to ask someone about that article I had read.

Kevin and I sat on the porch one evening, drank tea, and discussed Neanderthals while a kerosene lamp hissed, flickered, and slowly faded. I tried to recall the details of the article: The Neanderthals never developed language. Language could have made the crucial distinction, the single factor that allowed *Homo sapiens* to take over and to eternally smash the running dog Neanderthals. But Kevin said he wasn't so sure about the sequence of events. He thought that even though there was no archaeological evidence of Neanderthals after about 30,000 B.C. or so, they still could have been driven into isolated enclaves in Europe and survived there. They may have quietly mixed and matched with *Homo sapiens.*

Kevin said he thought the Neanderthals might have been blue-eyed and blond-haired, since, after all, they had adapted to a northern climate. It was true, he said, that their features must have been very distinctive, but he remembered one woman in one of his anthropology classes in graduate school who had a classic Neanderthal face.

But the brow ridge, I countered. The Neanderthals had a brow ridge! That for me would be the most distinctive feature. Markedly different from the flat brow of a human. So chimp-like! How could you avoid noticing the difference? "You obviously haven't observed this," Kevin said quietly. "People tend not to. I have a brow ridge."

Well, he did. In the upcast light of the kerosene lantern, its prominence was accentuated by a shivering, shadowy bar.

Every morning, Kevin would unscrew the brush top of a bottle of clear nail polish. Richard, bleary at the eyes and half naked, would turn around and wait patiently for Kevin to paint clear nail polish onto the pimples on his back and shoulders and arms.

Kevin and Richard looked like two chimps grooming.

The female mango fly lays her eggs in damp things, including damp clothing. That's why anything you wash at Kibale should be hung out to dry in the sunlight and, if possible, pressed with a hot iron. But if the female mango fly succeeds in laying eggs in your damp shirt or underwear, and if those eggs successfully hatch, little white worms emerge. The little white worms burrow into your skin and then undergo their ordinary transmogrification, nourished by the nutrients of your flesh, expanding there as bigger and bigger pimples until they become vigorous young mango flies. At last, fully adult, they crawl out of your skin, spread their wings, and then fly away, looking for damp shirts and damp underwear to lay their eggs in.

"What do adult mango flies look like?" I asked.

Neither Kevin nor Richard knew. There was one good way to find out. Let one of those little white worms grow into an adult under your skin. This was a sacrifice for science Richard was unwilling to make, however. He wanted to pop the little white worms out before they metamorphosed into adults. But the worms stayed inside their burrows very tenaciously while they were alive. So Kevin was killing the worms by painting fingernail polish over the holes where they had entered Richard's skin. The entry holes doubled as breathing holes for the worms, so painting them over suffocated the worms. Then all you had to do was squeeze the pimple until the dead white worm in the middle popped out. It was important to squeeze carefully, however, since if you merely crushed the worm inside it would fester.

I started to notice pimples on my arms, and looking in the mirror, I could also see them on my neck and back. This was just around the time a U.S. embassy employee named Steve arrived at Kibale. Steve was a beetle person with an interest in birds and a degree in forestry from a college in Kansas, and he spent time talking bugs and birds with Richard. Steve told me he had come to Kenya with the Peace Corps during the 1960s and then married a Somali woman and decided to stay in Africa. I said I knew someone who was in the Peace Corps in Kenya during that time: John McClure. Steve said he may have heard of John McClure, but many of the Peace Corps people in his group died. Several were killed in traffic accidents.

Richard and I were planning to leave Uganda at the same time, and Steve consented to drive us out from Kibale to Entebbe in his jeep. The drive took most of a day, and toward the end of the day the three of us stopped at the house in Entebbe of a British botanist Richard knew. Richard said he thought Steve could have a shower there, and he expected I could stay for the night. The botanist, Dr. Ian, wore heavy-framed glasses in front of hedgerow eyebrows.

Richard introduced us and mentioned that Steve was desperate for a shower. Dr. Ian consented. "Be careful with the water. We've not much, you know."

We had tea. During tea, as our conversational craft hovered inside a lull, Richard said: "We wondered if perhaps Dale might stay the night here."

Dr. Ian stretched two long, slender arms over his head and paused, as if thinking. At last he concluded: "Yes. It might be possible. Could be. Yes. Perhaps. It might be done. Possibly."

That may have been the British version of assent. Nothing more was said on the subject.

In the morning, Richard and I painted and popped each other's mango fly worms. Then we took a plane to Nairobi, where I stayed overnight at the Boulevard Hotel.

Next day, I caught a long flight to London and then another one back home to Boston, where I soon noticed an ache of the head and a weakness of the body. Cerebral malaria, my doctor said, and I spent four days in a hospital bed with quinine dripping from a bottle down a plastic tube into my arm.

10

Genius in the Jungle

An exploring expedition is daily exposed to a succession of accidents, any one of which might be fatal to its further progress. The cattle at any time may stray, die, or be stolen; water may not be reached, and they may perish; one or more of the men may become seriously ill, or the party may be attacked by natives. Hence the success of the expedition depends on a chain of eventualities, each link of which must be a success; for if one link fails, at that point, there must be an end of further advance. It is therefore well, especially at the outset of a long journey, not to go hurriedly to work, nor to push forward too thoughtlessly.

—Francis Dalton, *The Art of Travel*

It was dark by the time my plane settled onto the tarmac of a very small airport serving Banjul, capital of Gambia, West Africa, and I entered a hot, dry night thick with the sound of crickets. I was tired but happy to see, as I shuffled through the passport control line and into an open-sided baggage and customs pavilion, a young African holding up a sign with my name on it. I made myself known to the African, who pulled me out of the line and over to a wire fence beyond the edge of the pavilion. Cars were parked on the other side of the fence. Behind the cars were trees, high grass, and a black sky, and beside the cars were people. One of the people was a short woman dressed in gypsy colors, with long, wavy dark hair—Janis Carter.

My pack had disappeared, but finally someone found it. A customs officer drew a small circle on it with white chalk, and I walked through a gate.

I tossed my pack into the back of Janis's venerable car and sat in front. She started the car, and we drove away from the airport along a rough, dark road. Was I hungry? Would I like a Chinese meal?

I was very pleased to see Janis, whose letters had suggested some of the uncertainties and difficulties of meeting me there, and I was at that point happy to be taken care of. "I'm glad you could make it to the airport," I said.

She drove for a while in silence. Then she said, "I don't have visitors very often. I screen visitors carefully. For one thing, I'm real reclusive and don't like to talk to people. And then, also, visitors are a pain."

"How about Hippelwaithe? Was he a pain?" I said, referring to a British journalist who had once come to Gambia and written about Janis and the chimpanzee project there.

"Brian Hippelwaithe! Do you know him?"

"Not personally. I've never met him. Never spoken to him. But I was fascinated by his book."

"Hippelwaithe! God!" she said.

The car bounced along noisily, and I enjoyed the cool evening air passing through our open windows.

We came into town, dirt roads and wood fences, and a sign that said:

MY BAR. BASS SOUND SYSTEM BLASTING.

We parked in front of a modest Chinese restaurant with tables outdoors and paper lanterns strung overhead, walked in, ordered beer, tea, and a meal of shrimp fried rice. Dinner was served. As we began consuming the shrimp fried rice, I said: "Tell me about Lucy."

I had spent some time during the previous several months (back in the States) travelling around to look at chimps in cages—laboratories, zoos, circuses, shows, photographic studios, and backyards. In Tarpon Springs, Florida, I met a woman named Mae Noell, who with her late husband, Bob, had for many years run an itinerant carnival show featuring wrestling chimps. Chimps (wearing leather muzzles and boxing gloves) would wrestle with any people who dared enter the ring.

People always lost, of course, usually after the apes had humiliated them by pulling down their pants. After retiring from the carnival business, the Noells settled down in Tarpon Springs to run a small roadside zoo, Noell's Ark Chimp Farm, with a collection of apes that eventually grew to about two dozen chimpanzees, plus some orangutans and gorillas.

Mae told me that the famous talking chimp, Lucy, was born in her zoo, in 1964, then sent when she was two days old out to Oklahoma. I had already read about Lucy in Maurice Temerlin's book *Lucy: Growing Up Human*. Maurice Temerlin was a psychotherapist sometimes associated with the University of Oklahoma, who adopted Lucy as an infant and, as an extended experiment, raised the chimp entirely as a human child, providing her with two loving parents, her own pet dog, pet cat, baby-sitters, toys, clothes, bed, bedroom, TV, magazines, human food, silverware and dishes at the table, access to the refrigerator, and, when she was old enough—three years, in Temerlin's judgement—cocktails before dinner. Like several other chimps in the United States at that time, she learned American Sign Language, the language taught in American schools for the deaf. But Lucy was unique. Not only had she learned to speak in sign language, manipulating a vocabulary of some 120 word-signs to form intelligible remarks about the world around her, she also—and she alone—had been raised a human, to act human and to think of herself as part of a human family. She spent mornings playing with toys or people or her pets, and continuing her language lessons; afternoons fishing in the pond with Maurice or sitting on her living room couch, leafing through a favorite magazine; evenings in front of the TV or having an extra drink or two.

Later, as Lucy began growing up, things changed. Language-using apes no longer intrigued the scientific world. Maurice Temerlin and his wife, Jane, decided to end their experiment in humanizing Lucy, and so she was sent, accompanied by a human companion (Janis Carter, one of her former caretakers), to a chimpanzee rehabilitation project on the Baboon Islands of the River Gambia, in Gambia, West Africa, returning to a wild existence she had never known.

I had been planning the second leg of my Chimpanzee Travels, this time stepping into West and Central Africa. As my plans materialized, it became clear I might begin with a brief trip to the Baboon Islands of Gambia to learn more about the chimpanzee rehabilitation project sponsored by the government and managed with Janis's help. I was going to learn about the project. Only gradually did I begin to wonder, and then wonder increasingly, about Lucy, the chimp made human then turned back into a chimp. . . .

One thing that especially intrigued me about the story of Lucy was the character of her psychotherapist "father," Maurice Temerlin. Temerlin begins his book on Lucy with a promise to tell "my daughter's story," and his own, "with complete candor, regardless of how embarrassing to me it might be."

"Complete" is probably impossible, but I generally admire the degree of candor Temerlin achieves. He describes his success and failures with Lucy; reveals some potentially embarassing episodes, such as the time Lucy locked him out of the house when he was naked; considers with some apparent honesty his own changing relationships with his wife, Jane, and his son, Steve. Recognizing that this is more than merely a story of his new and exotic pet, Temerlin additionally details at some length the psychosexual development of Lucy. How she, reaching pubescence, began masturbating to the pictures of naked men in *Playgirl* magazine, squatting over them, scratching their penises with her fingernail, the various techniques she used for masturbating with the hose of their Montgomery Ward vacuum cleaner. "She runs it all over her body, chuckling with great delight, and puts it into her mouth and then onto her genitals, then reverses the sequence. The particular vacuum cleaner we have can be changed by a switch from suction to blowing. Lucy will sometimes blow air into her mouth or onto her genitals, and then reverse the machine, going from blowing to suction sensations at both orifices." The book even includes five photographs of Lucy interacting with said machine.

All very interesting. Well and good. But Temerlin's candor goes further. Maurice, we learn, masturbated in front of Lucy—in the interests of science, of course. Then, experimentally, he engaged in mutual masturbation with his wife in front of Lucy. Lucy didn't like it.

Temerlin ends his book declaring that the story is not ended. At that time (the book was published in 1975), the Temerlins had raised Lucy as a child for ten years. Lucy had become Maurice's "daughter." Now, although he and wife were "still committed" to the welfare of their "darling, virginal daughter," they also wanted "to live normal lives." So the last chapter discusses some of the options they considered for Lucy's future.

Finally, of course, Maurice and Jane Temerlin sent Lucy to a West African forest with the implied message: Stop being a civilized person, start being a wild ape. What I wanted to know was, why? Maurice

Temerlin remains, for me, a big mystery. I still can't figure out whether I like or dislike, admire or despise him. Was he insensitive? Was he uninformed? Was he cruel? Or did he and and his spouse do a brave and difficult thing in an imperfect world? What did it mean to nail Lucy, educated Lucy, talking Lucy, civilized Lucy, genius Lucy, into a box and mail her off to the woods?

"Lucy?" Janis said.

"Yes. I'm fascinated by her."

"You didn't say you were interested in Lucy in your letter," she said. "I thought you wanted to write a book about conservation."

"I do. But I think the story of Lucy might still fit in. I mean, it has to do with peoples' perceptions of chimps. Are chimps nearly human or are they just wild animals? Lucy became a bit of both. Didn't she?"

"You said you were writing about conservation."

"Oh. Well. But you know, I've heard so many strange things about what went on during the early years at Oklahoma, but a lot of people don't want to talk. One person even hung up on me. I met Mae Noell, who owned Lucy's mother. She told me she sent Lucy as a two-day-old baby out to Oklahoma with an agreement—a written agreement that she still has somewhere—that Lucy would be returned once the experiment was over. Why wasn't she returned?"

It was an issue I might have imagined to be historical. Janis thought it gossip. "I don't see what the personalities of Oklahoma have to do with anything. I'm not interested in mudslinging. What happened at Oklahoma might be important if you were writing a novel, a mystery novel. That all happened a long time ago. It's another world, and I don't even care about it. I'm just interested in the welfare of individual chimps!"

I said other things, raised other questions, pushed too hard, and Janis got fed up. She thought I was after gossip about the Oklahoma days—maybe I was—and so, finally, she concluded this clumsy series of exchanges with: "I don't know, and I'm not interested."

We finished our Chinese meal in an awkward silence.

Janis dropped me off at a bed-and-breakfast place just outside of town. This place was run by a retired British couple who thought they would try the African life for a while. They said their son back in Britain managed a "leisure complex," which I assumed was not a debilitating neurosis.

Next morning Janis picked me up and transported me into the center of Banjul. Banjul has some paved roads, I imagine, but I don't recall seeing them. I remember deep ravine gutters on either side of dirt streets, stucco buildings and tin shacks. We picked up and delivered mail, stopped at the airlines office, bought some food at a market stall.

We drove out of town onto a paved road at last and into an arid land with bottle-shaped baobab trees and many small mosques. After a few miles, we came to a fence, a gate, and a small forest. This was the Abuko Nature Reserve, a few square miles of land where water—a spring, a stream—had nourished forest against desert. There were some government offices at the Abuko headquarters, and I needed to meet Dr. Camara, director of wildlife conservation, and gain his permission to visit the chimpanzee project on the Baboon Islands, closed to tourists. Dr. Camara kindly gave permission after we discussed my purposes. I also met the former director of wildlife conservation, Eddie Brewer. Eddie and his daughter, Stella, began the chimp rehabilitation project a quarter of a century ago, first in Senegal, and finally, after that failed, on the Baboon Islands in Gambia. Stella has since left Africa and taken up married life in some other part of the world.

Eddie Brewer is a big man with white hair and an open, hearty manner. He said that one time when Stella had begun the chimpanzee project in Niokolo Koba National Park, Senegal, she was trapped by flooding rivers during the rainy season. Six weeks passed. Seven weeks, eight weeks passed. After three months, Eddie became worried. He mentioned his concerns to a friend who happened to have a small private plane. They flew out in the plane, found Stella's camp, circled overhead until she came out of her hut, and dropped coins wrapped in a handkerchief with a note: "Are you all right?" She gestured thumbs-up. They dropped eggs—well-packed—tins of food, powdered milk. But Eddie was still concerned, so his friend said they would land the plane at an old airstrip on the other side of a river. The old airstrip was covered with ten-foot high elephant grass, but the friend slowly lowered his plane down until they were flying through the grass. They came to a rough halt right inside the grass. Grass was thickly packed into the engines' air intakes, and the heat of the engines started to cook the grass. They began pulling it out. But they couldn't see anything. Stella's camp was some distance away, and they were afraid it was cut off by a flooded river. Ten minutes passed, twenty minutes. Then they heard the engine of Stella's Land Rover. She had seen them disappear into the grass, and she plowed through until she found them. . . .

I would have chatted with Eddie Brewer for much longer, but Janis had several other errands in mind, so we left Abuko. We drove around town, stopping here and there, and then Janis pulled in front of the bed-and-breakfast place, where we sat for a while and talked. Janis was still amazed and irritated that I had come with a curiosity about Lucy's background in Oklahoma. She felt deceived. She thought Lucy's story might serve as a tool for conservation education if written about properly, but, she thought, if I were to write anything, my apparently gossipy approach would doom it. "I'm not going to tell you about Lucy—or my relationship with Lucy. That's private."

She said she might meet me for dinner that evening. But then again she might not.

In mid-afternoon, I received a note explaining that Janis wouldn't be able to have dinner with me. We would leave for the Baboon Islands at eight o'clock the next morning, the note said. It also said I could buy a decent dinner at the big tourist hotel across the street.

I went early to the restaurant, early by African standards anyhow, so there were only two other people in the place, a white couple, who sat on either side of a candle and stared into each other's eyes. This restaurant was kept very dark, and it had a dark blue decor with some African themes. But the piped-in music played a whole succession of easy listening, non-African themes: Muzakified Beatles and Mamas and Papas tunes, for example, and, amazingly, Frank Sinatra singing his blandest version of "Ol' Man River." Frank sang, "Here we work while the white folks play," and I paid a reasonable sum of money for an ordinary baked chicken. The bird, flat on her back, arrived inside a silver mausoleum on top of a wheeled cart. The cart was rolled up to my table, the mausoleum was opened, and the waiter—dressed formally with a stiff white collar, a miniature white bow tie—bowed slightly and waited for my response. *Oh, yes, a dead chicken,* I indicated with a nod. The chicken was moved to my plate. A second waiter with a stiff white collar and a miniature white bow tie brought out a bottle of wine inside a silver ice bucket, uncorked the bottle, poured a sample, waited for me to indicate yes or no. Then another waiter in the same kind of outfit rolled out another table on wheels. He lit a fire on the tabletop and cooked up a sauce right there next to my table. The sauce was poured on top of the chicken. After everything was properly cooked and served, I began eating. But every time I ate two or three bites of food, one of the waiters would appear from somewhere and nervously ask me how it was. Dessert came at last, but not before someone set fire to it. A sizzling package of blue flames.

Next day Janis showed up, her hair woven into a thick braid down her back, wearing Rayban sunglasses and a red T-shirt that said, "Only elephants should wear ivory." We set out for the Baboon Islands. We drove east on a straight and narrow road, past mosques and men dressed in white Muslim caps and beautiful blue and flowing ankle-length shirts, into the Sahel. Janis said the country was 97 percent Muslim, but they liked Americans. However, the European women who come to the country and lie around topless on the beaches and at the tourist hotel pools do offend many peoples' traditional modesty, she said. Much more offensive were shorts exposing bare legs.

Janis said there were forty-four chimps on the islands, including more than a dozen who were born there. There are five Baboon Islands, but only three of them have chimps—living in four social groups—because the other two islands are seasonally inundated. "Socially, all but one group is closed," she said. "The last group I don't even know for certain if we can squeeze another chimp in. It will be a risk, a high risk."

"When is a social group closed? How do you know?"

"When they're not receptive to a newcomer. When they're typically very aggressive when they see a new chimp. When the chimps are younger and still forming social bonds, it's possible to introduce more chimps, but later on they get very uptight."

There were very few cars on this road, and I noticed that potholes were filled with an amalgam of seashells and tar. We drove past a line of young boys, perhaps seven or eight young boys, all dressed in white robes with peaked white caps—looking for all the world like walking penises, I thought. "Circumcision days," Janis said of the boys. The boys are becoming men, she explained, and they go through secret ceremonies that last for weeks.

The land was flat, dry, and dusty, covered with brush and scattered trees and some woodland in places. There were young green trees and leafless older trees, and there were very big baobab trees looking like fat fractals. It could be that baobabs *are* fractals. People walked along the road, women wearing bright wraparound clothing, and dusty cattle walked through dust. Goats hung out behind stick fences and sometimes inside woven grass corrals next to square mud houses with conical thatch roofs. Sometimes I smelled wood smoke. But everything was tinged with the taste, feel, smell, and sight of dust, a powdery dust in the air. The dust was as fine as flour, and it created a white, ominous haze and an artificial horizon at five hundred yards. Cars on the road in front of us disappeared into the dust, and the dust penetrated my clothing and clung to my hair. It insinuated itself into my eyes, ears, and mouth, and I felt it settling onto my skin. "*Harmattan*," Janis said finally. "Dust blown from the desert."

After a few hours, we turned off the road and followed a complicated track through burned earth and blackened brush, through a couple of villages, until at last we came down into some trees and then a dock and a river. There was a boat at the dock. I looked into the river and saw its color was an olive green. On the far side of the river, I saw dense and deep green forest.

A Gambian met us there. He wore dark glasses and a wide-brimmed khaki hat. He had a broad, wide-chopped face, and Janis introduced him as Bruno Boubane. We emptied the car of our provisions and then pulled the car over into some brush. We loaded our provisions into the boat, Bruno started the motor, and then we set off upriver. Or was it downriver? It seemed up at the time, and I think it *was* up, but during the days I spent on and along the River Gambia I first thought I was confused and then I realized that the current changed directions every once in a while. This was a tidal river.

The river sparkled, and as our motor pulled us out into mid stream, the air rippled against us pleasantly. We were no longer in desert country, I thought, but rather traveling into tropical forest. Both sides of the river were deeply forested, with thick vine tangles and many high and low palms. "Hippos!" Janis shouted over the sound of the motor, and she pointed to the far side where I saw in embankment shadows two overturned glazed ceramic bowls. The bowls slowly rose and then slowly lowered. Bruno shut off the engine, and we drifted. Then we could hear the hippos mooing and snorting and belching. Their belches started underwater and rose to the surface, bursting at the surface as belch bubbles. Eventually we thought we saw about ten hippos there. Sometimes we could see their heads or a set of ears twitching. Janis said there used to be many hippos in the river, but they have been hunted out. She believed there were still thirty left.

What I thought was the far side of the river, she informed me, was one of the Baboon Islands.

Bruno started the engine again, and we pushed through the water past that island, and then we moved slowly alongside another very long island until we finally turned away from the second island and beached on the mainland. The boat was tethered at a metal dock. We stepped out and walked up a steep and muddy slope, through a brief tunnel of vines and bush and low-hanging branches into the camp: some adobe cabins with tin roofs and screened porches and windows, dusty, a sleepy clearing in a lazy afternoon shifting in shadows and light beneath trees, with a rustling of olive-yellow vervet monkeys in the trees and a meowing of two young cats playing and pouncing in the dust on the ground.

Janis directed me to a room and a bed in one of the cabins, and then Bruno disappeared in one direction and she in another. There seemed to be no one else in camp at the time, and so I walked down to the river and looked across the river to the island. I heard insects everywhere and hundreds of birds crying and calling. I could see birds flying into and out of the forest on the island, and then, after a long time, I heard murderous screams coming from the island. Chimps! I fetched some binoculars from my pack and scanned the shore, but I saw nothing.

Behind the camp was a wall—an escarpment—and late in the afternoon I climbed it. About fifty feet above the camp and the river I reached the top and then entered desert again, or near-desert, a scorched moonscape of pocked laterite and black cinders and burnt scrub stretching back flatly to a flat horizon. This was the Sahel again. But from there I could look down to the camp and down onto the river, observe its wide and graceful turns, the deep green forests and the long islands stretching in one direction and the other.

Back in camp, I met a young Frenchman of Italian extraction. He had a small, compact body, sun-bleached hair, the start of a beard, and a broad sweep of a mustache; he wore shorts and flipflops, a bicycler's cap, thick granny glasses, and a single small gold earring in his left ear. He introduced himself as Philippe Bussi, and he said he was a veterinarian who had worked for some time at the ape laboratory in Gabon. He was on his way back to France to figure out what to do next, but in the meanwhile, he was pausing to offer his services for a while, perhaps six months or a couple of years, to the chimpanzee rehabilitation project.

I had heard various rumors about the Gabonese ape laboratory. I was even hoping to visit it later, but in the meantime I was eager to hear more. Philippe told me they had about seventy chimps and a dozen gorillas there, as well as a hundred and fifty macaques and forty mandrills. He said they were all from Gabon and all either confiscated or taken from another lab. It was mainly financed by the French oil company ELF until 1988, when Gabon took over most of the responsibility.

I said I had heard that the laboratory was primarily established to study human fertility with the hope of improving it, using apes as guinea pigs, because someone in Gabon was worried that other Africans were reproducing faster than the Gabonese. When he was there, Philippe said, they were doing mostly behavioral studies, studying hormones, collecting sperm. "I was masturbating the chimps. Nothing bad at all. We weren't doing any bad thing at all." But when he left, there were discussions of moving into AIDS research. "They were speaking about building these facilities infected with the virus. They have been quite criticized I think for the AIDS research. Are you a vegetarian?"

"I haven't decided yet."

"Would you object to eat bush pig for dinner?"

"I think I'll wait until I see the bush pig."

Philippe realized it could be controversial to eat wild animal meat at a wild animal sanctuary, but he was hungry for meat. A bush pig had been killed locally, and he had bought some of the meat. Philippe was supposed to take care of me, it turned out, and that included cooking my meals over the portable gas stove in his cabin. So that evening I did try bush pig meat, but only little pieces of it. I decided I would be a vegetarian.

My Chimpanzee Travels were eventually going to head south and east, into Gabon and Congo and the cities of Libreville, Brazzaville, and Pointe-Noire. Philippe had spent some time traveling around down there. He warned me that it would be expensive. "Brazzaville is the third most expensive city in the world," he said, "right behind Tokyo and Kyoto, I think," he said. "Libreville is fourth most expensive, I think."

Philippe said I should find Madame LeRoi of Brazzaville, the gorilla woman. "In three years she received forty-six gorillas. She lost most of them. One of my friends told me she received the gorillas after people in Pointe-Noire. People say that while she's doing a good job, she's kind of mad about gorillas. She cannot see one in bad shape without cracking." He said that I should look for ape smugglers in

Pointe-Noire. "Pointe-Noire used to sell chimps and gorillas, especially to boats from Eastern ports. One year ago, I was there and still heard about it. I had friends who saw them trying to sell them—chimps and gorillas."

We listened to a tape of Van Morrison, and then it was late. Philippe lent me his flashlight for the short walk back to my cabin. "When you go out at night," he said, "you must carry a torch. We have many snakes. You need to see where you are going."

My room was screened all around, with a screen ceiling overhead and mosquito netting tied from the ceiling and cast over the bed. I climbed under the mosquito netting, tucked its edges in under the mattress, used another piece of mosquito netting for a sheet, and then went to sleep. Everything was dusty in that room, but I didn't realize how dusty until I woke up in the middle of the night with a fine silt settling down into my eyes, my mouth, my nose, my hair, and in general my whole body. I woke up gradually, and sleepily I began to wonder what had caused the sudden dust storm over my head. Something. Something was moving somewhere in the darkness directly above me. I could hear it moving. Slowly it moved. Then it didn't move. I knew it was real, but then I didn't. Perhaps I'd been dreaming. Then the thing moved again. Something *was* up there! I remembered the warning: *When you go out at night, you must carry a torch. We have many snakes. You need to see where you are going.* Slowly, I reached my arm outside of the mosquito netting. Slowly, carefully, quietly I pawed at the dark floor where I had left the flashlight before going to sleep. I found the flashlight, slowly brought it back into bed, and ever so carefully, without a sound and without turning on the light, I aimed it toward the source of the noise overhead. Then I flicked on the beam of light. Ah! Something was up there, I could see. Ah, it was an animal, a small mammal. I saw fur, a body, legs.

A cat had crawled onto the top of the screen that served as a ceiling for my room and she was now lying curled up above my bed, trying to get some sleep. With the flashlight, I jabbed at the underside of the screen—a whole avalanche of dust suddenly dropped out of the screen into my face—and dislodged the sleepy cat, who very, very reluctantly walked and then bounded away somewhere, and I, choking, coughing, sneezing, spitting, cursing, imagined it might be possible to go back to sleep.

•   •   •

Next morning, Janis showed up, and Philippe cooked breakfast for the three of us. I asked Janis if she thought chimpanzees were intelligent. "I don't like the term," she said. "It's too human-centered. All animals are highly intelligent in their given environments. You mean in terms of cognitive functions? Well, yes."

But then she left, disappeared somewhere—"Work to do," she said. That was about all I saw of Janis for the rest of the day.

After breakfast, Philippe and I went out in a boat to find the chimps. Philippe said there were six chimps on the small island, ten on the middle island, and twenty-eight, in two social groups, on the large island. In the river, he said, there are manatees, crocs, and epos. "Not a lot of them left—the crocs. I saw a big one four months ago, four meters long."

That was interesting, but I couldn't figure out what epos were. Epos? A few minutes later Philippe half stood up in the boat, pointed, and shouted out: "Epos!" A dozen hippos floated in a social conglomeration, only ears and eyes and the tops of their heads above water, their eyes coming to attention as we drew closer, their ears flickering.

We motored alongside one very long island, edged by palms and filled with vines. There was a muddy rim at the water's edge, and the island emitted the noises of birds and insects. The island included a big swamp, Philippe said. "There's a few chimp nests you can see," he said. "There's a nest there, a nest there. But now they just stay in the sun. They don't make nests too much."

Philippe cut the motor. We drifted. "Usually they come when they hear the boat," he said. "All the young chimpanzees here: ten chimpanzees. But two females have babies. But there's no real dominant male. There's few males about eleven, twelve, but no one is having the dominance now. There is no one showing a strong character right now. So now we are introducing chimp one month ago on this island. This is the only island where we can still make introduce chimpanzee."

We drifted toward a short dock leading to a red and white steel cage and a red and white danger sign: the provisioning area, where they tossed food to the chimps. Not enough food to keep them dependent on the source, but enough to tempt them to show themselves, so they could be monitored.

But no chimps were there. Philippe lit a cigarette. "Freddie! Freddie! Freddie!" he called. "Tina! Tina!"

We waited. "When it's very windy like that, if you are on the other side of the island, you can't hear a thing," Philippe said, cigarette dangling from his lips. He took the cigarette out and started making chimp hoots. But there was no answer, only the lapping of the water and the soft coo-hooting of a wood dove, like a faint echo.

"Freddie! Hooo hooo hooooo!!!!"

We sighted a pied kingfisher.

But eventually Freddie galloped out of the forest, slapping the ground, hair raised on his shoulders, screaming and screaming, hooting, drumming on the ground. He climbed down the bank and then sat down on a huge driftwood log, caught on the bank at the river's edge. He sat with his knees up, elbows resting on knees, and watched us with a quiet and thoughtful expression on his face. An older female—it was Tina, Philippe said—came slowly out after that, followed by a young male, and she climbed down and sat on the log not very far from Freddie. "The young male is Tez," Philippe said, "and he is the son of Tina, born on the island." Two other females, Emma and Kirsten, appeared out of the vegetation now, followed by Jan. Freddie became agitated. He began hooting. The hair on his back and shoulders bristled, and he stood up and chased Tina and Emma back into the underbrush. "They're not used to seeing us when the river is low, and when they don't get any food, they get upset," Philippe said.

He started up the motor and we plowed off, into the center of the river, and finally turned into a minor channel off the mainland, where there were swarms of tsetse flies, a swampy smell, and milky green water. We saw palms with vines dropping down at the river's edge, some flowers, and a goliath heron, tall, with stilt legs and a periscope neck, walking a loping walk.

We beached the boat and climbed up the escarpment onto a windy hilltop, where we could look with binoculars down into the river sparkling below and at the islands, and see mist rising from the channel on the far side of the islands. We saw a fish eagle perched at the peak of an isolated palm, looking regal, and in the river we saw two submerged brownish shapes that must have been epos, a mother and her offspring probably. The hill we stood on was covered with dry, yellow grass, and some yellowed, scrabbly trees. Then we saw two baboons running, looking over their shoulders and cough-barking. Pretty soon we recognized a whole troop of baboons scattered across the hillside, hidden and then emerging. They had brown fur with an olive sheen, and they ran like dogs. "Usually there's a big group, sixty. There are baboons everywhere," Philippe said. "They get to be quite big and are afraid of nothing. Gambians don't like them at all. Baboons they are good swimmers. When there is no food on the mainland, they swim to the islands. They are competitors with the chimps for food."

After dinner that evening, I went out with Boiro. Boiro was slender and very dark, with fine features, a sweet smile, decorative scars on his cheeks, a soft, minor mustache on his upper lip, and matted hair beneath a black leather cap. Boiro Samba was his name in French; the Gambian version of Boiro was Buwaro. He is a Fulani from Senegal, I learned, and like many Africans he is a linguist. He speaks Mandinka, Fula, Wollof, Jolla, French, and English.

We took the boat out, along the river through warm air and a smell of wood smoke. I sat at the bow and dangled my feet over the front. The air trembled the laces of my sneakers. At the edges of the river, now, baobab trees, entirely black in the dusky light, stretched out branches and twigs in a perfect rigor mortis. An eagle circled overhead, gray with white.

We docked the boat at a small town, walked for some time into the center of town, and Boiro negotiated with great seriousness—with smiles, wheedling, pretend insults, bluff offers—a taxi. He talked the taxi driver down from a hundred twenty dalasis to seventy-five dalasis, but it took the better part of an hour. Finally we climbed into a taxi that took us out to a house where we picked up a generator, slide projector and slides, a sheet and a can of petrol, and then it took us out to a village. In the village, we had a dinner, which was a meat stew, in someone's house.

During dinner, an American Peace Corps volunteer named Jim Zinn showed up. Jim was from Davis, California, and he had thin arms, thin legs, and a long, good-looking face with an aquiline nose. He wore a green sport shirt, yellow, ragged shorts, and he carried himself with youthful optimism, which I enjoyed. He said that two young Peace Corps workers of the opposite sex, living in a small African town, went out to the beach for a swim. They took off their clothes. As the sun set, their attraction for each other rose. One thing led to another. They embraced, kissed, made love. It was the first time for both of them, but while they were enjoying this momentous occasion someone stole their clothes, so they had to run back home naked. They were observed running naked through town, and the resulting scandal shook the Peace Corps to its veritable foundation. Jim said that the local word for white person was *toubob,* but he couldn't explain the origin of the term.

After dinner, we walked to the center of the village, placed a white sheet on a wall, started up the generator, and showed slides. I understood very little of what was said, since all of Boiro's lecture took place in Mandinka, but Jim Zinn explained a lot. The slide projector spurted out pictures of African animals: giraffes, lions, leopards, buffalo—and chimpanzees. "These are animals that used to live in the Gambia, but are now gone," Jim said. "Boiro is asking, 'Have you ever seen it in the bush?'" The lecture introduced ideas of conservation and explained the importance of the chimp project.

I stayed at the camp for five days, traveling on two evenings out to villages on the river while Boiro gave his slide shows and lectures. But I seldom saw Janis. Was she avoiding me or was she just very busy? I had by then accepted the fact that she didn't want to talk about Lucy.

Janis tells her own story in the June 1988 issue of *Smithsonian* magazine. She arrived in Africa with an eleven-and-a-half-year-old Lucy in September 1977, her expenses paid for by the Temerlins, thinking that the chimpanzee would require some adjustment to a new life, expecting to stay a few weeks to help out.

Lucy was placed in a large holding cage for orphaned chimps at the Abuko Nature Reserve near Banjul. After the Temerlins left, Janis and Lucy became ill. There was no question, in any case, of placing the still young chimp in a wilderness somewhere. It was much too soon.

A complication arose. Stella Brewer, who had originally begun the rehabilitation project, was during this period camped out in Senegal's Niokolo Koba National Park with several chimps, trying to return them to a wild existence, discovering how difficult such a process would be, realizing furthermore that the wild chimps already living in Niokolo Koba would most probably kill the semi-tame chimps she had hoped to release. Wild chimps had in fact already attacked some of her chimps, and so Stella pulled up stakes and returned to the Gambia with them. Eventually, the project selected the Baboon Islands of the River Gambia National Park as a second potential release site.

While Lucy was slowly adjusting to life at Abuko, meanwhile, several new chimps came. Typically, they were orphaned by hunters who shot their mothers, tied them up, and transported them to a city somewhere, to be sold as pets or, in some instances, research subjects

for the European laboratory market. So when Stella returned from
Senegal with her group of chimps, planning to release them on one of
the islands, Janis was preparing to release a second group onto a second Baboon Island.

In 1979, Janis moved Lucy and eight other chimps out to one of
the islands. What would they do there? How would they find food?
Some of those rehabilitated chimps probably had memories of living
in the wild and knew something about wild foods. All of them were
reasonably expert at climbing trees. All except Lucy, who knew almost
nothing about indigenous food plants and showed very little interest
in climbing trees. Thus, Janis moved onto the island too, along with
the nine apes. She had a wire cage built and placed her own tent inside,
to protect her belongings from the chimps. For the next two years,
Janis lived on the island, "more as a chimpanzee than as a human," as
she writes in the *Smithsonian* article, and did her best to teach the
chimps how to survive. "I taught them how to build sleeping platforms
high in the trees. By gnawing on green figs and live ants, I showed
them how to forage for wild foods."

Lucy was the problem. Lucy didn't want to be a wild chimp.
"Each day I spent hours teaching her, responding to her needs and she
responding to mine as though she were another human being." Lucy
didn't want to drink directly from the river; she wanted to drink from
a cup, just as Janis was doing. Lucy didn't want to climb the baobab
trees, to get the best fruits, flowers, leaves, and bark. Indeed, one time
Lucy sat desperately beneath a baobab tree while her ape companions
climbed in it and feasted, and then used sign language to beg Janis for
help. "More food. Janis go," she said. Finally, Janis retrieved a long
plank of lumber from the camp and placed that against the tree, making a ladder that Lucy then climbed.

In the end, Janis stopped talking to Lucy. She cut her off, linguistically, emotionally. Lucy became desperate. She would sit around
Janis' tent, whining, pretending to be injured, creeping forward, saying
in sign language: "Food . . . drink . . . Janis come out . . . Lucy's hurt!"
Janis would tell Lucy to go away; Lucy would move away, then slowly,
slowly creep back. The struggle continued for three months until,
Lucy "just broke." She started moving on her own, foraging for her
own food.

After two years on the island, the chimpanzee had adjusted well
enough that Janis felt able to leave, returning in a boat only occasion-

ally to check on Lucy's progress. Lucy grew up, adopted a son, seemed slowly on her way to becoming a socially and sexually normal member of her group—and then one day in late 1987 she disappeared. Her remains were discovered a few days later, near Janis's old campsite, her hands and feet brutally severed, her skin simply stripped off. "We can only speculate that Lucy was killed—probably shot—and skinned. Because of her confidence with humans, she was always the first to confront newcomers to the island."

Lucy was buried in a simple grave on the island.

What about Janis? Janis spent two years on that island, *two years*, living alone, in punishing isolation, separated from her own species. I can only admire completely her strength of character and her dedication, or whatever it was that sustained her—but what did sustain her? Why had she done it? What did Lucy mean to her? Clearly, Lucy was her closest companion during this time. What was the nature of their relationship, their friendship: chimpanzee and human? What did Janis read in Lucy's eyes? How did they communicate? How did Janis satisfy the ordinary human need for ordinary social intercourse? I know how Lucy survived. She became an ape. How did Janis survive?

"To those of us who knew her, Lucy was an extraordinary creature, sensitive, caring and gentle," Janis Carter writes: "she was the thread that joined my days, weeks, months and years."

The last day I was there, Janis and I sat in chairs down at the edge of the river. She said a Liberian hunter told her that the one time he shot a chimp and watched the ape die, he decided never to do it again.

She had gone to Liberia seeking chimp habitat. An American research laboratory in Liberia wanted to release some lab chimps that were all tested out, and Janis was trying to help find suitable habitat within the country's remaining forested areas. (The lab's chimps finally went to an island in the Ivory Coast.) Wandering around in the Liberian backcountry, sometimes she saw chimp hands floating in people's soup bowls.

One time, after a chimp died, Janis became distraught. She had never experienced a death before, person or chimp. "I'm not religious," she said. "Well, I am religious. Put it this way: I don't believe in organized religion. I do have a reverence for life." She finally talked to the top religious leader in the country, the Imam of Banjul. Did he think it strange that Janis could mourn the death of an animal? "No," he told her. "There is a traditional belief that the chimpanzee is the only animal that, if you find it dead, you must bury it."

I was amazed by this story—and I thought to myself: *That must have been Lucy.* Janis had become distraught and sought the Imam's advice over the death of Lucy.

Another African religious leader told her: "Chimps are like us because they try not to get their hands dirty. That's why they walk on their knuckles."

We were sitting in wooden chairs near the river, and light, reflected from the wavering surface of the river, softly wavered into the trees around us. Janis had olive green eyes, illuminated by sunlight flickering off the surface of a river that was exactly, I suddenly noticed, the color of her eyes.

"So," she said at last, "what are your questions about Lucy?"

11

Technology and the Ape

*Common bullets of lead, whether round or conical, are
far inferior to those of hard alloy; for the
latter penetrate much more deeply, and break bones,
instead of flattening against them. A mixture of
very little tin, or pewter (which is lead and tin), with
lead, hardens it: we read of sportsmen melting up
their spoons and dishes for this purpose.*

–Francis Galton, *The Art of Travel*

Although I haven't mentioned it yet, some people were preparing for a war during this phase of my travels. It seems that the ruler of a small desert nation had instructed his army to move from one place in the sand to another place in the sand. This second place in the sand was already claimed by others, and it possessed great economic value because underneath the sand lay a big coagulation of rotten plants and animals. Many people were unhappy. The United States and several allies sent planes, tanks, troops, and so on, to the area with plans to push the ruler's army from the second place in the sand right back to the first place in the sand. Metaphors, insights, and religious conversions became necessary. President Bush began talking about "a line drawn in the sand." Vice President Quayle quietly observed his golf schedule turn into a gulf schedule. The ruler of the small desert nation miraculously found himself to be a devout Muslim. He offered glorious martyrdoms as an ultimate bonus to the nine hundred thousand men in his army, and he threatened his opponents with "the Mother of All Battles."

While I boarded a plane in Banjul, Gambia, and flew to Abidjan, Ivory Coast, planning to continue my Chimpanzee Travels, many others were flying a little farther to the northeast to commence the Mother of All Battles. There was no solid reason to imagine the two endeavors might intersect, but the Mother of All Battles in any event dominated many people's imaginations at the time.

I was thinking about it, too.

Perhaps I was thinking about it too hard. In the Abidjan airport, I passed through immigration and looked up from my thoughts just in time to notice a very large man pull my pack out of the luggage area and waddle right through customs with it. I ran after him, into the airport lobby, and furiously wrestled my bag out of his grip. He wrestled it back. We struggled until, finally, I gave up and let him toss my pack into the back of his taxi. I climbed into the front after he told me he knew how to get to the Centre Suisse.

This taxi was a technological nightmare. It looked to be constructed from six hundred spare parts: almost all upholstery gone, no glove compartment, hollow doors, broken windows. Only the saint on the dash seemed whole and sound, a center of spiritual magnetism holding all the rest together. As we drove out of the airport, the driver said the trip would only cost me a few thousand West African francs. I was just figuring out how to compute the equivalent in dollars, but it already seemed too much. "C'est cher!" I said.

When we arrived in downtown Abidjan, he stopped and innocently explained to me—repeating the French many times—that what he had thought was the Centre Suisse was not actually the Centre Suisse I wanted. Together we puzzled over the directions in my letter a second time, and then he declared it would be a little out of town. He knew where it was now. It would cost many more thousands of francs.

I was beginning to feel cheated, and I started to tell the driver so, but I didn't know the French word for "cheat," so I was left inarticulately fuming and sputtering—"C'est trop cher! C'est trop cher!"—with no real sense of whether I was actually right or wrong or even where, precisely, we were driving right then, or how far I had to go. Was I being cheated? Perhaps. Perhaps not. We drove, and as I stumbled with the rough arithmetic over and over in my head, this began to seem a very expensive taxi ride indeed.

But I knew what to do! I would not pay him until we reached my destination, where I would be able to ask my Swiss hosts whether the price was fair. Then I could haggle over it with the help of someone who really spoke French and who knew what the ride from the airport ought to cost. Just as I had formulated that plan, however, my driver pulled up at a gas station and declared I had to pay him right then. His machine was out of essence. It could go no farther until essence was purchased. I considered climbing out of the taxi and walking away without paying him a thing—but I looked around. This seemed like a rough part of town. I had no idea where I was. I saw no other taxis. I looked at the gas gauge: empty. I paid.

The driver bought only a tiny amount of essence, however, and the gauge still showed empty as we drove off. After a long drive out to the west of the city and down a country road, we came into a beautiful place that looked like a college campus, past a turnstile and guard-house, into the Centre Suisse. As we pulled up in front of the house of my hosts, the taxi driver began asking for a gift—un petit cadeau—for taking me so very far.

I laughed at his nerve and stepped out of the cab.

My hosts were Christophe and Hedwige Boesch, who study chimpan-zees in the Taï Forest National Park of western Ivory Coast. Taï Forest is probably the single most important piece of chimpanzee habitat remaining in all of West Africa, well protected by the Ivory Coast government, and the Boesches' work was particularly interesting to me because they had been observing chimpanzees who were using a stone and wood technology. Nowhere else in Africa do chimpanzees use stone and wood tools—only within a small corridor of West African habitat, west from the Sassandra River in the middle of Ivory Coast, through Liberia and Guinea and into Sierra Leone. I wanted to see those paleolithic chimps.

Christophe and Hedwige were there when I arrived. She was stay-ing home with the two children. He was soon going to be on his way out to the Taï camp. But I would ride out to Taï slowly, and check out chimpanzee habitats elsewhere in the country, with two other Swiss researchers, Paul and Natalie Marchesi, and a third researcher who was Ivoirean and a member of the Guéré tribe to the west, Denis Lia.

We all had dinner together that evening, and I was happy to be among friends. Dinner conversation zigzagged between French and English. Christophe told me that French has no word for "ape." Mon-key is *singe,* and an ape would just be *grand singe.* I also learned that the

British journalist Brian Hippelwaithe had recently been out to Taï—he was doing an article on apes for a major magazine. Brian Hippelwaithe again!

"How was Brian Hippelwaithe?" I asked.

"Fine," Christophe said. "We had some conflict, but that was solved in the end."

After dinner we listened to the radio, which told us things had come to a breaking point with the leader of the small desert nation. That night I stayed in a room in an old hotel, virtually empty and abandoned for one reason or another, on the grounds of the Centre Suisse.

Christophe was younger than I had expected—I had been corresponding with a "Dr. Boesch," whom I imagined belonging to a more formal generation. He had a quarter-moon mustache beneath a prow of a nose, and I found him to be very analytical. The next day, for example, as we stood out by Paul's truck, Christophe looked me over slowly, from head to foot, and said at last in a cool voice: "I am just wondering if you are fit enough to keep up with me in the forest."

I said: "We'll find out, won't we."

Foolishly, I had imagined his statement to be an ingenuous expression of gratuitous ungenerosity, but Paul and I spoke about it later, and Paul set me straight: "The chimps can move very fast, and it is important to stay with them. Sometimes you'll be running. They can go twelve kilometers in a day. Oh, Christophe is a wild man. He speaks his mind."

Paul and I went shopping that day, gathering our supplies for the big trip, but we listened to the radio whenever we could, and we all turned in that night with the conviction that things were grim indeed.

The next morning Paul woke me up, saying: "The war is started." We both walked over to the Boesch house to hear more news on their radio. Hedwige was clearly upset. "So, it has begun!" she said fiercely. "The Americans and the British have started bombing Iraq. Ah! They are so pleased with themselves, these pilots! We heard them interviewed on the radio. So very pleased!" She looked at me. "It is very bad, yes? I think they could have negotiated. No? They didn't really try! Ah! It's horrible. They could have negotiated!" She said this with a grim smile, her face flushed, speaking with such passion I was immediately won over: *Yes, of course,* I thought. *They didn't really try. They could have negotiated.*

We had breakfast, and then Paul, Natalie, Denis, and I left the Centre Suisse at half past nine after learning all we could from a French-language radio—not much.

Paul had a Caesar haircut on top of a broad face, but his main feature was his smile, which was predictable but warm. Already he had deep smile crinkles at his eyes, and he was only thirty years old.

He drove. I rode shotgun, and Denis and Natalie sat behind us. We stopped in town to buy a pair of high rubber boots for me and a single cigarette for Paul. "I gave up cigarettes six months ago," he said, "but I think I'll have one now. Just one." And then we drove south out of Abidjan. It was a very humid day, and we drove into a broth of haze along a straight road through many miles of oil palm and rubber plantations. At dinner the night before, Christophe had said that a French scientist once told him that a palm plantation had the same ecological value as a primary forest. The French scientist said, "But we are planting trees, which is good for the primates." Nothing could be further from the truth. Tree plantations have their virtues, obviously, but in a biological sense they are deserts. We stopped the truck and briefly looked inside a rubber plantation—absolutely geometrical plantings, splotched trees, latex slashes, cups fixed below the slashes. We listened for birds and heard one.

We stopped for Cokes at a bar alongside the road. There was a bus outside the bar, piled high with luggage, with people popping out of the windows. Zairean music was emanating from the bar, fast and nervous, with a tinny guitar. Paul bought some cigarettes at the bar and said he hated Zairean music: It reminded him of mosquitoes. Three women were cooking mango slices in pots of boiling oil over wood fires, outside the bar.

We crossed the Bandama River, clear and still, cutting briefly through a piece of chaotic forest: bursts of leaves high and low, a shattering pattern of palm, white herons sitting in a tree over the river. Early in the afternoon we located a rural government building serving the Eaux et Forêts department associated with the D'Asagny National Park.

We wanted to see the island chimps just outside D'Asagny.

The Eaux et Forêts officers wanted a fee at first, but after we explained that we were not tourists, they settled for a written note about our intent and then invited us inside the stucco building to watch TV: the news, a little footage on the war. So we watched TV with the chief of the Eaux et Forêts while he ate his lunch in an armchair to one side, a big pile of rice and meat. The lesser functionaries of Eaux et Forêts also sat in armchairs and also watched the news on an ancient black-and-white TV. One of them could hardly contain his glee at how the Americans and Brits and Saudis had apparently just crushed the enemy. There were exciting shots on TV of sleek American fighter planes roaring off the runway. We all engaged in an extended palaver about life, the war, the forests, the chimps, with lots of handshaking.

Finally we left, accompanied by one of the Eaux et Forêts officers, who sat with us in the truck, navigating down a road until we came to a small fishermen's village next to the river. The village was deserted except for several lizards with gray bodies, yellow heads, and red wattles. The lizards crouched on sticks and in small bushes, and then they jumped to the ground and did push-ups.

We walked through the village, down a bank to the river. There was an old dugout canoe there, at the river, with a long tin patch nailed on the bottom, and in the middle of the river we saw the island. The island was small and had one very large tree in the middle, green and arching, with brown chimpanzee nests in it. There were other trees on the island, some green, several completely stripped, white and bare, and a dense green underbrush. Pretty soon a few chimps appeared out of the underbrush, walked to the edge of the island, and quietly looked across the river at us. They loosely swayed and slowly bobbed their heads. The island and the chimpanzees looked sad. It was like looking at lepers in a leper colony or schizophrenics in an asylum. But eventually the chimps got bored and disappeared back into the underbrush.

Paul said these apes were castoffs from the American laboratory in Liberia, retired from their research careers and now marooned here. The original plan, so I learned later from the laboratory director, had been to place them into D'Asagny itself, but then, too late, it was discovered that D'Asagny already had its own population of wild chimps, and as a last resort one dozen laboratory chimps were left on that island. The government paid local people to go out to the island every day and toss food: coconuts, bananas, all kinds of fruits. Paul said he would go find a fisherman to take us in his boat out closer to the island, so we could take photographs, and he left with the Eaux et Forêts officer.

Natalie, Denis, and I sat at the edge of the river. Fish jumped in the water, and I could look way across, beyond the island, far enough that the haze in the air dulled the green, and see the giant trees of D'Asagny National Park. The heat of the afternoon rose, and I sat at the river's edge and listened to the heavy buzz of insects. It was a slow afternoon, a thick sky, a bit of a breeze coming off the river. And then I heard a smacking noise, and I looked up to see a big male chimp who had just appeared out of the brush at the edge of the island. He was standing up, like a man, and slowly smacking his hands, clearly trying to get our attention. He stood in the shadows and shook his head back and forth, back and forth, and he smack, smack, smacked his hands. There was a sound of the rising breeze in the trees brushing leaf against leaf, and I saw above me an eagle, circling high.

Paul and the Eaux et Forêts officer returned some time later, and the officer was holding nine small crabs bound together in a row, a train of crabs bound with palm fiber, all eighteen claws very neatly wrapped, the crabs tied together into a single carrier, like an instrument case almost. The Eaux et Forêts officer stood stiffly in his khaki uniform, with silver epaulets and a green beret, and he held up the wrapped crabs for us to see. "The fisherman said his pirogue was too broken, too dangerous to take us," Paul said. "He didn't want to take the risk."

We left the river and the village and the island chimps, and we drove west, through winding dirt roads and forests, past small villages, over wooden bridges that had to be rebuilt before we could cross them. We eventually entered some very nice forest. The road turned into a narrow passage, and it converged and diverged with other narrow passages for an hour or two until suddenly we broke out brightly onto an open sky, smashed trees, the smell of fresh sap, and the huge racket of five bright giant bulldozers, clawing and roaring, plowing the earth and tearing up trees. Paul talked to one of the workers, a barechested man with the hair on his chest knotted into circles. "It's a beautiful forest, isn't it?" Paul said. "The trees, the fresh air, the monkeys."

One of the bulldozers cleared some trees out of our way, and we continued driving, this time on top of fresh red clay through a wide and chaotic passage and bright sun. We came to another group of workmen, including one man who carried the tail of a flying squirrel. Paul greeted them, chatted, and then, as we were driving away, said to me: "Many of these workers are only here to hunt, to get bush meat for the others." But Paul was more concerned—perplexed, actually— about the building of the road itself. The formal understanding, as he understood the understanding, was that the World Bank would support building the road a few miles to the north of where we were. We were driving inside of one of the last remaining pieces of primary forest in the country, theoretically protected, the final habitat of chimpanzees, many monkey species, elephants, even leopards. It was sacred to the local people and an important hunting resource. Now this road was being smashed right through. It would eventually cut cleanly in a forty-yard swath over hundreds of miles. Paul had no idea why it was being cut here, in the middle of the forest.

We continued driving, and after a time we came to the end of the construction area and turned back onto the old road, the narrow, winding passage in the forest. We drove along that for some time, perhaps an hour, until the road descended to a river. We parked the Toyota and walked down to the edge of the river. A young boy was standing there, at the edge of the river, with a two-foot-long catfish at his feet in the dust. There was a panga—a big knife—in the boy's hand and a bloody slice across the head of the catfish. The catfish was dead all right, its skin dry, clumps of dirt sticking to the skin, its whiskers curling back. As I looked at the boy and the catfish, a childhood image unfolded inside my mind: a giant fish, a dream fish perhaps, stretched right across the railroad tracks at the edge of the Chemung River, back in my hometown of Corning, New York. Did I see the giant fish? Did I dream it? But the boy was looking across the river, and then I saw a cable stretched across the river. On the far bank, connected to the cable, was a rough ferry—an old steel hulk with drive-on flaps of steel on either side—that would take us to the road on the other side. That ferry had just left the far bank and was moving our way. Three barge-men, an old man and two younger men, pulled laboriously, heaved and hauled on the cable, drawing the barge back across the river to our side.

But as we watched this great labor and the barge slowly moving toward our side of the river, we saw beyond the far bank a car appearing, raising a high tail of dust, appearing and moving fast, so it seemed, toward the river at the barge landing. But instead of pausing and descending down to the river, this car veered to our left. Five seconds later it was on our side of the river, stones spinning under its wheels, dust rising, and it disappeared down what we suddenly understood to be the cut for the new highway. There was a highway over there—and a bridge! Someone had just finished building a bridge!

Laughing—as the three bargemen still hauled that old hulk over to our side of the river—we all raced back to the Toyota, leaped inside, slammed the doors, turned it on, spun around, pulled out to the new highway, still dirt, not yet paved, and drove across the new bridge, with the old bargeman shouting after us.

Paul said: "He wanted money! He wanted us to think that was the right way!" It was comical. I couldn't help laughing, nor could he, but after a moment's reflection, tears of laughter still in his eyes, Paul added: "I think that barge is a family business, for very many years a family business. That bargeman and his family are now out of business. It probably happened today or yesterday. The highway is here, now, and the bargeman has just lost his profession."

Just as it was getting dark, we came into a town big enough to have electricity. We passed the electrical generating station on the edge of town and then came into a place with two streets, some shops, and a couple of small eating joints.

We stopped on the street before one shop consisting of three stucco walls and a roof. The fourth wall was open to the street out front—two square openings separated by a single supporting square column. Above the openings hung two rolled-up metal shutters. At night the shop was closed by a dual portcullis, a pair of rolling-down metal shutters. But it was early evening yet. The shop was still open, and the inside was illuminated by weak yellow light. Outside, a single neon tube up high spread blue light feebly into the air and across two concrete steps rising from the dirt of the road to the concrete floor of the shop. Insects spun around the blue light. From where we sat in the truck, looking across the road into the shop, it seemed at first to be deserted. Then orange peels began flying out of the shop and landing in the dust at the base of the steps. I saw a moving hand and an arm. Someone was indeed sitting inside the shop, his back against the square column, eating an orange and casting the remains behind him out toward the road.

We got out of the truck, went into the shop, and found the energizer of those orange peels, a Lebanese man with a purplish face—bad-ticker sort of color—overweight, wheezing, bald save for a hair horseshoe, his shirt wide open revealing the pallid drum of his great paunch. He was listening to news about the Gulf War on his radio.

We exchanged pleasantries in French, ordered Cokes, and casually looked the place over. It was crammed to the ceiling with everything from soup to boots. The Lebanese man said, "Good evening," in English. I was the only native English speaker of our group, and the comment may have been directed to me. I ignored his English not deliberately but automatically. I had already gotten used to making social exchanges in French. But later on, as we drank our Cokes in the shop and thought about what else we might need to buy, Paul discussed some of our plans with me in English, and the Lebanese man pounced: "So, you do speak English!"

Paul smiled and explained that he and Natalie were Swiss, Denis was a Guéré, and I was—he thought fast, no doubt considering possible sensitivities generated by the Gulf War at that moment—a Canadian. "Don't all Canadians speak French?" the Lebanese asked suspiciously, in English. By this point all our talk had switched into English.

The Lebanese said he had lived in the United States for ten years, in Detroit. But then he decided to come back to Africa. He had spent a total of forty years right here, on this road, here in Africa. He had seen a lot of changes, he said, a lot of changes.

Meanwhile, the radio news about the war continued in the background. Paul commented: "Bad news today."

The Lebanese said: "Bad news? It's good news! Now the war has begun! But it's not going to end soon, my friend!"

The Lebanese said he was happy, because beginning today the man would finally show the world. He would punish the Americans and the British and also the Israelis for their arrogance. They would be beaten—and they would suffer—just as the Arabs had been suffering for the last five centuries.

This was not the sort of conversation I enjoy. I said nothing, but Paul, always ready to engage and debate, merely paused to light a cigarette, which bobbed loosely at his lips as he talked and caused one eyebrow to rise. "But you must admit," he said, "the man has done wrong in invading another country. He has gone in with his army, taken everything. It's not right."

The Lebanese: "My friend! You don't understand! You have to know a little history. A long time ago the British stole a piece of the desert and called it Kuwait. They took these silly people out of the desert and said to them, 'Now, dear boys, you're the rulers of Kuwait!' "

Paul: "That may be, but now we have national boundaries that people have agreed are there. You cannot expect the rest of the world to do nothing when one country invades another."

The Lebanese: "My friend! Where was the rest of the world when Israel invaded Lebanon?"

So went the conversation, Paul and the Lebanese continuing on and on in this vein. Finally Paul concluded with: "I don't think that it's so simple. No, I don't agree." And the Lebanese, apparently pleased to have had this long and forthright argument, invited us to have coffee with him in the morning. "I have good coffee," he said.

But we missed him the next morning. We slept in a cold-water hotel and left early with plans to find elephants in an oil palm plantation by the sea. Paul had heard about the elephants somehow, and the story he told me was that before the oil palm plantation there was a forest. The forest is gone, but some of the elephants are still there, wandering around the plantation and protected now by the government.

We drove onto the plantation, which was huge—rows and rows and rows and rows and rows and rows and rows and rows of oil nut palms, along with some broken-down areas and lots of dense brush and thickets—and after a couple of hours located the plantation patron, a big, barefoot man with small eyes and a broken fly, who was casually supervising some sort of work project at the beach. The patron said that a couple of years ago there were about two hundred elephants, but now he didn't know how many there were. The elephant is protected in this country, he said, and it's not right. Someone started shooting at the elephants. Now the elephants are spooked and dangerous. They are afraid. We could see them if we could find them, he said, but we should be careful they don't trample us. He said some of them had crossed the Bolo River and entered farmland, where there would be trouble.

We thanked the patron for this information and went off looking for someone to help us find the elephants.

After a time, driving through the plantation once again, we came to a small market alongside the road: a meeting of people and dogs and chickens under the shade of a tin roof propped on crooked poles. Paul got out of the truck and soon had a large group of curious people milling around him. He leaned against an old table, legs crossed, smiling, and after a few minutes had hired a middle-aged local man to help us. This man had a heavy jaw, a mustache, and a goatee. He carried a machete, and he wore orange flip-flops and a bright yellow-green shirt with baccarat designs in gray.

He squeezed into the front seat of the truck, and we drove around the palm plantation for some time before parking and climbing out. By this time, the sky had become dark and heavy, with big clouds moving fast; we entered the plantation with a rising wind. The rising wind rustled the palm fronds with a sharp, metallic sound, and the fronds themselves were clustered tightly, sharp and curved, dark green with a silver tinge—like hissing racks of knives. We stepped into this hissing wilderness, silvery hissing trees in rows for as far as the eye could see, complicated by lines of high and thick brush.

We found big trails blasted into the brush, and we walked through areas dense with barnyard smells and paused to consider big dumps of fresh elephant dung. After an hour we thought we were close, but how close we couldn't be sure—and we didn't want to stumble on the elephants. Our guide shinnied up a high tree, looked around, saw nothing. We walked some more and came across broken coconut shells and very fresh dung. The trail turned into a maze in eight-foot-high brush, and the maze led us into a part of the plantation where most of the palms were long ago destroyed and replaced by a total chaos of low secondary growth. What we saw first, through the dense and high brush, were white birds. Someone said: "Les hérons qui guardent le boeuf"—cattle egrets.

Our guide climbed a stunted tree, then climbed a termite mound, then an old, overturned stump (fire-blackened and covered with vines), and then pointed. The rest of us tried the tree and the mound and the stump. I could see, perhaps twenty or thirty yards distant, a puddle of gray at the base of a tree. Through binoculars I saw a big, dark ear lifting up, flapping down. Then a spurt of dust was tossed up, and another, and a long, dark appendage lifted and tossed dust, which rode out on the wind.

The elephants seemed nervous, and they moved, after a time, deeper into the brushy chaos. The sky was turning darker. We followed them, finally coming upon an intact tree, not a palm, to climb in. The tree was just about big enough to hold five people, and all five of us wound up in different parts of it, looking over a group of six elephants inside a small, rough copse of trees and brush fifty feet away. Their ears moved rhythmically, wavering back and forth like gills. A trunk rose like a snake, and then became a periscope, straight up save for the tip that, bent from the vertical, pointed this way, pointed that way, pointed in our direction, sniffing—a sniffoscope. Then a great gray head turned our way, ears flat back, massive and gray.

After several minutes, we climbed down and began wandering through the dense brush, unable to see anything but imagining we were headed toward an even better vantage point. But out of nowhere there was an explosion of crackling brush and a rumbling and a shaking in the ground. I had been behind everyone else, but suddenly I was ahead of everyone. They were running behind me and in the opposite direction. I turned and ran after them. I ran like hell!

Or, rather, I tried to run like hell. But it was like running in the invisible molasses of a nightmare. There was no actual trail in the brush there, only a series of potential weaknesses where a person might or might not squeeze through, and as a consequence, we all frantically squeezed ourselves in different directions. The elephants would have been at a great advantage in this sort of environment, had they chosen to follow us, but I believe they were running like hell in other directions, scattering elsewhere in their own pachydermic panic, and after a while the five of us found each other once again, breathless and laughing. Paul said: "You have just seen some of the last forest elephants of West Africa."

It started raining then, and we walked back to the road, climbed into the truck, and returned our guide with the yellow-green-with-gray-baccarat-designs shirt to his house. Pretty soon the rain cleared up, and we drove out of the palm plantation and continued on our journey, west and south now, along a narrow highway and then a dirt track through some thick forest and out to the ocean.

We came out onto a beach and parked the truck in the sand. The beach seemed deserted. It was late in the afternoon by then. We were all hot and mucky and sweaty, and the vision of those great rolling breakers pounding onto a high slope of sand was very exciting. We tore off our clothes, hopped into bathing outfits, and ran across the beach, down the sandy slope, and dove into any convenient wave of the ocean.

The water was as warm as anything, and the waves were huge, and they lifted you up and let you down and then crashed over your head. The four of us dove and tread water and rode the surf out there, Denis spouting water through his mouth and laughing with sheer pleasure—Paul said that Denis had never seen the ocean until last year. Denis and Paul went swimming along the surf in one direction, while Natalie and I remained where we were, bobbing up and down next to each other. The top of the beach was high enough that I could only see the truck when a wave lifted me up high—when the wave let me down, the truck was out of sight. As we bobbed up and down there, I began to observe, as in a sequence of snapshots, two young men walk toward the truck and then stand next to it. What were they doing there? I asked myself. I became suspicious. "Is the truck locked?" I said to Natalie. No, she didn't think so. "Should we worry about our things?" I asked. No, she didn't think so. There was a village just down the way, and they were known by the village chief, so everything would be protected. Last year, she and Paul and Denis had been out here looking for chimpanzees. They camped for two weeks on the beach and nothing was stolen—except for a portable refrigerator. The chief investigated and got their refrigerator back, nothing missing from it. It had been stolen by the son of the chief in another village, so he couldn't be prosecuted.

After a while, we climbed out of the ocean and walked back to the truck. The two young men knew Paul, Natalie, and Denis, greeted them heartily, and wondered if we needed anything. We gave them money for some locally brewed wine, and then lay out in the slanting sun on towels on the sand to dry ourselves off while they ran off to get the wine. The sand was pocked with a billion holes, and inside the holes were sand crabs. They hid completely under the sand as long as you stood up or moved around, but the minute you lay down and ceased moving, they came out. I lifted my head and one shoulder, and all the crabs around me instantly disappeared, but several yards away they were surrounding Paul, who by then looked to be asleep. They were sand-colored and stealthy, and their eyes stuck out on sticks. Their robotic bodies were entirely rigid—only their legs moved—and they looked like earth-moving equipment. In fact, they acted like earth-moving equipment.

It was just about time to cook dinner, but before dinner, Paul said, we had to greet the chief in the village. If I looked down along the curve of the beach, way down, I could actually see that village from where we were, near the truck, and Paul and I changed back into our clothes and then, carrying two bottles of the local wine, walked down the beach. We walked past a lagoon. Paul said the village was called Dagdego. It was a fishing village, mainly, net fishing in the lagoon. They didn't fish in the ocean, he said—only Ghanians did that. And we came to the village, quite large and really beautiful, I thought, with a couple of rows of planted coconut palms out front, between the village and the sea.

The village itself consisted of a whole series of houses and lots fenced with palm fences, and the lots were mostly contiguous, like lots in a city block, but there were also a few wide paths running through the village, defined on either side by lot fences. The houses were very simple and seemed perfectly functional: stick constructions, no walls to speak of, thatched roofs. Paul said that when, at certain seasons, it became too mosquitoey to sleep in the houses, the people slept next to the ocean, where a sea breeze swept away the mosquitoes.

By the time we began walking up one of the paths into the center of the village, several adults and a couple dozen children had already met us. They accompanied us until we finally came to a gate at the fence of the chief's house in the center of the village. The chief opened the gate and shook our hands. He was a short, powerfully built man wearing a blue toga. He had a long upper lip with a few unshaven white hairs in the middle, a small chin, a deeply furrowed brow. The white hair on his head had been cropped just about down to the skull. He wore dark glasses, and beneath the glasses, I thought, he was blind in one eye. A short pipe was clenched in his teeth.

We entered the chief's yard, which was a large black sand rectangle behind a stick and thatch house, and sat in a couple of chairs in the yard. The chief had his own stool, and he sat on that, while through the gate passed several village elders including the village president, whose name was Denis. We shook many hands, and then everyone sat down, in chairs, benches, and the chief on his stool, and then Paul presented the wine to the chief. There were several women visible from where we sat. They stayed back in the house or on the peripheries of the yard. One woman spread out a towel in the yard and lay down on the towel, comfortably observing from there our palaver, and another woman produced a half dozen glasses from somewhere, washed them in front of us, and then we began pouring the wine into the glasses. There weren't enough glasses to go around, so some of us shared a glass with a neighbor, but pretty soon the wine warmed our throats, and we began talking. The chief knew Paul from last year, and so Paul's explanation was partly a formality—he said we had come to look for chimpanzees in the village forest, that we were there for scientific purposes, that I was a writer of books, and that he hoped someone from the village would help us find chimpanzees tomorrow. The chief chewed on his pipe, and the village president said that they didn't eat chimpanzees. He said he had been telling his people to protect them. He said several other things I didn't understand (this whole conversation was conducted in French), and he concluded by discussing with the chief and the other men who would be the best person to help us find chimpanzees the next day.

Someone brought into the yard a gigantic sea turtle carapace, and someone else said that turtles came to this beach to lay eggs, which were eaten as food. Paul asked if they preserved any of the eggs so that the turtles would come back next year. Everyone laughed at the idea. Daniel Abrou was the name of the man designated to help us tomorrow.

After dark, Paul and I shook everyone's hand and walked back from the village to our little encampment. Dinner was cooking by then. We ate dinner, and then, while a major portion of the Milky Way quietly exploded right above us, Natalie twisted the radio dial for news about the war. She located a crackling voice in French, which went on and on with news I could not understand. Paul told me that a hundred thousand soldiers had been killed. "Are you sure?" I said. I couldn't believe it. "Are you sure it wasn't just a hundred thousand casualties? That seems high. The war has only been going on two days. It took ten years in Vietnam to kill fifty-three thousand Americans . . . and half a million Vietnamese."

We were a lot closer there to the war than I had been in the United States. It was just a short distance—that's what the stars seemed to say. All those bombs and rockets were exploding just on the other side of a few trees and a single desert. If I looked hard enough, perhaps I could see them lighting up the sky. You didn't need much more than a camel to get there from where we were: *Take the main road to Timbuktu, left fork at the first sand dune, right fork at the forty-seventh, then straight on. You can't miss it.*

With a deep foreboding, I climbed inside the pup tent I shared with Denis and went to sleep.

At dawn, a small wooden boat appeared on the ocean with the rising sun burning right behind it. The boat ran into the surf and hung out there, with the engine turning a choked swallow. A man and a boy jumped out of the boat into the surf and soon had climbed up the sand slope and were walking toward us, the boy holding by the gills a foot-long barracuda. "Ghanians," Paul said. The man wore green shorts and a red baseball cap that said "Old Fart" on the front, and he offered the fish to us for a certain price that was eventually negotiated down to five hundred francs. They left, and we cooked the fish for breakfast.

After breakfast, the four of us walked down the beach to the village, looking for our guide, Daniel Abrou. But there was a fete going on, and people told us Daniel was at the fete. We walked to the far end of the village and finally came to a very large fenced yard, a communal area. Someone opened the gate to this area, and I looked inside to see several people and a fearsome face, black with two round white circles for eyes. Someone saw me look in and said, "It's all right: It's a dance mask"—meaning, according to Paul's later explanation, that it was a dance mask not a magic mask and that therefore I wouldn't be struck dead on the spot. Anyhow, through the open gate I heard drums and singing and saw a crowd of people and a dancer dressed in billows of grass, a headdress of feathers, and that black mask with the white eye circles. The dancer danced for a few minutes, and at the end of his performance, the feather headdress and the mask and the grass costume swirled and spun off the dancing, twisting person underneath. The person collapsed and vanished utterly while the costume seemed for just a moment to take on its own swirling quickness, until it too rose, twisted, heaved, and collapsed.

People came to the gate. We shook hands and were told by someone that Daniel Abrou wasn't there.

Paul went off looking for him, while the three of us—Denis, Natalie, and I—walked out toward the beach, where we watched a village puppy wrestling mightly with palm fronds and listened to the surf and the drums of the fete. The drums were superb, syncopated, asymmetrical, point and counterpoint in two pitches, and in the background someone shook seeds in a hollow gourd and a singing voice repeated over and over and over the same three-note phrase. The drumming continued brilliantly and then broke at last into cracking rimshots. A voice cried out: *Ahhhhhhhhh!* And another voice answered: *Tah ta-de neh!*

Pretty soon, Paul arrived with Daniel Abrou, a gaunt, middle-aged man with a receding hairline and a slight mustache. He was dressed in rags and wore flip-flops on his feet, and he led the way for a long walk along the beach, the surf crashing on one side and the forest rising in low hills on the other.

We walked until we came to a lagoon and an obscure trail into the forest. We took the trail and entered a darker, quieter world, with shadows and splashed sunlight and birdcalls and a muffled rhythmic roar from the ocean. We walked along a trail up a hill, and after a time I began noticing giant land snails. They had spiraled shells about the size of a fist, and the shells were of two sorts. One was widely striped in brown and nicotine yellow on the outside, with pink and violet on the inside; the second was narrowly striped in shades of olive drab on the outside, mother-of-pearl on the inside. Paul told me these were two species of the *Acatina* genus of giant land snails.

In the shadow of a towering tree with roots as big as culvert pipes, we found a flat rock and broken snail shells scattered among the leaf litter: pink and opal and violet and mother-of-pearl fallen into a matrix of brown and green, yellow and olive. The flat rock was laterite, dark and deeply pocked, and when we examined it closely, we found small scratches on the surface and, embedded in some of the pocks, tiny pieces of snail shell. This was evidence, Paul thought, that the shells had been smashed on the rocks. But he was disappointed. "When we came here last year, it was a big mound of shells—twenty, sixty. It was crazy."

During the next couple of hours, we found other flat rocks also surrounded by scattered shell shards. Typically, a very large proportion of shards would be scattered to one side of the flat rock, suggesting that whoever or whatever broke the shells sat or squatted to one side of the rock, broke the shells methodically with a hammering action on the stone anvil, and then tossed the broken pieces away. We found several shells that were nearly whole, except for smashed ends at the spiral tops, suggesting a preferred technique for getting at the snail inside: break open the top, reach in with a finger, and then push or pull out the meat inside. Altogether that morning, we found nine anvils with broken shells around them. We reassembled the shells and found enough shell fragments to account for perhaps half a dozen to a dozen snails cracked open and consumed at each of the anvil sites. Paul and Natalie took photographs and notes; with Denis, they measured and sampled. Natalie asked Daniel if any of the villagers ate land snails in the forest. But of course not, Daniel said, in French; they always take the snails into the village and cook them. "Only wild animals eat meat without cooking it." In West Africa, the generic word for "wild animal" is "beef" or "meat"—Daniel literally said, "Only meat eats meat raw." Natalie asked Daniel if he had ever seen chimps breaking open snails on these rocks. Oh, yes, he had seen the chimps do this.

We sat down to eat a lunch of oranges and boiled eggs. White butterflies flickered and turned brilliant in a pool of light. "It's a pity," Paul said, "because last time there was plenty. Plenty! We found twelve of these sites, twelve different rocks, and not all here, but some three kilometers away. Last year at each site we found up to sixty snails. Shells. We could recognize sixty different snails." We were not yet in chimpanzee nutcracking territory—that was a little farther west—and no one had ever written about chimpanzee snail smashing anywhere in Africa. If chimps in this region did crack snails on stone anvils, it

would be an important discovery of a new chimpanzee behavior.
"But," Paul cautioned me, "don't write about it until we've published
our data. First, I'm not absolutely sure about this behavior, and I
would like to make it a surprise."

"It must be chimps."

"I am trying to think of other animals that could do this, but I
cannot."

"But, it's so similar to the nutcracking. It has to be chimps doing
this."

"Yes, but I want to be . . . prudent. Is that the word?"

"Careful? Thorough?"

"Prudent."

"Oh, prudent."

We rested after lunch, lying on the forest floor, listening to the
dreamy woodwind and percussion of the forest and the rushing and
brushing of leaves. Paul took two cigarettes out of a pack, gave one to
Daniel, lit it, and lit one for himself. "I have been feeling like smoking
lately," he said. "I guess the taste goes and comes."

Daniel said he had only one wife but sixteen children. Denis asked
him if he took an aphrodisiac. "No, it's not necessary," Daniel said
modestly.

But our rest was interrupted with a burst of hooting. "Chimps!
Very, very close!" We crept slowly forward, listening to the sound of
wind brushing in the leaves, an occasional cracking of branches, once
in a while the calls of some monkeys in trees way behind us. Daniel
stepped out of his flip-flops and began stalking barefoot; and then we
heard the whimpering of a baby chimp, then an adult scream. Then
there was nothing, and we found ourselves listening to the hypnotic
sounds of the forest and looking into a wavering pattern of green and
brown, light and shadow, trunk and leaf. The chimps were gone.

We returned to camp soaked in sweat and then jumped into the
ocean and swam. Then we ate dinner and, after dark, listened to the
BBC news on the radio. The man had bombed Jerusalem.

We traveled west the next day and paused to look at the Sassandra
River. "This river," Paul said, "is the eastern limit for chimpanzee
nutcracking."

We crossed the river and, after several miles, came to a town with
a gas station, a bar, a small market. We bought food at the market,

essence at the gas station, and then we thought about air for our tires, which were soft. Right next to the gas station was a small wooden shack, tin-roofed. Several tires on top held the roof down. A sign out front said, VULCANIZATEUR. We located the vulcanizateur, and for a fee he poured a little essence into a one-cylinder air compressor on his front porch, cranked it up, ran a rubber hose across his yard into the gas station lot, and filled our tires with air.

We left the truck in the station and walked over to the bar for a drink. The bar was a twelve-sided building with a tin roof and a sand floor. There was an old concrete lion on a concrete pedestal situated right in the middle of the floor, facing the door and sinking into the sand. The old lion had hollowed eyes with white eyelashes. It had a pink face and white body and a magnificently coiffed black mane. A curled wire with a light bulb socket at the end came out of the mouth, which was open, toothed, tongued, and roaring.

Paul said, "It's awful!" We looked at the lion and drank Cokes.

We drove south now, back down toward the ocean, and stopped at a tiny village hidden in the forest. This village consisted of a few mud-daub houses and some stick furniture. It was deserted except for one young man who said we could draw water from the village well. We paid for the water and then drove farther south through forest down to the ocean, a bay, a beach, and a village on the beach. This village was actually Ghanian. Ghanian sea-fishers came here and took the spot on a rental basis, paying rent in fish to the nearest Ivorean village.

We spoke with one of the Ivorean villagers about the situation, who said that there were about three hundred Ghanians, that they arrived even before he was born, twenty-five years ago. He said that the relations between the Ivoreans and the Ghanians were getting worse, because there are now so many Ghanians, and they don't give the fish free anymore. They still give fish, but now the Ivoreans have to ask first. He said that the Ghanians stay there to get as much money as they can, and then they go back home to Ghana.

We camped on the beach.

It was raining in the morning, and I looked out from my tent into the green bay where a long wooden fishing boat was anchored. It was a Ghanian boat, and it was painted a turqouise blue above the water-line, with red, yellow and blue stripes in the middle, and several strange pictographs with some words in English: "Good Dey" and

"When?" The pictographs were as cryptic as Egyptian hieroglyphics: a dog on a pedestal, a snake curled around a stick.

Later in the day, Paul, Natalie, and Denis took me to a hidden spot deep inside a forest—a dark and steep glen protected by high, old trees. Thick lianas and vines grew up and hung down from the trees, and thick roots snaked all around us. We came across an anvil-like flat rock. On top of it were two rounded, grapefruit-sized rocks that looked as if they had been carefully placed there. The anvils were marked, deeply pocked with golf ball–sized indentations. We stopped for a moment, listening to something crashing through the brush toward us; when the sound ceased, we continued walking across the steep and forested hillside, finding during the next half hour perhaps fifty hammer and anvil sets. Typically, the anvils were flat but deeply indented, with anywhere from one to perhaps a dozen golf ball–sized dents. The hammers were all roughly the same size and shape, rounded and clearly worn with use. Most impressively, the hammers were often placed quite neatly on top of the anvils. Paul told me that the chimpanzees carefully placed hammers on the anvils when they were finished cracking nuts. Appropriately sized and shaped rocks are not easy to find, so the chimps value these hammers; they don't want to misplace their tools. The golf ball indentations in the otherwise flat anvil surfaces puzzled me at first, but as we examined the broken nuts scattered in heaps all around us, I began to realize that the chimps, when cracking the nuts, placed them in favored spots on the anvils, where they would least likely dislodge from an imperfect hammer blow; over time, these favored spots were carved deeply into the anvil surface. Most of the anvils were laterite, comparatively soft, but we found at least one solid granite anvil that had nine indentations deeply worn into the surface. How many chimpanzee generations of nut cracking were required to pound those dents into granite?

We found a wasps' nest. "How do you say when they needle you?" Paul asked.

"Sting?"

"Some of these species, they can sting very hard."

But I was left impressed by the age of those anvils. The chimps had been coming here for a long, long time. And I was intrigued by the idea that the stones were valuable to the chimpanzees. Were certain stones favorites? I wondered. Did the chimps think, in some pre- or non-linguistic fashion, upon entering the nutcracking zone with some uncracked nuts in hand: "Now where is my hammer? I thought I left it over there." Did the chimps give names to their favorite stones?

These days every piece of significant human technology is given a name. It's a marketing ploy. You drive a car? It has a name. It could be a lemon, a disaster, but it has a name. In medieval Europe, true, swords were given names—but only certain swords, only very special swords. Europeans did not begin to perfect the art of tempering steel until the nineteenth century, and as a result, most medieval swords were brittle. But by some combination of sheer accident and the persistence of skilled swordsmiths, a very small number of swords came to be well-tempered steel: heated to precisely the right temperature, the working iron accidentally exposed to precisely the right amont of carbon from burning charcoal in the furnace, then the combination cooled by quenching in cold water at precisely the right time and to the right degree, and—ping!—the carbon was suspended evenly within a crystallized lattice of iron. These were very special swords, and their bright ringing resilience must have surprised swordsman and swordsmith alike. It must have seemed almost magical, for these few special swords had an amazing virtue: *They could break almost any other sword they struck.* They seemed almost to have personality, character, charisma, soul. They became legendary, and they were given names. Excalibur!

No, of course—no Excaliburs beneath nut trees in West Africa. Still, there must be favorite hammering stones, good stones, well-rounded stones with just the right heft and feel.

It was getting dark as we drove along a rough track into the Taï Forest. Outside of the forest, it had been hot and dry, but the minute we were surrounded by trees we became enveloped in a bath of humidity. After dark, we turned into Christophe's camp. This camp must have been rough at one time, but now it included a rather nice main building with stucco walls, thatched roof, an extended porch, even running water via a rainwater cistern on the roof.

Christophe had company—a couple of zoology students, Edward and Pascal, who had come out to study the chimps—and they cooked enough dinner to include us. Christophe said to me: "So what you like to see tomorrow?"

"Chimpanzees."

"Chimpanzees? You've seen chimpanzees at Gombe."

I went to sleep surrounded by the rhythmic singing and scraping of a million insects and woke up before dawn. I dressed, had a quick breakfast, and then Christophe and I entered the forest and walked fast through dark and twisting passageways for a mile or two or three before sitting down on a log.

Christophe said, "The chimps are not as habituated as they are in Gombe. So try not to speak. If you can, whisper. And try not to break too many dead branches. I know it's difficult. But if you do too much, then they display. It upsets their mood." We could hear the chimps up there above us, still inside their nests, and then they slowly woke up. They made some sleepy noises, urinated out of their nests and off branches, and began moving around in the branches and leaves. Christophe, whispering, told me what to do if we became separated: I should make a certain call; he would find me. We listened to other sounds of the forest. A turaco. A three-note whistler. Rising waves of insect noises. We sat there as light gradually filtered into the forest, and then we watched human-shaped silhouettes moving through the trees.

They started coming down to the ground, climbing down, riding down thin and bending treetops, jumping down–chasing each other down. We heard screams and grunts and chorusing cries, the thump thump thump of feet running across branches, a surfy bursting through leaves, and, for a moment, we watched two very big males sit side by side on the ground and eye each other warily. "It's the alpha male," Christophe said, nodding his head toward the larger one who, seemingly in response, stood slowly, began swaying and vocalizing with noisy inhale-exhalations, and suddenly burst through some vegetation on the ground and flew into an ancient, half decayed tree trunk that exploded, while the male simply continued on his flight, landing in an area of vines and other vegetation and then tossing himself into a tree over our heads.

The day was beginning. A half dozen chimps started, slowly and in a disorganized fashion, walking along the forest floor. Christophe and I turned in behind to follow them, but they hadn't traveled for more than a few minutes, a half hour at most, before they all suddenly stopped and started whimpering and screaming. What was it? Other chimps appeared around us now, moving into the branches overhead, some on the ground, and they all leaned over and looked at something on the ground and started screaming. After several minutes had passed, the chimps stopped screaming and began moving again, so Christophe and I were able to approach the interesting spot on the ground. He pointed. I looked but couldn't see anything. What was it? I saw only a matted area of ground, a dried green and tan conglomeration of old sticks and leaves and grass. Really, it took at least a half minute before that pattern seemed to reassemble itself until, at last, I saw the heavy pile of a thick, curled and scaled reptile. It was a viper, Christophe thought, probably a rhinoceros viper.

We walked around the snake and caught up with our chimps, who were still passing through the filter of the forest at a leisurely pace, weaving in and out of our vision, disappearing, becoming only a rustling inside vegetation and then becoming nothing at all. We would hear screams and commotion, some loud drumming on trees, and then silence.

Toward the end of the morning, we stopped and listened to a light thumping sound. Down a hill, then, I saw a large dark ape, a female, squatting beneath a big tree, lifting and dropping, lifting and dropping one end of a large, irregularly shaped reddish log. She was hammering. The tree was a nut tree, I saw then, and I could see several nuts on the ground. I watched her gather nuts, put them into a spot beneath the one end of the red log, then regularly, methodically, pick up the end of the log—it worked like a lever—and hammer away at the nut, which eventually cracked. When the nut cracked, she would reach under her log, pull out the whitish meat, and eat it. Then she would place another nut in the spot beneath the one end of the log and start hammering again.

Soon there were other sounds of hammering from other spots in the glen: from the far side of the same tree, a mother, as I could see now, infant clutching at her breast, was cracking away at some nuts; and from a third and fourth spot in the same general area came more of these industrious sounds. The glen sounded like a small factory, but after several minutes, the chimps had stopped cracking nuts and left, so Christophe and I trotted down the brief hill and examined the big nutcracker log beneath the big nut tree. This cracker was a piece of hard and heavy wood with an irregular shape, perhaps a yard long, and beneath it we located the nut holder: a worn dent in a twisted root.

Christophe had some green nuts in his pocket, and he pulled a few out and handed them over. I placed one of the nuts in the dent, picked up the log, held it with both hands, just as the female chimp had done, and began hammering away. Sure enough, after six or seven hammers, the nut cracked open with that satisfying telltale sound. I picked out the white meat of the nut and ate it.

I put a second nut in the root dent, picked up the log, hammered away, but this time nothing happened. Those nuts were hard, and this one wasn't about to crack, so in the end I tossed it aside and placed a third nut down, at which point Christophe commented: "Typical infant behavior."

"Really?"

"That's just what the chimp infants do when they're first learning," he went on. "If it doesn't crack you blame it on the nut and try another nut. The nut is not the problem. It's your technique. Aiming is very important."

We followed the chimps again, and they continued through the forest for some time, seeking out food, climbing trees, and then resting: sprawled out, or sitting down and grooming each other. Once, I sat next to a bush that shook from laughter. It was astonishing. I never knew before that chimpanzees laugh. They do, and I listened to fifteen or twenty minutes of a gleeful and hoarse kind of wood-sawing—whuuu! whuuu! whuuu!—and watched on occasion as the two frantically playing juvenile chimps fell out of the bush, ran around, wrestled, chased each other, and then fell back into the bush again, laughing all the while.

In the early afternoon, we all reached a siesta place, a gigantic hole in the forest where a big tree had fallen down and the sun was pouring through. Around twenty chimps appeared at this patch of light and simply relaxed. Christophe and I did, too, and we watched some of the apes fling themselves back on the ground and sack out, with sun warming their faces; some sit or sprawl and wait for someone else to groom them; and others—almost always young—roll and tumble and play. There was also, in this particular group, an old male with a gray spot on his back, who had adopted a young orphan. We watched this old male chasing his adopted child around and around a tree, the young chimp laughing wildly, while the old male closed in and finally caught and tickled him, and playfully chewed on his foot.

An hour or so later we were up and moving again, and the group of chimps seemed to have grown bigger—though it was often hard to tell, since so much was obscured by the forest around us. But we were moving fast, now, and finally, we followed the chimps across their own international border. "They've entered the territory of the neighbors,"

Christophe·said, and it seemed as if our chimps were nervous. They approached a monumental tree and, making a tremendous racket of hoots and screams, grabbed onto some hanging lianas and just climbed right up, up perhaps eighty feet before entering the crown of the tree and disappearing inside. I don't know what they were doing up there. I couldn't see. And Christophe and I just stood patiently beneath the tree and looked up, while dust and sediment drifted and settled down into our faces.

Our walk through the forest was like a journey through an extended underground cavern. We wound through obscure passageways, into dark places and narrow places, out into small openings or great room-like glens, and then we tunneled back into winding passageways. Toward the end of the afternoon, Christophe and I followed what seemed like a large movement of chimpanzees, both sexes, all ages, into one great open room in the forest, relatively clear at ground level except for many columns of nut trees—and soon about a dozen chimps were hammering away, using log hammers on log or root anvils.

Hammering filled the air and mingled with the late afternoon chorus of insects, while the fingers of sunlight passing through trees reached low and then withdrew, and the light turned soft, then, and gentle. We had entered a factory, but it was a nursery, too, and I turned to watch a mother playing with her infant, tickling his toes with little playful nibbles and then looking into his laughing face and eyes with the most amazing gaze of adoration. Elsewhere, three adult females had situated themselves in a tree and were surrounding a single lucky infant. They were kissing and tickling the baby, who writhed with apparent pleasure, when, suddenly, their faces, which had taken on remarkable glowing expressions of adoration, registered in my mind as utterly comprehensible and entirely human-like. I was looking at intelligent faces experiencing an emotion I could only imagine to be love.

One commentator has said that the big difference between humans and chimps (intelligent though those apes may be) is that humans can invent great wonders of technology. "I considered the differences between men and animals," this person wrote. "Some were vast. A chimpanzee could be taught to drive a car. It could even be taught to build parts of it. But it could not begin to design it. . . . Our intellect is incomparably more sophisticated than any animal." One hears that sort of argument often, and, to my mind, it is mere self-stroking puffery. Could you or I begin to design a car? Has any single human being actually designed a car? Has any individual person really invented a steam engine, an airplane, or an F-117A Stealth fighter? Could any one person, abandoned at birth on a desert island somewhere—without pictures, communication, education, or artifacts—even invent a tricycle or a child's kite or a mouse trap? Obviously not. No, left at birth on a desert island, you and I and that commentator would be lifting and dropping chunks of wood or rounded stones onto hard nuts—and be damned glad we had figured that one out.

The great accomplishment of *Homo sapiens* is not technology, which in any case has become bigger and scarier than we are, a mixed blessing. The great accomplishment is language, which has enabled us to accumulate and coordinate our achievements, insights, and minicreations. Our big technologies are collective efforts, cultural products, all and always made possible by language. Even the supposed "milestones" of technological advancement—the use of movable type, to take one example—were collective events. Gutenburg didn't think up movable types whole, in an isolated stroke of genius. His partner was a goldsmith; his father was a mint employee, entirely familiar with the properties of soft metals. Printing presses were all around Europe by then, producing wonderful reproductions of woodblock originals. Gutenburg's great genius was to assemble, revise, and modify already long-established traditions in metallurgy, goldsmithing, and woodblock printing, not to mention papermaking and levered-press design.

If our great accomplishment is language, our great hope predates language in the timeline of ape evolution: the internal compass that may enable us to guide ourselves and our technological powers into the future: our glowing capacity for adoration of our own kind and for at least some empathy beyond our kind. The hand lifting and dropping the stone or chunk of wood is less impressive than the eye that gazes with love.

A Japanese scientist, Yukimaru Sugiyama, was studying some nut-cracking chimpanzees at a village called Bossou, in Guinea, that could be reached by driving north and west out of Ivory Coast. I had Sugiyama's permission to go there, and I even had a visa for Guinea. I was

especially interested in Bossou because I had heard the villagers regarded those chimps as totemic. I looked at the map longingly. Bossou
was only three inches away. But a good deal of those three inches
wiggled into the mountains, and Paul and I finally decided there
wasn't enough time.

Paul said there was an Ivory Coast village, Yaélé, at the foot of
Mount Nimba, where chimpanzees were also totemic. "They don't kill
it. They respect it. Like in Bossou." Paul said that Hedwige knew the
full story, but as he understood it, a family in Yaélé had a daughter
who one day went into the forest to gather nuts and became lost. She
was seen later in the forest with a group of chimps, half a chimp by
then. Since the chimps saved her, chimps became a village totem. I
looked longingly at Yaélé on the map, too, but Paul convinced me it
would take too much time.

Anyhow, first we had to go visit Denis's wife and children, who
lived in a village not far from Taï. The village seemed large to me and
disappointingly geometrical—very methodically laid out. Denis's
house was a mud daub construction with a thatched roof, and there
was a rabbit hutch to one side. Denis had been trying to breed rabbits.
He had started with three, a male and two females. Unfortunately, the
rabbits had been stolen, possibly by Liberians, Denis thought. Because
of the recent civil war in Liberia, many refugees had migrated across
the border and were taken in by Ivorean villages. Denis's own village
had taken several Liberians, he said. Not very long ago, he added,
before the Liberian war began, he and his cousin had gone into a
Liberian village to buy a shotgun. A Liberian took their money, promised to deliver the gun, and then never did. They went to him several
times to get the gun or their money back, but the Liberian had been
dishonest. Then, one day, the same Liberian became a refugee and
fled across the border with his family—and wound up at Denis's village
pleading to be taken in! He and his family were turned away.

Denis's wife was pretty and looked very young, possibly a teenager. They had three children, and the oldest son, perhaps six years
old, became angry toward the end of our visit. He didn't want his
father to leave again, and he cried and said angry things.

We stopped that afternoon in the village of Zagné and looked over
the edge of a bridge into brown water. Denis told me to drop a piece
of bread into the water, and when I did, the water swirled and then
solidified into fish—it was like watching a venetian blind close—catfish
with gray and whiskered wide heads, almost climbing on top of each

other to get the bread. We spoke to some villagers. Fish in this section of the river were totemic, one villager said, so no one was allowed to eat them.

Altogether, we took five days getting back to Abidjan, and on the way we stopped and looked inside several forests to see if there were chimps. Nonhabituated wild chimps are nearly impossible to find, so our technique was this: With machetes and a compass, we would walk absolutely straight into a forest for a particular distance and count any chimp nests we saw along the way at a certain distance on either side of our transect. Supposedly, then, we had taken a random sample of chimp nests over a certain area of potential habitat. If we knew the full area of potential habitat for that forest, we had a way of estimating the number of nests for the full habitat, and from that number we could estimate the number of chimps.

Mostly we camped along the way, but one night a local Eaux et Fôrets officer said there was a spare house we could stay in. We unlocked the door into this dusty, deserted place, but it stank of batshit. We cleaned it out, swept and mopped and opened all the windows, but it remained unbearable, so in the end we decided to find a hotel in town. The hotel was very dark inside, lit by a single blue fluorescent bulb in the lobby, with a plastic beach ball hanging from the ceiling as a bit of decoration, and our rooms swarmed with mosquitoes, but it was nice to have a shower.

The next day we ordered Cokes on the patio of a small restaurant. Across the way, a sign painted on a brick wall said, in French: FORBIDDEN TO URINATE HERE. Every two or three minutes, a man came and urinated on the sign. Some stood. Some squatted and somehow urinated out between their legs. A man in a business suit set his briefcase down before urinating on the sign. When our Cokes came, the waiter opened them in front of us, and Denis commented: "They always open the bottle in front of us because in Liberia people will put poison in it. And if you are in a village and they offer you water, they always drink a little bit before you do." Denis wore a T-shirt that said: "Yachting. Harry Sanders League America's Cup Diary."

We drove north for a couple of days to see what savanna country looked like, and so came to a hotter, drier region, a place of grass fires and brown leaves, with young boys pedaling old bicycles with huge bundles of firewood fastened to the back, and an old man riding his bicycle and carrying a big yellow and white dog under his arm. A woman carried a single large yam on her head. The yam looked like a hat. And in the towns, people hung around on the streets, sitting around a cooking pot, lying down in the shade, or sitting in an open tin shed and drinking beer.

We stopped in a town, at a bar, for a few drinks toward the end of a hot afternoon, and we asked for information about hotels. There were no hotels, we were told, but there was a factory where we might be able to sleep. We were given directions and so drove off the paved road onto a straight dirt track, riding in a cloud of red dust, driving for several miles through a dusty air and into a lingering smell of smoke.

This was a softly rolling land, wild, with only occasional signs of human habitation, a few baobab trees, brush and brown grass to the horizon, and, as the sky dimmed into dusk, a full moon rising.

We came to a crossroads and found the factory.

But it seemed desolate out there, so isolated, a blasted moor beneath a translucent moon—and then we found the factory, giant and modern, lit up now with halogen security lights, patrolled by uniformed security guards from the local village, a square mile of factory surrounded by a high fence topped with barbed wire. There were two gleaming, cathedral-sized buildings inside the fence, interconnected with covered conveyors, and more buildings spread out from there, along with sheds and guardhouses, giant hoppers, giant machinery, wheels, tractors, and gas pumps. There was a vast storage yard, filled now with grazing sheep and perhaps a hundred or two hundred steel shipping containers with vines growing around and into them. Nearest the road, there were two single-story administration buildings. The once manicured lawn out front had turned into scrub, and the glass door entrance to the main administration building was smashed. The parking lot in front of the main building was disintegrating, but we drove into it and spoke to two uninformed watchmen standing there.

They told us it was a sugar factory. Shut down in 1984. They said we couldn't sleep inside the factory without permission from the chief of security, who lived down the way.

They gave us directions, and we drove out along a straight road marking part of the factory's perimeter and then onto a winding track, past three shanties with laundry and chickens outside, down a road, past a village of open mud huts, out to the security chief's place. The security chief, a big and pleasant-mannered man, sat out in the backyard of his bungalow, chatting quietly with some other men. Chairs were brought out from the house for us.

We sat and palavered with the security chief and his friends in a Miró dream under a pasted moon, with two young girls in soft cotton dresses laughing and playing, with goats, chickens, a stucco bungalow and tin roof, rusty steel drums, and the muted colors of dusk settling onto a dirt landscape. It was really a lovely evening, cool, with the melancholic smells of a distant grass fire, the drifting sound of childish laughter, musical and beatific, and a strong sense of rural peace.

Water was brought out in four glasses. Paul smiled and apologized for not drinking. He explained that white people have weak stomachs and get sick on well and river water. Denis drank his water with gusto.

The security chief gave us permission to sleep at the factory, and so we drove back. A key was rattled inside a keyhole of the broken glass door entrance to the administration building. The doors were unlocked, drawn open, and we walked inside. The power lines to the factory had long ago been cut, so there was no electricity other than an emergency supply lighting up the security lights, and so we made our way through the adminstration building with flashlights. Paul had a coal-miner's lamp strapped to his forehead, and it was so dark inside there it felt like we were exploring a mine. A door with a sign on it saying CENTRE DE GESTION was unlocked, and our lights swept inside—desk there, shelves and cabinets, a red curtain over a window. The curtain was pulled back, the window pried open. We looked into a second room and then a third room—SALLE DE CONFERENCE—with a beautiful long wooden desk and records stacked everywhere. Our lights illuminated piles and piles of correspondence, memos, statements of rules and policies and procedures, debits and credits, long explanations regarding this and that. We opened all the windows we could, but the offices were still hot and stuffy, and in the end we moved out to where the truck was parked, in the executive carport. We hung mosquito nets from the braces of the carport, set up our gas stove, kerosene lanterns, tents.

The security guards were there, of course, and so we simply left our things out in the open, under their protection, while we made a quick trip down to the local river to bathe. A woman stood in the river, a half-full pan of water balanced on her head, holding her wraparound dress with one hand and, with the other, scooping water from the river with a calabash and tossing it into the pan on her head. And then, cool and clean with sand on our feet, we came back to the factory and cooked dinner.

The news on the radio said that bombs were being tossed onto the man's capital city and that the man was squeezing off missiles into Jerusalem. But that was the news we had heard yesterday and the day before. The grass fires were closer now, so I judged from the smoky haze in the air and the sudden swarms of winged termites—and the thin and wavering voice on the radio news took on a remote and surreal aspect. We ate our cache of chocolate for dessert, and Natalie looked at her final piece of chocolate and said, half in jest, "It's because we have this that the forests are gone." Paul smoked a cigarette and wanted to know if I had gone to Woodstock. I hadn't. "It was a famous event in Europe," he said. He played some tape recordings of monkey calls, and then he played an Eric Clapton tape. And, as that dog-howler moon rose overhead and turned the night black and silver, I fell into a melancholic fit. This night reminded me of balmy summer nights in California, the sweet smell of dry, golden grass and the dark scattering of live oaks on the hills. I had been young in California! Eric Clapton sang about all the terrific things that were going to happen after midnight, and I wondered: *How has my life gone so fast? My mother is dead. My father is dead. The forests are going, and the world is dying.*

President Bush had begun comparing the man to Hitler, and some people were objecting that the comparison was exaggerated and that it inappropriately personalized the war. The man, in turn, began comparing President Bush to . . . President Bush, which may have been exaggerated and inappropriately personalized as well.

But really, this was not a war between leaders. Nor was it so much a war between generals or between opposing ranks of hard, heroic warriors. No, this was a war of technology. And, if I were to personalize the techology a little, I might say that it was a war between technologists: between opposing phalanxes of the awkward, understated blokes and birds with the pencils in their shirt pockets. This was a war of engineers. Were the engineers who had labored so hard and long to invent, design, and assemble the man's technology any match for the engineers who invented, designed, and assembled the coalition's technology? It came down to that.

My father was a civil engineer, and he always liked to think about bridges and factories and public works. The one time he went to Europe, he entertained himself by looking over European sewage systems. When he was an old man in a nursing home, he could recite the precise number of paces from his room to the dining hall and other points of interest, and the average times walking there.

It must have been with a memory of my father that I so doggedly requested permission to walk through the inside of the factory the next morning. The security chief agreed that I could, as long as I didn't take any photographs, and so one of the guards accompanied me, and we walked past a shed still filled with sacks of sugar, past a series of huge conveyors leading into the largest factory building, an edifice rex covered with corrugated aluminum and fiberglass panels. We entered the storage and packing building and from there passed through a high overhead pipe, along a catwalk with conveyor belts on either side, into the main building. It was as high as a forest inside, with four levels of catwalks, with furnaces and wells, outlets and inlets, power switches and control panels, cooking vats and mashing vats and mixing vats, a high and hollow place filled with thick dust and a few flickers of life—a single iridescent blue butterfly fluttering aimlessly into and out of a shaft of light, a few pigeons dropping white pellets from the top vents—like a forest in height and light, but still and dead, as quiet as a desert, with only the echoing pong of our footsteps on the catwalks and the lonely chirping of a couple of lost birds.

The guard explained everything to me in French. "And this is where they mash the cane," he said. I understood, and I responded politely and, given the inadequacy of my French, primitively: "Very big. Very big."

The guard said: "And this is the control board." I said: "Ah!" He said: "And this is the hot water." I said: "Yes. Yes." He said: "This is where the cane comes in trucks and the machinery unloads it and flips it over there." I said: "Yes. I understand!" He said: "Here is the storage area." I said: "Very big. Very big."

The place was very big, very big, but it was very sad, too. Like so much technology that comes, poorly planned, to untechnological places, it had quickly been rejected. It was already an artifact. Technology is a fossil, a footprint, an echo of human passion: the sword fits the hand and slices the body. But in this sad and whispering place, this already abandoned and lost engineer's dream, I thought I would have engineered a new kind of technology, something farther from the hand and fist, and nearer to the breath and the heart, something less of a rounded stone and more of a loving gaze. If I could I would have engineered a small device, a tiny Stealth of the mind or soul that would take something fragile and fleeting—the soft laughter of a wild chimpanzee in a disappearing forest, for example, or the murmur of one stricken soldier, *I didn't mean this, I hadn't planned to be here*, as his body gasps and sucks and separates into twenty-seven useless pieces of flesh—would take that laughter, that murmur, and amplify it beyond our imagining until hypothetically at least it could rise and expand and explode with an urgency of thunder around the world, and break hearts. It would break every human heart.

12

Leaders and Heroes

*It is perhaps just worth while to mention a trick that
has been practised in most countries, from England
to Peru. A traveller is threatened by a robber with a
gun and ordered to throw himself on the ground, or
he will be fired at. The traveller taking a pistol from
his belt, shouts out, "If this were loaded you should
not treat me thus!" and throws himself on the ground
as the robber bids him. There he lies till the robber,
in his triumph, comes up for his booty; when the
intended victim takes a quick aim and shoots him
dead—the pistol being really loaded all the while.*

–Francis Galton, *The Art of Travel*

The more I travel, the less I like airplanes. Airplanes are heavier than
air, not lighter, and it's a fundamental violation of nature for them to
go up there. I particularly dislike big jets, the way they roll and rage
along the runway, creaking and wobbling like an old house, and then
they suddenly pull up and ascend far, far, far, far too steeply. Then
there's the dipping feeling, minutes later, as the plane levels off. *Oh, no,*
I think, *we're dropping!* I hear the engines fade. I feel the loss of
forward motion. The whining pitch of the engines lowers, then stabi-
lizes, then rises again. *Why is the pilot doing this to me? Who is up there
fiddling with the controls? This thing could drop like a stone!* And then, sometimes, when the turbulence is suspiciously better than usual or omi-

nously worse, and when we're up so high there's no point in looking
out the window, I remember those famous disasters—the airliner
turned into an oil slick by a Soviet fighter pilot just following orders,
the one bombed into nonexistence by an unhappy someone or other—
and I think, dropping all pretense of rationality now: *It's going to explode!*
I can see the plane exploding. I'll hang on to my backpack—it's got my
notes inside. I'll see if by spreading my arms and legs like a skydiver, I
can slow my fall enough that a crash landing in the trees can save my
life. Or maybe we'll land in the ocean. Somehow, I'll have to keep my
notes above water. *God!* I cry out in my mind, *Let me live!* And I grip
the handles of my seat and press an overhead button for the
stewardess.

Love and death are closely allied, as any English major will tell
you, and as I sat there, quivering and mortal, strapped inside a vibrating metal prophylactic pushed by only three jet engines high into the
cold, thin air above Central Africa, my mind delinquently jogged back
and forth between the spiky grotto of Thanatos and the soft bower of
Eros.

It all began that morning when I woke from a dream. I was in
college. A gorgeous, flame-haired woman of indeterminate age and
identity, a stewardess perhaps, came to see me to fulfill certain long-
ings. She herself was disturbed about a strong feeling of rootlessness.
We agreed to meet and discuss these issues further as soon as a time
could be arranged. We would meet in a padded room, which I went
off to find. I came to a corridor full of fresh cut, luscious fruit: mounds
of strawberries, pineapples, peaches. *So this is where the university stores its
fruit,* I said to myself. *I'm glad to know where I can get some in the future.*
The meeting was arranged, the room was well-padded—and I woke
up, bathed in a benign and luxuriant mood.

I was one of the first to board the plane that morning, and I went
directly to my seat near the front. Two stewardesses were managing
my section, both French, one slender and one huge. The congestion
of the crowd sweeping into the plane, pressing into places everywhere,
forced the huge stewardess off to one side of the aisle, against my seat,
where she pressed a buttock the size of a basketball, the texture of a
very ripe melon, into my face. She persisted in that posture for, oh,
half a minute; and then she turned around to apologize, in French. I
could only smile and say, in English, "It's all right!"

Then there was the other stewardess, the slender one—with short
hair, bright red lips, an upturned blouse collar, a blouse that pulled

open between buttons when she stood in a certain way, a big Gallic nose, and terrible English: "Ladies and cattlemen, please toss your seatbelt and place your seat upright to piss in." And when she sat down, strapped herself into a seat alongside the steward, and they turned to smile chummily at each other, I burned with jealousy!

I knew I was in trouble now. I was headed for a place where French would be very important. Even the stewardesses didn't know English, other than a few stock expressions they had memorized by rote in stewardess school fifteen years ago. I thought back to my high school French teacher, Reba Masterson, bless her dear, dear soul, shouting "Écoutez!" and rapping her desk with the knuckles of one hand while holding up a pencil in the other. "Écoutez! Alors! Qu'est-ce que c'est?" she said.

"C'est un stylo," we said.

Having reviewed with suave verve my French lessons, and now that we were looping up into the air, I pressed with a certain je ne sais quoi the overhead button, and the slender stewardess with the red lips and the big nose bent down to me. I said, with bourgeois insouciance: "Avez vous quelque chose en Anglais à lire?"

She said several quick French sentences in return, smiled, and then half an hour later brought me a French newspaper describing the situation in Le Golf. I screwed up my eyes and stared at the words on the page, but what I read was what I already knew: a war going on, bombs dropping, people dying. Oh, yes, George Bush was saying something, only it was in French–so I couldn't figure out what he was *really* saying. But wait a minute! I never knew what he was *really* saying anyway, even when it was in English.

It is true that George Bush would not have allowed himself to be distracted by stewardesses, and he early in life overcame his fear of flying. He was a hero, in fact, and I do very much admire his record as a young man: one of the youngest American pilots of World War II, shot down flying an Avenger bomber over the island of Chichishima. He was a brave pilot and a hero–but the war produced many brave pilots and many heroes. (Among them, John F. Kennedy, who also emerged a hero after swimming in the Pacific during that nonpacific time.) Why should this particular one now clutch the controls of an airship carrying a quarter of a billion passengers? Did anyone ever imagine that heroes may not make the best leaders? Did anyone ever think the man was too enthusiastic? That he loved the surge and dive and rising flak of international conflict a little too much?

Pretty soon the newspaper had given me a headache, and when the plane tipped nose down and descended like a rocket, I was ready to crawl out the window. First it was cold. Then, after the doors opened, it was stifling and steamy.

My ultimate destination was Gabon, Central Africa, but I had discovered an extra dozen days on my schedule and so was taking a short side trip to another place where, according to rumors I had heard, plans were afoot to establish a new biomedical research laboratory that would use chimps. But without any good contacts or solid leads in this country, the rumors remained rumors, and after a couple of days I found myself sitting at a table of the Death Bar in Hotel Too Expensive, watching on television an inaudible image of George Bush alternating with other inaudible images of chaos, drinking beer and socking myself in the head for having been so stupid as to come there in the first place.

Bolted to the walls of the Death Bar were big stuffed crocodiles, a stuffed gar, the socket-eyed skulls of a huge buffalo and a tiny duiker, a varnished sea turtle carapace, and the head of a sea bass, its mouth gaping wide enough to hold a sewer pipe. Tucked in between the skulls and trophies on the walls were two dozen photographs of happy campers: A white man sitting on the back of a dead male lion, pulling the lion's head back and up by tugging on the mane; other white men stroking their erect guns and sitting next to dead buffalo, bongos, a big male baboon, more lions; and two more white guys standing next to a tipped-over elephant. A huge gun with a telescopic sight had been propped up against the corpse of the elephant, and the two white guys were modestly trying to restrain proud grins that said: "We done this! It was beautiful and wild and alive, and we put holes in it and made it dead—all by ourselves!"

These guys no doubt saw themselves as heroes of the old school, sword-slingers and chaos-conquerors: Beowulf victoriously displaying the head of poor Grendel. I had trouble deciding whether they were pathetic poseurs or stupid bastards.

While I was looking over the Death Bar decor, an African came over. "Oh, there you are!" he said most eagerly. "I saw you at the airport! I was your immigration officer. You remember me? Immigration?" He shook my hand wildly and invited himself to sit down.

I smiled at him: "Okay, you're the immigration officer! Do you remember my name?"

No, he didn't remember my name.

"Buy me a beer," I said. He did, and after two more beers, I found him to be much less obnoxious. When I said I was traveling around Africa trying to learn about chimpanzees, he said he knew just the person to help me: Abu.

I met Abu at his house the next day. He was big and extroverted. He had a round face, a powerful smile, and a real interest in wildlife. But he was currently vexed because his Toyota had broken down. I looked beneath the hood and discovered, to my delight, that this problem I understood: leaky water pump gasket. I fixed it, cutting a new gasket out of an old piece of cardboard, and stayed for dinner.

Abu could be described as a leader of the loyal opposition. He was an important person, I began to realize, and he had a sense of humor to go with it. He stammered, on occasion, but once his sentences began they were completed precisely in whichever of five languages he was using at the moment—for me, excellent English. He kept the fingernails of both pinky fingers very long, and after we became friends I asked him why. He said it was to pick his teeth after a good meal, though I never actually saw him picking his teeth. We got along. We shared some interests, and pretty soon he had decided to take a week off, drive me out into the bush, and show me himself where he thought chimpanzees might be.

Thus, one morning, I pushed my pack and a few other essentials into the back of Abu's Toyota and took off. There was actually a good-sized forest just on the edge of town, and we drove by it and saw some of the trees, but Abu didn't think it was worth looking into very deeply. "There were chimps in that forest about fifteen years ago," he said. "But now it has no apes and no monkeys. In fact, no mammals at all. But it's good for insects."

A couple of hours outside the city, the road turned into a winding track through primary forest, and an hour later we overtook two hunters walking along the road, one with a double-barreled shotgun, the other with a single-barreled shotgun. We saw their dog first, a little black and white affair with a whipping white tail, trotting along the road, and when we saw them, we stopped and talked to them briefly but learned very little. As we drove off, Abu said: "This is supposed to be protected forest, where hunting is illegal. The fact that they didn't hide, didn't jump back into the forest when they heard our car, tells me that the Forest Department rangers haven't been around lately." He thought about that one for a moment, and then added: "Actually, the rangers never go into the forests. They don't like the forests, and they are afraid of the poachers."

Abu said that every rural village had at least one hunter, a person who would provide meat for everyone else. He said that the best way to find chimpanzees was to walk into any village and ask to meet the man who knew the forest best—that would be the hunter. We stayed that night in town, at a small hotel, and the next day we went from one village to the next, asking to meet the man who knew the forest best.

In that fashion we met Stephan, a middle-aged man who never actually said he was a hunter, but claimed to know the forest very well and declared that his family owned twelve hectares of it behind the village. Abu commented later: "But this is a protected forest. Typical situation: The government claims ownership, but the village has been here forever. The people say, 'This has always been our forest.' There's still a lot of forest left, but I have a feeling his way of life is doomed. And he will be one day, possibly, hungry."

We met, and had dinner with, Peter the Little Hunter, young, handsome, and built like an athlete. He told us he was the only hunter of his village, eighteen adults. He hunts meat for himself and his family, but when there is some left over he gives it to the other villagers. He said he uses a flashlight to hunt duikers and other small animals at night, and during the day he hunts monkeys, most often dianas and mangabeys. Red colobus have already been pretty much hunted out of his area, he said, because they are so easy to hunt. Yes, he hunts chimpanzees, too, he said, and manages to bag about ten per year. It can be dangerous, hunting chimps. One time, for instance, he shot a mother and her infant, and a big male showed up and began to attack, so he was forced to shoot the male as well. On occasion, he manages to get living chimp babies, after shooting their mothers, and sometimes these can be sold to white people.

And we met Alain, a slow-moving man with a slow smile and missing teeth, a single-barreled shotgun slung over his shoulder, panga in his hand, on his way along a path into the forest. We asked him what he hunts. He answered: Duikers, monkeys, and chimpanzees. He showed us his cartridge for chimps. It was white. His usual cartridges were red, but the white one had a bigger grain of shot. Abu said: "You leave the chimpanzees today, because they are my brothers"—and he thumped his fist over his heart to emphasize the concept. After Alain had walked away, Abu said to me, "He will not hunt chimpanzees today. If he does, I will go to the police."

We came to a river and walked down to the edge. A few hippos were there, raising and lowering themselves in the water. They were huge, the size of trucks and shaped like storage tanks, and they made the noises of big cows: heavy breathing and an explosive, half-submerged moooooooooo! The water was green, the hippos gray, and more must have been submerged under the water, because big bursts of air kept breaking up to the surface in big watery explosions, like gigantic bathtub farts: Poooooot!

Then we drove on a highway that was only a couple of years old, paved and following a straight gap cut through the forest. High green walls on either side smelled sweet and fecund. We saw several hunters walking alongside the road, and Abu said, "I never saw so many guns! It's crazy!"

We parked on a bridge and looked at a river, but while thus engaged a Forestry Department officer with a gun at his hip approached us, began smiling and saying friendly things. He had decorative scars on his forehead, cheeks, and around his eyes. He was very friendly, but after a while, I understood that he was too friendly. "It's February," he said. "The New Year. Give me a little gift to celebrate the New Year." Abu smiled and agreed that perhaps a gift would be a good idea. He reached into the backseat and drew from an open sack of vegetables a limp zucchini. He handed the officer the limp zucchini, smiled brightly, and put the Toyota into gear.

We entered a part of the forest that had been designated as national forest, legally protected from hunting and unauthorized logging, and we walked slowly along a narrow trail, looking for chimpanzee nests. Two old people overtook us on the trail. The old man came into sight first, a man with rotten teeth, white stubble on his face, plastic shoes falling apart and tied together with twine, who sighed tragically as he walked. He was carrying a panga in one hand and a jug of water in the other. About five minutes after him an old woman appeared on the trail, dressed in a brown-patterned wraparound, barefoot, carrying a large aluminum pot on her head. "This old man and this old lady are the workers of the forest," Abu said. "They will cut the forest today. The president says, 'When you plant coffee, the earth belongs to you.' So it means that, if the Forestry Department comes here, it is not easy to chase these people—even if it is a national park. You have to arrest them before they've planted anything. It's much easier then."

Indeed, we eventually caught up with the old man and old woman resting inside a small stick and palm house within a very large, rectangular hole in the forest. There was bright sunlight, dry air, a few still standing trees, some fallen ones, and coffee plants all around. "You see this encampment?" Abu said. "One day the whole family will move here, and it becomes a village. I have looked at the satellite maps now, and I see just irregular patches of forest left—islands of forest. Some of the boundaries are still sharp—a very clean edge between plantation and forest. But other boundaries are moth-eaten, as people move in, illegally, and begin to poach on forested land. In Europe you have cut all your primary forests already, except in Poland. So if you want Africans to save primary forests, perhaps you will have to pay. . . ."

We drove along a road to the end of one forest and entered a region that looked like a war zone: dead trees and scrappy bush, then weeds, grasses, denuded soil, and tree skeletons. "This road was built ten years ago," Abu said. "Ten years ago, this was all primary forest for hundreds of miles, and now, in the north, people actually have to buy wood. Ten years ago, you used to see trucks coming on this road carrying only one big tree. Now the trees are not so big anymore. The trucks carry five or ten. There used to be big crocodiles in the river here, but you cannot see them anymore. White people are still killing crocs for fun in this country, and so the big ones are not common. Buffalo are still common. They like degraded forest, and they are very dangerous to hunt, so it's only specialized hunters with big guns—who also kill the elephants."

We drove north, then, stopping for a moment to talk with two boys standing along the road, offering a dead monkey for sale. The monkey was a spot-nosed guenon, limp, blank-eyed, tongue hanging out, and the boys said she had just had a baby, which they also killed. They offered the monkey to us for the equivalent of eight dollars, which Abu said was the price for white people. He said a fair price would be more like four dollars.

We drove onto a country track and stopped at a trail leading to a village. Two adolescent boys came out from the village trail. One wore a red baseball cap with the Coca-Cola trademark in white; the other was dressed in brown pants so raggedy he had to wear another pair of pants beneath to preserve his modesty. The brown pants had a back pocket, which held a slingshot. The two teenagers ushered us into this village—mud-brick and mud-daub houses—and directed us to sit down in a wood-pole and thatched-roof pavilion. We sat in tripod stick-chairs and waited. At the other end of the pavilion, an old woman and a young girl were sitting, talking, and cooking in a pot over an open fire. Pretty soon, the chief's son appeared, a hulking man who seemed perhaps thirty-five or forty years old, and he said that we couldn't go into the forest without permission from the chief and that the chief was out making *bangie*—palm wine.

The two teenagers agreed to take us to the chief. We exchanged pleasantries with the young girl (lovely, about eight or nine years old, wearing a worn and simple cotton dress, a sweet face, her hair in snaky plaits, sitting facing us, knees slight apart, modestly holding the hem of her dress shut) and the old woman (gregarious and toothless, in a baggy dress, who held out her wrist rather than her hand to shake, indicating with eyes and a wry facial expression that her hand was dirty from cooking) and walked back out to the Toyota. The teenagers piled into the backseat of the Toyota, and as we drove back down the track, they directed us to turn here, not turn there, until we stopped again on the track. We got out of the car and walked up a path that was marked with an entrance: a well-manicured palm frond, looking like a wide-toothed comb, arranged between two trees as a lintel for the door of the path. Hanging on this lintel were twigs, leaves, and a single curved horn, closed at the end with a small piece of cloth. We came to a small clearing. The clearing had a few logs placed in a manner that clarified their function: benches. One of the teenagers explained that this was where the men went to drink their palm wine.

The chief appeared, along with three or four other men. The chief was old, with grizzled short hair, and was dressed in a brown shirt and brown pants. He was sweating, and had a pug nose and a nice smile that showed teeth as yellow as corn. He was both dignified and impish, and he wore a full straw hat. We shook hands. We sat down. Abu turned to the chief and began explaining, in French, why we were there. But the chief looked at Abu blankly and waited while one of the men turned Abu's French into the local language—a tonal language that sounded vaguely Chinese. Then the chief said something in the local language, and the interpreter put it into French for us. The chief was seventy-two years old. He had been to Europe, and he knew many

Europeans. For two years he fought against the Germans during World War II. Abu said something back, in French, and, while the chief gave us his blank look, the interpreter dutifully turned it into the tonal language.

This interpreted conversation went on for about ten minutes until the chief became tired of his ruse and began speaking directly to us in French. I suppose I must have been looking my usual vacuous self, because after a minute he said to me, "Monsieur Dale, quel age avez vous?" I understood what he said, but it took me so long to formulate a response in French that he switched to German: "Sprechen Sie Deutsch?" Abu later said he thought the chief was trying to find out if I was German. Perhaps he hated Germans.

The chief showed us how to make palm wine. The tree is dug up at the root, toppled, and then a square hole is cut near the top of the palm, removing the heart. The heart (tender and delicate, with the texture of celery root) is eaten, and then a slow fire is burned in the square hole. The fire melts and draws the sap, which drips through a hole and bamboo nozzle into a jug or bowl and then is left to ferment. Several liters a day will flow out of a single tree, the chief said.

A couple of days later, we visited the northern edge of a national park, and sat on some rocks overlooking a beautiful open stretch of grassland. We watched about two dozen forest buffalo trot out into the open, followed by a hartebeest buck, and then we heard a gunshot, over to the right. Upon investigating, Abu and I discovered the source of that gunshot—poachers, perhaps two or three—inside a small copse. Very stupidly, we chased after the poachers who, surprised and confused by our fake, unarmed attack, fled. But a few minutes later, we discovered more poachers over in another direction. Then, as we drove into another section of the park, we sighted the rising plume of smoke from a poachers' fire, probably smoking meat.

Hunters had taken over this national park. I thought it might be useful to go talk to some, but Abu was afraid they might shoot us.

"There have been people here in Africa for millions of years," he said, "and only in ten years we are killing and destroying everything. This makes me crazy!"

Late one afternoon, we visited a local Forestry Department building. After various minor formalities, we were shown into the office of the director. The director's office had green-painted stucco walls, one of which supported a detailed map of the region. On top of the director's desk was a plastic rose wrapped in cellophane and placed in a wooden vase. There was a small metal Statue of Liberty on his desk; a postcard showing a Ford flatbed truck carrying a single giant tomato had been propped against the Statue of Liberty. The director, a slight young man with a dent in the right side of his forehead, wore a tan leisure suit. He said he had only been on the job six months and thus had not yet been out to see any of the forests. He thought there might be elephants and chimps around, but then again he wasn't certain. He looked through his files to find any information about possible elephants and chimps, and then he called in his assistant. The assistant, wearing a green leisure suit, was bigger and more forceful. He said he had been in the forest once or twice, although he wasn't sure where it was on the map. He didn't know if there were elephants or chimps in the forest, but it was all right if we wanted to go out and look for ourselves.

And so, the next day, Abu and I went out to that protected forest to look for ourselves. We started just outside of the forest boundary, as we understood it from the map, where there was a good-sized village, and we asked in the village whether there was anyone who knew about the forest. We were directed to sit on a log in a dirt clearing in the middle of the village, in front of the chief's house and under a persimmon tree with a few ripe persimmons in it. A pole lay on the ground beneath this tree, and pretty soon someone came over, picked up the pole, and knocked out three persimmons: one for Abu, one for me, and the third for himself. A nail had been driven into the trunk of this tree, and on the nail hung a portable radio and tape player. That and a week-old newspaper on the ground (with the headline: BAGDAD BOMBED) were the only signs of modern life in the village.

It was a simple place, I concluded, but peaceful, and some men came over and visited. They said the chief was gone somewhere. One villager, dressed in shorts and a clean white sport shirt, looking healthy and prosperous, untwisted a piece of newspaper: flecks of gold! "We get this in the river," he said. Later, he showed us something inside another wad of newspaper: uncut diamonds. "We find them at the river." And then, at last, the village hunter appeared.

He was a tall beanpole of a man, and he looked dissolute. He had wild hair, a scruffy beard, and the whites of his eyes were orange. He held a shotgun in his hand, and he carried, in a black leather sheath at his waist, a long knife. He wore Levi's, white plastic sandals, and a purple cotton hunting shirt. This shirt had two shotgun cartridges, one red, one green and white, tied with string at nipple position and hanging there, like big magic nipples; a big gray cartridge pouch had been sewn to the belly. There was also a small knife in a black sheath tied to the shirt, beneath one of the nipple cartridges. The hunter's name, we were told, was Akka Kareem, but he didn't speak any European language or any of the three or four African languages Abu understood, so he wanted to bring along another villager who spoke a little French. Abu said that was all right, but no guns—we weren't going to shoot anything—and so Akka disappeared and soon reappeared minus his shotgun plus an interpretering pal.

The four of us climbed into the Toyota and drove down the road toward the protected forest. This was a very dry forest. The leaves of the trees were more brown than green, and there were large spaces between trees where the sun poured in. We crunched through the forest, walked across some grassland, and came down to a river. Akka said (as we quizzed him through the interpreter) that he sometimes hunted chimpanzees, and that he had killed three of them. We weren't sure that he meant what we meant by "chimpanzee," so we asked him to describe them, and he did accurately. But he seemed impatient with us, and he walked fast.

We rested by the river for a long while and ate some eggs and oranges. There was a midday calm on the water, with twenty white herons sitting on rocks in the middle. Boat-shaped brown and yellow leaves floated slowly down in the slow current at the river's edge, and inside the water I could see several small fish.

We came to the poachers' camp belonging to Akka and his friends. The camp included three rough huts and several wood racks for smoking meat. In front of one of the huts I saw a large steel trap, and off in the grass to one side an old blue motorbike had been leaned against a short tree. Inside one of the huts, a man with a very big nose was lying on a rough mat, stripped to the waist, his two feet sticking out in our direction. We must have woken him up. Akka began talking with this man, and then, through the village interpreter, Akka said this was a hunting camp, of course, but they didn't actually hunt very much. Just enough for themselves. Abu commented quietly to me: "Before, he said they hunt a lot. They hunt everything, I think."

It was a very hot day, and the hunter and his interpreter led us at their quick pace here and there, through high, dry grass and through forest so dry everything cracked and crackled. We walked through burned areas, where hunters had set fires I was told, across charred and bitter-smelling grass and long white stripes over the black where fallen trees had slowly dissolved into white ash. I don't believe Abu liked Akka the hunter very much, and I do know I stopped trusting him. Perhaps it was the way twigs and leaf fragments stuck in his chaotic hair, or perhaps it was his manner of smiling, very slowly, as if he were being careful not to sneer. Perhaps it was the covert way he would look over to his cohort, or perhaps it was their long, quiet talk in a tongue neither I nor Abu understood. I imagined Akka to be a bachelor: He seemed unkempt, uncared for, incomplete. And I could imagine those eyes—onyx irises surrounded by orange—turn, with that slow smile, crazy.

Chimpanzees (so the experts tell me) live in a "fission-fusion" social system. Largely in response to environmental or physiological circumstances—availability of food, for example, or the presence or absence of estrous females—individual chimps in any given community tend to disperse or to coalesce.

Beyond that general trend, other forces operate. The smallest, most stable, and most important social unit exists between mother and offspring. Mothers stay with their offspring for many years. Young chimps need their mothers for many years. They need their mothers first of all for nourishment, for milk and, after weaning, guidance to the best food sources. They need their mothers for transportation and physical protection. Perhaps most significantly, they need their mothers for psychological sustenance.

Young chimps never know who their fathers are, nor do the adult males in a community appear to recognize their children. Typically, the mother will have mated with several males during her time of estrus, thus obliterating any clear knowledge of paternity. As a result, typically no adult male in a community will single out young for special, parental-style attention. Adult males, in other words, are not typically the nurturers of a chimp community. On the other hand, the confusion of paternity means that no male can be certain that a youngster in the community is *not* his offspring—and probably as a result of this confused paternity, the adult males are protective in a generalized fashion of the community young. (In distinct contrast, gorillas live in harem societies: one "silverback" adult male mating with several adult females. Gorillas are not confused about paternity, and when, as sometimes happens, a resident silverback is driven out by some powerful upstart, the victorious rival celebrates his victory by killing all the infants of the group and then, as they become fertile again, mating with the adult females, thus insuring his own paternity for all the infants in his new group.)

If the smallest chimpanzee social unit is the mother-offspring bond, the largest unit is the community: the larger group of chimps, perhaps fifty altogether, who generally live together in a single territory, individuals who behave sometimes as friends, sometimes as enemies, but who always act as if they recognize each other. The larger community operates like a nation, of sorts, and typically it exists in an uneasy truce with other chimpanzee communities inhabiting territory in the surrounding forest, sharing common and often clearly defined borders.

The borders are defined by adult male chimps who regularly join together in all-male coalitions and patrol the edges of their home territory, moving around the perimeter, testing the quality of the neighboring community's defenses, testing the fluidity of the borders, ready to recede if they accidentally stumble upon male chimps of another community who happened to possess superior numbers—and sometimes ready to attack if they stumble upon inferior numbers of foreign male chimps. When they do attack, the results are often both brutal and lethal. Attacking gangs of male chimps have been known not merely to beat up poorly defended males of another nation-community, and not merely to kill, but to break, tear, and dismember.

The situation resembles human warfare—and, in fact, only two species, humans and chimps, live in these sorts of societies, with these kinds of uneasy, international or intercommunity territorial relationships, this perpetual state of war or potential war mostly organized and led by highly aggressive coalitions of adult males.

Inside the chimpanzee community, the same coalitions of adult males exist in a hierarchical yet politicized harmony. There are chimpanzee leaders and chimpanzee followers, and perhaps the simplest way to describe this pattern is to consider that some chimps are dominant over others. A dominant chimp has first access to the goodies of chimp life: food and sex. And it is true that dominance is partly achieved by physical force. A big and strong chimp is likely to become dominant over a smaller chimp—and, because males are physically bigger and stronger than females, adult males tend to achieve dominance over females. (Males may also be more preoccupied with the dominance struggle in the first place. Females think of other ways to entertain themselves.) But among chimps, at least, real dominance is achieved and maintained over time not solely through force and intimidation but through politics. Chimpanzees develop important friends and allies, within any community, and the overall leader is going to maintain his position over time because he is smart enough to keep his rivals disorganized and his allies organized.

I once knew a Saudi Arabian well enough to ask him the following personal question: "What's it like to live in a kingdom?" His answer surprised me, but it shouldn't have: "It depends on the king." Of course, the quality of life in a democracy depends on the president or prime minister—as well as the coalition of leaders behind that personage. But in a democracy, even if your president or prime minister is a crook or a fool, at least every few years you get to try your luck with another crook or fool.

Chimpanzee society, it seems to me, combines the qualities of kingdom and democracy. There is a hereditary element. Although the chimpanzee leader will never know who his offspring are, he does know who his brothers and sisters are, and his authority and dominance tend to spread along family lines. Siblings, male and female, tend to become allies. On the other hand, chimpanzees have good memories. The alpha male, the dominator of any chimp community, may have first access to the goodies of chimp life, but he also serves an important community role. The alpha male is also a leader, a bringer of order from chaos. For chimpanzee life is not merely a series of isolated violent interactions perpetrated by aggressive individuals, followed by rigid and predictable realignments in hierarchy and privilege. No, as Frans de Waal has argued and documented so thoroughly in *Peacemaking Among Primates*, chimpanzee social life is more a dynamic and ongoing series of conflicts followed by reconciliations. There will be realignments in hierarchy and privilege, over time, but the leaders ultimately achieve leadership through political skill: "The law of the jungle does not apply to chimpanzees," De Waal has written. "Their network of coalitions limits the rights of the strongest: *everybody* pulls strings." Chimpanzees fight and then make peace within the context of a highly politicized community, and to the degree that the big cheese dominates through physical and political power the social life of his community, so he tends to be the big stabilizer. A chimpanzee leader who is not enough of a stabilizer, a peacemaker, and who does not cultivate his subordinates, is likely to lose allies and in the end to incite successful rebellions.

Heroes, among humans and possibly among chimps, become heroes in the foreign and not the domestic sphere. While the good leader brings stability to the domestic community and as such is a peacemaker, at the edges of the community and looking outward into foreign affairs, the good leader is a warrior. Ideally, among humans and perhaps among chimps, he is a war hero: an individual tested in battle to the limits of physical and psychological endurance, who has bathed in chaos and returned, alive and whole, with (figuratively, most of the time) the head of a fearsome enemy in hand. Beowulf, John Kennedy, and George Bush all share that heroic history, and for the most part I admire all three. What worries one, of course, is the tendency of ersatz heroes and hero wannabes to create their own little pools of chaos in order to bathe in them.

Next, I flew to Gabon. I checked into a hotel in Libreville, Gabon, at three in the morning, checked out at seven, and took a taxi out to the train station. There were already three lines in front of the three ticket windows at the train station, and I placed my pack off to one side where I could keep an eye on it and stood in one line. The woman in front of me said they would start selling tickets at eight o'clock. But soon it was ten minutes after eight and no one was selling tickets. The ticket sellers inside their three cage windows were shouting at each other, arguing about whether or not they should start selling tickets. The three lines began to press forward in anticipation. Five minutes passed. At last there seemed to be motion. The first person in my line got a ticket, turned, pushed, and extricated himself from the crush. But, from what I could see over heads, the second person in my line had been abandoned. Our ticket seller had disappeared! Ten minutes later he returned; a second ticket was sold. By this time, our line had turned into a crushing crowd, and, as the most aggressive members of the crowd socketed themselves deeper into this heaving, swelling swamp of bodies, I became aware that the ticket seller was writing each ticket out individually, in duplicate: date, price, destination, number of people, ticket number, tax, class, et cetera. The crowd pressed.

Fifteen minutes later, the train rumbled down the track and hissed to a halt on the other side of the station, and the crowd surged forward madly. A man behind me started trying to press himself in front of me, and I deliberately blocked him with my shoulder, hip, and leg. The man started to laugh, and began saying to his neighbor (in French): "He's blocking me! He's blocking me!" I turned around and started laughing too: "Of course I'm blocking you! I'm ahead of you! Ça va? Ça va?" But the crowd was getting nasty, pushing, pushing, and the ticket seller continued slowly, laboriously, deliberately, studiously writing out each ticket. Arms reached forward, fists of money were raised in the air, voices cried out destinations: "Franceville! Boué! Ayem! Abanga!"

Then a white man, short and stocky with gray hair, gray eyes, big jaw, a button-down sport shirt with green and white stripes, approached the edge of the crowd and looked inside—I was crushed right in the middle—and he called out to me, in French: "Buy a ticket for me! Lopé!"

Just because we're both white, I thought, *doesn't mean I owe you a favor*—but he was going where I was going, Lopé, so it wouldn't be inconvenient to buy two tickets instead of one, and besides, he could watch my pack. I told him to watch my pack, which was leaning against a railing just outside the crowd. Meanwhile, the ticket seller had turned away to write out three tickets for someone inside the office who just walked in—this was maddening—and the crowd surged forward. Now it was ten minutes before the train was due to leave. I was crushed, breathless, against the ticket cage, reaching out with a wad of bills like everyone else, my arm among a dozen arms waving a dozen handfuls of money at the cage, and the ticket seller remained as poker-faced and slow as ever. But I had observed that whoever managed to slap money down on the counter right in front of him, right at the cage, seemed to get his attention. So finally I slapped my money down and cried out: "Lopé! Deux billets! Première Classe!"

It was nine o'clock then. Hurry! The train will leave without us! The prognathous Frenchman—his name was Charles de Jaw—and I stepped onto the train, and then waited an hour in our seats before it left.

We walked into a first-class car, past a couple of compartments, until Charles de Jaw said, "Here! We have friends! Here!" And so we entered a first-class compartment with a big dirty window and a middle-aged Belgian couple inside. No one spoke English, and the Belgians warned me in French about the razor experts of Libreville: They will slash open your pack and steal everything.

All three of my companions had hair coming out of their noses, little tufts of hair hanging down like tiny puffs of Spanish moss. They were all neatly dressed. The woman wore a thin cotton dress, white with pastel yellow, pink, and blue brush strokes, and a navy blue blazer.

At last the train strained and jerked into motion, slowly, and began rolling . . . past train yards and boxcars (barn red with OCTRA painted in white), past three women sitting on a rail in the space between two boxcars (shaded by the cars and eating a lunch spread out before them), through an area of tall grass and weeds, laundry hanging on a line, red soil and yellow soil, shacks with corrugated tin roofs held down by rocks, and one shack on a hillside with four huge armchairs situated on the grass outside. Quickly the train racketed past those signs of urban existence, and then we entered a region of farm bush—high trees and thick brush, small manioc plantations, fern fields, and some recently cleared areas (dead trees crooked and silver and a floor of green), some blasted areas (blackened trees and an orange clayey soil), and then a hillside covered with the soft green lace of manioc. Now we came to bursts of palm, and then some tree that seemed like a holdover from the Devonian, rising on wavering stilts with a small crown of wrinkled and shiny, teardrop shaped leaves; and another tree with many clustered leaves in round, daisy-shaped clusters of fingery green leaves; and vines always and everywhere, sometimes spread across the ground, sometimes cast over an entire tree, top to bottom. There were still a few signs of human presence—an orange road, some sheds, rusted and battered tin roofs in a market—and then we slid back into bush again.

Meanwhile, Charles was yakking in French and scratching his crotch at the same time, talking to the Belgian couple about his meals during the last two days. He had a dinner that was shit—he frowned deeply with the distress of that memory—but the buffet he had yesterday, it was terrific! Perfect!

We left all signs of settlement. High bushes had grown up right next to the railway, and their leaves slapped the side of the train as we passed. Then we came to another area of tree skeletons, sunlight passing through, and a swamp with a green and brown surface textured like a kitchen sponge. We stopped at a small station—M'Bel—and then proceeded. We crossed a flat, muddy river with a surface shiny and barely wrinkled, like flattened aluminum foil, and then Charles de Jaw began telling the Belgian couple how I had saved him from the crowds at the Libreville station. It would have given him a cardiac—he patted his chest in a heart-thumping style—to fight through that ticket line.

But the couple, by now, had settled into their reading. He with *Paris Match*. She with *Femme Actuelle*.

The air-conditioning on the train didn't work very well, and so our air-conditioned first-class compartment with the big dirty window became a suffocation box. I left the box and soon discovered my error: Second-class was much better. In the second-class car right behind us all the windows had been pulled wide open, and a wind was rushing through the car, lifting the blue curtains and pouring into faces and nostrils a wonderfully cool and clear air.

A cluster of dirty gray clapboard shacks with tin roofs whipped by, and we stopped at a station: Dyan. Vendors hawked in front of the second-class windows with claw-like clutches of green bananas, bushels and pots of various cooked goods, and ten loaves of bread wrapped in paper. The train whistled, people ran and climbed aboard, and we began rolling again.

I returned to my seat in suffocating first class.

We passed through a swamp of creamy green water, green-brown reeds, and the pale green medallions of lily pads. We came to logs: heaps of logs beside the tracks, logs gray and inert, sliced at either end, numbers written on the ends in white. We passed a small stream, sunlit into a milky green, and then slid inside the forest again. And as we passed through this forest, with our sealed window and filtered air, on springy red seats inside steel and rolling on steel, the green—this forest!—flickered only the vaguest shadows across the vacant faces of my companions. They absented themselves inside *Figaro* and *Paris Match* and *Femme Actuelle*, their eyes lowered, hair drifting out of their nostrils, and they swayed like dreamers to the swaying of the train.

The husband managed a logging company not far from Lopé. This was explained to me in pantomime since my French comprehension was so bad—Charles de Jaw looked up from his *Figaro* at one point, made a motor noise with his mouth, moved his hands back and forth as if wielding a chain saw, pantomimed a tree crashing, and then pointed to the other man: He does that. "Oh, he's a forester," I said, in French. Charles laughed and said: "No! He doesn't cut the trees himself. He's a manager!"

The car swayed, the train whistled, and we passed into dark wells of forest, beautiful and deep, like shadowed rooms obscured by vine

curtains. The logging manager licked his fingertips, pushed the crin-
kling pages of *Paris Match*, and we hurtled inside a green tunnel
through dark and mystical places, shapes, patterns, shadows and light,
past a brown pool of water, glistening; along a river, mud-brown tinged
with a spill of green at the edges, white roils and wrinkles on water
with a sheen of glass (brown glass with depth and shadow, smoky
glass illuminated by sunlight into insubstantiality), into forest darker
and fuller now, a bursting of leaves and a propagation of wood, with
great upreaching arms of giant trees and tossed and spilling sinews of
vines, with a dripping of vines above and a spreading of ferns below,
carpets of ferns following the land down into a sink of green, down to
a pond, a swamp, a brown rivulet or stagnant pool, a mantle of ferns
spreading over the ground like snow and moving across the lower
vegetation like a sea, rising and falling with the earth, lapping and
splashing into low trees and bushes.

The train whistled—to-tooooo-tooot!—and we came to a giant yellow scar: a road with deep erosion gullies and canyons on either side,
and we stopped at Abanga.

Someone was offering a dead squirrel for sale at Abanga. The
owner held the squirrel by its right hind leg, slowly swinging it back
and forth. Someone else was selling strings of small river fish, a dull
brass color with whitish bellies. A man carried on his shoulder a squat
tank of cooking gas.

We moved again, through forest for most of the morning. The
train whistled its whistle in two pitches, first a lower note, then higher
with a low toot at the end: like a hunter's horn: to-tooooo-tooot! The
stations along the line were identical: small, rectangular stucco buildings the color of pancake batter, with steel bars on the windows and a
white sign with blue lettering naming the place.

Later, we rolled and racheted into hills and across rippling grasslands with patches and galleries of emerald and malachite forest. We
passed timber yards and giant timber boles on railroad flatcars; we
passed hills scraped clean and eroding into deep gullies. We came to a
very wide river complicated with great rocks, islands, trees, sandbars,
half-submerged trees, disturbed with cataracts, whirlpools, wells and
swellings and eddies, rushing and then rolling nearly flat with a bright
surface moving slowly with great smooth slabs and scales of surface,
under a sky of giant clouds.

We came to Ayem, where the Belgian logging manager and his
wife tucked away their *Paris Match* and *Femme Actuelle*, said goodbye,
and got off. I watched them through the window as they climbed into

a mud-stained Japanese truck. They suddenly looked bright and alive for the first time.

And then we came to Lopé, a small station in the middle of nowhere. I said goodbye to Charles de Jaw, who worked in some capacity—I never understood exactly what—with the logging operation at Lopé. We both stepped off the train and turned in opposite directions.

Only a half dozen people had stepped off the train, so it wasn't very hard for Caroline Tutin to find me. Caroline was quiet—terribly pleasant and direct, British, with a face tending to freckle and long sandy hair that was braided and tossed across her shoulder like a rope. She smiled an Englishwoman's smile: Mona Lisa with warmth. And I said, "Bet you thought I wasn't coming."

"I thought it'd be a miracle if you did," she said. "The trains weren't running at all last week. They've been on strike. Last year they were on strike for more money. This year they want to get rid of their bosses. Anyway, I don't think you can stay until Sunday: no train. There'll be a train on Thursday, I hope, and you'll have to take that."

We climbed into her truck—Japanese, with a World Wildlife Fund panda on the side—and drove out along a long dirt road.

I was glad to be with someone friendly who spoke English, but quite disappointed to hear my stay would be so short, so I sniffed for any bone of positive information. "Brian Hippelwaithe—has he been here?"

"No, actually, and he's not coming."

"Why not?"

"Well, he wrote me just about the same time you did. I wrote back in the same way. In fact, I wrote him the same letter I wrote you: 'Send more information.' Apparently, he became hostile, irritated that I should question his purposes. He pulled some strings, tried to have pressure placed on me through various sources—but he never wrote back."

"Oh, that makes me feel better," I said. "I've been so jealous—everywhere I've gone in Africa just about, Brian Hippelwaithe was there first. And I know how well paid he is! All expenses taken care of! It just burns me up! Okay—simple jealousy! I admit it."

We were quiet for a while, and then Caroline said: "We had a debate about whether you were male or female, actually. I decided you were female."

"Oh?"

"Well, your name is the sort that could be either."

"I know. It's bothered me all my life."

"But your reply to my letter—it was charming. I decided it showed a feminine sense of humor."

"But didn't you look at my signature? No woman scrawls like that."

We chattered in that fashion until, finally, we stopped at an Eaux et Fôrets building and met the dignified director, Josef Maroga, and an assistant, a live wire whose name was given to me as, simply, M'Guema. Then we entered the Lopé-Okanda Forest Reserve, a pristine wilderness in one of the most remote parts of Africa. Well, the area *was* remote until about five years ago, when the trans-Gabonaise railway was finished. But it was, in any event, wonderful: rolling grasslands interrupted by huge rocks and patches and galleries of rich deep green forest, the edge of the great Gabonese forest rolling all the way south into Congo, all the way west to the ocean. Our dirt road wound and wound through these grasslands and forest patches, and gradually took us up to the research camp on top of a small hill of grassland.

This was a very civilized camp, I soon discovered, with a few gray, weathered, clapboard buildings, and electricity, running water, and even air-conditioning in the computer trailer and a real flush toilet in the outhouse. The electricity powered a refrigerator with Cokes and beer inside and, when you pressed a button, turned overhead fans in the great open porch of the main building and inside the smaller cabin where I was to sleep. The electric generator automatically turned off at midnight, Caroline said, and the running water was piped in from the river we had just driven across. The person who had, during the last few years, installed all these amenities was Michel, her husband. Caroline said that some other field scientists felt strongly that a research camp should be Spartan. She mentioned a couple of names. But she happened not to agree. "When you're out here for years . . ." she began, without finishing the thought. She said Michel spoke good English but pretended not to because he preferred that people spoke French.

Michel came out to greet us, shook my hand forcibly, and said some things in French. He had a high forehead, a prominent jaw, and narrow, colorless lips. And he was worried: Rebecca had not called in for three hours.

Rebecca was a Canadian researcher visiting Lopé to study something about mangabeys. Anyone going into the forest took along a walkie-talkie and regularly checked back with Michel, who sat at the base camp, but Michel hadn't heard from Rebecca.

"I need to find Rebecca. Want to come along?" Caroline asked. I certainly did. So, although it was late afternoon, we walked through the high yellow grass toward the forest. "Is this a natural savanna?" I wondered. Caroline said she thought it may have been created by pastoralists a few centuries ago, but the forests, she thought, had remained in a stable equilibrium more or less since the Pleistocene—with a high density of leopards, and duikers, bushbucks, elephants, apes, and monkeys. She said that one day she saw a group of perhaps four hundred, probably more like five hundred mandrills walking across the grass here—she stopped counting at a hundred twenty-six.

We came to the forest wall, passed through a door in the wall, and entered a different world, humid and noisy. We descended to a clear stream, crossed it, and then walked along trails in a thick undergrowth until finally—around a corner—Rebecca appeared, her eyes open wide with alarm for a second. "I thought you were gorillas!"

Rebecca was young and pretty, dressed in a clean khaki outfit, tall with a rather long face, clear brown eyes, bright brown hair, and a youthful timbre and thrill to her voice, as if it were wonderful just to be alive, as if she were in love. Rebecca said she was sorry. She had simply forgotten to radio back to the base; she had been following the mangabeys.

We returned to camp and ate dinner—soup, fish pie, and beer—out on the communal porch at dusk. A second researcher was visiting Lopé as well, an Englishman named Lee White, who was studying the effects of selective logging on chimps, gorillas, and elephants.

So the five of us ate dinner, out on that open porch where your eyes could only resist for so long the hypnotic relaxation of gazing across those great rolling grasslands out to the forested horizon. As it became dark, the insects started swarming, and the two overhead fans whirling above our dinner table raised a complex turbulance of up and down drafts that sent waves of small and large insects scattering helplessly into my beer, my soup, my fish pie. In the end, I gave up picking them out, except for the large moths, and contented myself with the extra protein—but it was a superb meal, reminding me that I had missed lunch.

During dinner, Caroline said she got started in Gabon in the following way. She had studied the reproductive behavior of chimps at Gombe, under Jane Goodall, and spent time in Senegal working on another project. Then one day, the Gabonese ape laboratory in

Franceville sponsored a meeting of primatologists, both lab and field scientists. A number of people came, including Caroline, and at one meeting—was it a dinner?—the director of the ape lab said, "What's the great ape conservation project most needed in this part of Africa?" After some discussion, the answer came: "We need to know what's there. We need a census." So the lab director said, "Well, who would like to do it?" Caroline raised her hand. "Okay," he said. "You do it."

She and Michel conducted a census across Gabon and concluded that the country was still one of Africa's great reservoirs of chimpanzees and gorillas. Gabonese forests, they concluded, harbor perhaps sixty-four thousand chimps, plus or minus 20 percent, and perhaps another thirty-five thousand gorillas, with the same variance. "Gabon has the most gorillas, chimps, and elephants of any country in Africa. The reason is simple: It's got an incredibly low human population density."

After the census was complete, she and Michel set up this research site in one of Gabon's richest areas, Lopé, with the idea of conducting a number of research projects in tropical forest ecology. The Lopé-Okanda reserve itself, she said, covers approximately five thousand square kilometers and probably protects fifteen hundred to two thousand chimps and the same number of gorillas, as well as several thousand forest elephants. The whole of Lopé is protected from hunting but, unfortunately, permits have been given out to log the entire place. The train was financed partly by logging concessions, she said, so the Gabonese government was unable to revoke permits for Lopé. The European Community had sponsored some plan to prohibit logging in a thousand square kilometer core area of Lopé, but the reserve is very attractive to loggers because it's so close to the railway. "Distance to the train is very important in calculating the value of timber," she said.

In the morning, a light fog hung over parts of the forest, creating a smoky glaze in some places and, in other places, wisps of white.

Caroline and I went out together that day looking for chimps. What I now remember most about Caroline is that she used a pair of small, red-handled gardening snips, modestly snip-snipping at blades of razor grass and other vegetation intruding along the trails as we walked. She wore olive khaki pants, a tan khaki shirt, a walkie-talkie attached at her right hip, a small canvas bag riding on her left hip and suspended with a strap from her right shoulder. Her hair was braided in that thick rope; and in her right hand she carried those red-handled gardening snips, with which she was snipping away at the forest.

Snipping away at a tropical forest with gardening snips seemed such a calm and reasonable thing to do, and Caroline maintained such a calm and reasonable demeanor as she did it. Snipping was a feminine approach to the forest, I concluded (as I followed her along the trail), entirely opposed to the male bluster and mayhem of a machete or chain saw. *The forest is a mirror*, I thought: *One comes as visitor or destroyer.* But then a second voice said, *Don't be so pompous. Snipping may be good for the touch-up. It's not so good for carving a new trail.*

Caroline would stop, pull out her walkie-talkie, and say very quietly: "Romeo to Charlie." And she would chat with Michel back at the base camp. Sometimes she would call to Rebecca, who was somewhere else in the forest: "How are the mangabeys?"

We looked at plants and animals, dung and insects. Caroline showed me a small plant she called *Barteria.* "It's not to be touched. It's almost always protected by ants that have an incredibly painful sting. This is a good instance of coevolution, incidentally. The stems are hollow, so it provides a shelter for the ants. It even has little entrance holes for the ants, and the ants cultivate a fungus in the sap. But the ants keep off any herbivores that would otherwise eat the plant— even elephants don't like it. Will you recognize it when you see it?"

We saw a shape high up, dark and moving within a filigree of leaves and branches in front of a light sky. "There's no ape in there. Just monkey," Caroline said. And we heard monkeys calling and then splashing into the leaves. We heard some chittering from the monkeys, then splashing sounds, and we saw swirling leaves and a tailed body moving through the swirling leaves. We watched monkeys placing a whole tree, even a corridor of trees, into a swirl—the leaps of many dark bodies from branch to branch and tree to tree, the dipping and swaying of leaves and branches.

This was a forest of gray trunks splotched with cream and some blood-red lichen stains, and a comparative sparsity of high leaves, which left the sky open and powered a profusion of vegetation on the forest floor. We came to a sea of ground plants, in fact, chest and head high, with broad, boat-shaped leaves, lightly ribbed: *Haumania liebre-chestiana,* according to Caroline. "Gorillas eat it—the pith at the base of young leaves. Elephants eat it as well."

We watched a big green predatory insect tentatively stick one foot into a formicating mass of ants.

Late in the morning we rested on a large rock in the forest. Caroline smoked a cigarette. She said it helped keep away the sweat bees— and when those tiny insects began to spin around my eyes and land on my eyelids and try to drink the sweat around my eyes, I tried a cigarette, too. The smoke didn't seem to bother the sweat bees, but at least you imagined it might. We chatted away about various things and people. Caroline told me the story of the Crocodile Man, a Frenchman who gave local people a flashlight and shotgun and asked for crocodile skins in return. Three truckloads a week of crocodile skins were going out to Libreville every week. Now no crocodiles remain in Gabon. Caroline said she wanted to study the behavioral ecology of gorillas, but it was hard to keep track of them. She had thought about radio collars, but silverback gorillas don't have necks, and you can't dart any of the group unless you catch the silverback.

She said that chimps would be very hard to find. "A needle in a haystack, searching for chimps. The area they're capable of covering is absolutely enormous. I know there are chimps and gorillas not very far away, but the chimps are very quiet unless they're in a big group. And the gorillas are always quiet." She had thought about habituating the chimps to human observers—but that is very, very difficult to do. Jane did it. Christophe did it. To a degree, the chimps at Kibale have been habituated. But really, why should chimps not flee at the sight of people? "People are never a nice thing. All we can hope for is to be neutral and not nasty. But, fortunately, they're great apes, and so they're curious."

I think we were still sitting on that rock, talking about various things, when we heard a tremendous crashing and crunching behind us, inside a big area of trees and bush. We stood up. "Something big," Caroline said. "But now it's leaving." Carefully we moved closer and walked through some brush until I saw, behind tree trunks and leaves, a big gray shape, like a smooth boulder. Then I saw a thick tail, whipping once, twice. Then great ears, tablecloth-sized, flapping loosely. I thought I saw the trunk rising into the air, sniffing. "Mother and baby," Caroline decided, though I never saw the baby.

But we were too close, and so slowly we began backing away. When we reached a certain point, we heard a distant crashing. "That's the elephant deliberately making noise," Caroline said, "saying, 'Don't follow us.' I think it's deliberate. Very often they'll stay quiet until they've worked out where you are. Then, if they decide to move away, which these did, they'll make noise while moving."

The cicadas were extremely noisy in that forest, and we stopped to look at one of those noisemakers: primitive-looking, jeweled and armored, with eyes like brass rivets and making the shrilling noise of a bad ball bearing.

We came to a watery glen at a twist and curve of the creek, with rocks so worn by the water they had taken on their own flowing and eddying patterns. The creek had a yellowish sandy bottom, and the water splashed and rushed past a fallen rotten log with small leafy plants glowing with sunlight and some purple, daisy-faced flowers, and then receded into a tunnel of vegetation.

Later in the day, Caroline told me to look up. I saw a tree with a thick and high and dark cloud of branches and vines, dark inside like a house. This tree was almost wholly overtaken by vines, the bole surrounded and doubled in size by a furred coating of vines and vine leaves. But there was a slight rustling, and a dozen leaves rained down from out of the dark, leafy house. "Chimp!" Caroline whispered. "It's a baby, and its mother is over there." I saw nothing. We watched for a long time. Everything had gone quiet—even the insects. At last, I saw inside the shadows a dark shape and a few shifting speckles of light, and I heard a rustling. Then, from out of the middle of this dark cluster about forty feet above us, I saw an adult female chimpanzee—with a baby clinging—climb out, dash and leap madly fifteen feet across an open gap into an adjacent tree. From there she climbed up higher, now about sixty feet up, and frantically climbed out into a high, open part of the tree. She was entirely visible now, and in apparent desperation to escape she tossed herself down thirty feet into the lower branch of yet another tree and—craaaaaaaaaaack!!!—that branch suddenly broke and fell, she and her baby with it, but on the way down she caught herself in the crown of a lower tree, and then climbed down that tree trunk, hand over hand, foot over foot, baby still clinging at her breast, until she had disappeared entirely.

"You see what I mean?" Caroline said. "They don't like us."

"I didn't even see her at first."

"She knew we were there. She was trying to figure out how to make an escape. What was happening during that long quiet period was they were getting together—then waiting for a moment before making their escape. When danger hits, young chimps run straight for their mother."

But the chimp could easily have dropped her baby in that fall, I knew, and I was relieved she hadn't. I would have felt responsible for such an accident, and even as it was I felt uneasy about the whole incident.

On the way out of the forest, we came across a cobra skin—long, thick, translucent, with a woven pattern—stretched right across the trail, as if the snake had used the rough and broken vegetation at the trail's edge for help in slipping that slough.

When we returned to camp, Michel (wearing a purple T-shirt that said, in white letters, "Authentic") greeted us with very bad news. The Americans and their European and Middle Eastern allies had been bombing military sites in and around Baghdad for some time now, with laser-guided smart bombs. But smart bombs are not much smarter than the people who fire them, and today, according to the news Michel had heard on the radio, a bomb had demolished a building with civilians inside and killed more than a hundred women and children. Michel was very upset.

Our argument began after dinner, in French, and I don't remember it all. Michel's comments may not have been directed my way at first. The Americans were criminal, he was saying, and President Bush had made a purely political decision: trading the lives of Iraqi civilians for the lives of American soldiers. It was a purely political move. Bush was merely concerned about votes for the next election.

I thought this was a misreading of Bush's character. I said I didn't think he was so cynical.

I didn't want to become involved in an argument. I knew very little about what was going on in any case, having heard only fragments of news during the last few weeks. I had not actually formed an impermeable opinion about the Gulf War. President Bush had forgotten to consult me before calling in the troops. In fact, I hadn't even voted for Bush. I had voted for that other guy.

But Michel began sliding quickly from the subject of George Bush in particular to the subject of Americans and American policy in general. And, since I was the only American within a few hundred miles of our little camp in the wilderness, it began to appear that I would serve as the principal authority on and representative of Americans and American policy.

Michel continued: "This is a deliberate American policy: to kill Iraqi civilians! It's immoral. The Americans have no right, and the French resent being associated with this absolutely immoral decision. When it's a war, French soldiers expect to fight and die. That's their job. The French are ready to fight right now—so why are we still bombing defenseless Iraqi civilians?"

I knew the bombing had to have been an accident, but even as an accident it was not defensible. I saw some logic to Michel's now forceful comments. But, damn it, I was not going to back down. A Line had been Drawn in the Sand, and it seemed to me some sort of significant principle was at stake.

"If the French don't think the American decision is right, then they should go ahead and start the land war right now," I said.

Michel glared. He said more things; I made more replies and counterstatements. I knew the argument was becoming less fun, now—especially when Caroline abruptly stood up and walked away, followed by Rebecca. Only Lee White remained with us then, and Lee only because by that time I was speaking in English, Michel still in French, and we had insisted that Lee sit there between us to interpret.

Michel: "We have agreed to operate under the American leadership! We can't break away from the coalition and fight on our own now! But why are these Americans such cowards? If you're a soldier, you should be ready to fight a war! Not bomb civilians! The French are prepared to die! Soldiers take that risk when they put on a uniform!" He was shouting now, his jaw and mouth tightening, his forehead bulging with anger.

Me: "When the land war does begin, you can be sure the Americans will take the bulk of the casualties."

Michel: "That's not the point! It's degrading for us to be associated with the American policy of bombing civilians!"

Me: "Well, if the French resent American leadership, they should have taken the lead. I think Americans would be delighted if someone else, the French for example, took a leadership role in this enterprise. We find this role a burden. We'd be delighted if someone else took it on. Why didn't the French provide the leadership in this?"

By this time, I saw, even Lee White was backing off. It seemed as if he had begun to shorten and ameliorate his interpretations of what Michel and I were shouting at each other.

Michel screamed: "The French take the leadership? It's impossible! That's absurd! It's impossible, that's why!"

"Wait," I said. "Let me understand this. On the one hand, you can't be the leaders. On the other hand, you hate being the followers. What would you like? To continue as you were, supplying Mirage fighters to Iraq?"

When I took the train back to Libreville, I bought a first-class ticket. Force of habit. First class was only marginally more expensive than second. But the only first-class compartment not crowded or stuffy with cigarette smoke had a dead admiral in it. The dead admiral wore a white uniform with epaulets on the shoulders and arcane medals and badges on the chest. His eyes were closed and his body was propped stiffly into the middle seat. I tripped over his mirror-polished shoes and took a window seat—and within two minutes made up my mind to try second class.

It was late afternoon then and very hot in second class. But the windows were open. You could look outside and smell the air. A man three seats in front of me had a cardboard box with a chittering monkey inside, an almost furless infant, and the man fed the baby with a baby bottle.

Toward dusk, the train came to a big logging village, N'Djole, fringed by ugly and eroding hills, with a whole trainload of logs parked on a siding along our stopped train. Insects vibrated away. Zairean music played on a radio. A neon edge cast a weak blue highlight across the station, and the sky turned dark gray with an edge of nacre. We had a long wait there, an hour or more, and I was told the wait was because of the prisoner. *What prisoner?* I wondered. There was a good deal of beer drinking in the car during this wait and then a repetitious argument over who owed whom two thousand francs. "J'ai vous demande . . . ," said a drunk man with a thick tongue. And a man carrying a dead duiker in a cardboard box—four little legs sticking out of the box—passed through and offered meat for sale.

At last the prisoner, shirtless with muddy pants dropping low on his hips, shackled at the wrists and ankles, was escorted by two uniformed officers and a small crowd of onlookers across the station and onto the train.

The train rolled again, and after a time it became completely dark and started raining. Through our open windows, the rain raised a sweet, wet smell—wet vegetation and mud—and the smell of the train brakes, like flint on steel, rose up and through the windows as well. The wet air sucked and billowed our pleated, dingy blue window curtains, and they rippled and flapped. The yellow lights from the train brushed against high vegetation outside, along the tracks, and the vegetation bowed and nodded from the wind of the train's rush or slapped against the sides of the train. Passengers stood up and hung out the windows to see and be enveloped in the smells and reveries of the forest, until the rain came down harder and began splattering in through the windows. Then the windows were shut and began reflecting images—my own face, the young boy across the way. And then the baby monkey in the box three seats ahead started crying wildly, as if he sensed, finally, that he was in a hard, hollow, steel world, an envelope of steel rocketing insanely through his lost and pliant plant world.

When we finally arrived in Libreville, I was fast off the train. The taxi driver who opened the door to the train grabbed my pack. I grabbed it back. He said, "Taxi?" He was obviously the very taxi driver I should have avoided most, but I hadn't learned my lesson yet. I thought, *I can handle this one this time.* So I nodded assent, descended from the train, and became surrounded by the crowd spilling off the train. Someone crashed into me from behind, and I turned around to see a wild face, a madman's face, raging ebony eyes, wild and ragged hair—the man stumbled, lunged at me, his hands behind him, growling something nasty in French, and then I recognized at last: the prisoner! And I moved out of his angry, lunging way, the gendarmes teetering along behind him, trying to keep up.

The taxi driver, of course, didn't understand the name of my hotel, and our discussion of the price drowned in a swamp of bilingual gibberish. At last, at the hotel, he wanted six thousand francs. I paid it, but not happily. "C'est trop, trop cher!" I scolded him—but I was no George Bush, and in the end I wimped out.

The next day was my last day in Gabon. I was flying out that evening. So in the morning I went into town and practiced my karate escape moves on the sidewalk souvenir merchants. I rested at midday, and in the late afternoon, left the hotel again to mail some letters and go to the bank. But outside of the hotel, a crowd had formed. I saw a soldier holding a submachine gun and directing traffic. More crowds appeared. An armored jeep with a very big gun mounted on the back and pointing at the crowds came tooling down the highway, followed by a truckload of soldiers and, overhead, a helicopter. The helicopter crossed the highway toward the sea, then dipped and banked and began swooping back, spinning in the process and only slowly recovering from the spin so that for a few seconds it was moving sideways and coming down, about to crash, it seemed. I heard sirens, and when I actually got out where I could look down the highway, I saw huge crowds of people along the highway looking expectantly to the north. A man nearby wore a uniform that had *securité* written on the left breast, and so I asked him, in French: "What's happening?" He replied in English: "Mandela is coming!"

Sure enough, a few police cars came down the highway, then one smoked-glass limousine, and then I could see coming my way a convertible with Nelson Mandela and two others standing up and waving! Mandela was waving! He was beautiful: his white hair, that soft coffee skin, those hooded eyes, that gentle smile. "Mandela! Mandela! Mandela! Mandela!" the crowd chanted and cried out wildly, waving back. And I, swept away with the fervor myself, waved wildly. Then I saw, as his car moved toward me, a running mass of people following the motorcade, a flood of people bearing down. I looked for shelter and saw just in time a car parked at the edge of the highway. I moved into the lee side of that car, and the crowd surged against it and parted like flowing water against a rock, and merged again behind it. "Mandela! Mandela! Mandela!" the cry went, and I was reminded of Bobby Kennedy when I saw him in 1963: handsome, bright, glowing with the light of a hero's reality combined with and elevated by celebrity. It was a jubilant, dazzled crowd, running along the motorcade with tremendous excitement, crying a continuous hallelujah of joy: "Mandela! Mandela! Mandela!"

I saw his famous bright face up close now, sensed his calm courage. I knew he represented the best of the African spirit. Here was a leader and a hero, a real hero, and I cried out, entirely caught up in the emotion of the crowd: "Mandela! Mandela! Mandela!"

13

Snippets

When climbing a steep hill hang on to the tail
of your horse as you walk behind him.

–Francis Galton, *The Art of Travel*

I wasn't sure exactly what I was looking for in Brazzaville, Congo. Fortunately, Jane Goodall had powerful friends there who, I hoped, would help. She was close to the American ambassador and his wife; and once I got into southern Congo, Jane had assured me, the president of Conoco Congo would take me under his wing. I had written to the American ambassador, a generalized sort of letter, not asking for anything special but incidentally mentioning the time and date of my arrival in Brazzaville, just in case anyone wished to find me at the airport at midnight. I had also written to the president of Conoco Congo—once again a generalized sort of letter. And now, as the plane wheeled and lurched toward a thin stream of light in the otherwise utter blackness, I repeated my own personal mantra: "Nothing can go wrongo, I am in the Congo."

Once our plane had parked on the tarmac, passengers and crew descended into a lake of hot night air and swam slowly over to the airport. We waited outside. The airport was closed. No one had the key. We were standing on one side of the airport's glass louvres, and a worker from inside the airport yelled through a broken glass louvre, in French: "We don't have the key! This is Africa!"

Eventually, the key was found and the doors opened. We proceeded through immigration and customs. My turn came at last. The

219

immigration officer, a strapping man, scowled at me and said–demanded–something I didn't understand. He demanded again. I said, "Je ne parle bien le Français." He demanded a third time, louder, in case I was hard of hearing. Someone in the crowd translated his demand: "What's your purpose?" "Purpose? Ah, tourism. Tourism," I said. The demand was repeated a fourth time and again translated by someone in the crowd: "What's your purpose?" "Tourism–tourisme!"

He checked "tourisme" on his little slip of paper and then demanded something else I couldn't understand. So it went. And if all that suggests I should have paid better attention in Reba Masterson's French class thirty years ago, consider this: Those immigration and customs people got sick of me fast. After that minor delay, I zipped right through. Unfortunately, no American ambassador was waiting for me, but that was all right. I had actually made reservations for a hotel–a first for me–the M'Bamu Palace.

The M'Bamu Palace was an absurdly expensive erection in one of the most expensive cities in Africa–Cokes cost the Central African franc equivalent of five dollars per bottle at M'Bamu–and I was running perilously low on cash. I had little actual credit to speak of, either, but who else knew that? So I checked in, utilizing an already overdrawn Security Pacific Visa card, stepped into an elevator playing snippets of Simon and Garfunkel that had been Muzakified and translated into French, and found my room at last on the seventh floor. I slid my key into the keyhole of room 737. From my window, I could see the Zaire River and far away on the other side of the river the lights of Kinshasha. I cracked open the window a couple of inches and, at last, fell asleep listening to a long drawn mournful duet of foghorns on the river.

I woke up slowly the next morning, had a nice, long, hot bath, and, while sitting in the bath, decided not to worry about my finances. I had already slipped into Bankruptcy Canyon, and the only thing to do now was enjoy the fall. I ordered an English language newspaper (for the equivalent of five dollars) and a good breakfast from room service (for the equivalent of twenty-five or thirty dollars).

The newspaper was three days old, but it said that all seventeen Kentucky Fried Chicken franchises in Kuwait had been taken to Baghdad. A spokesperson for Kentucky Fried Chicken was quoted: "They ate all the chicken and stripped the places of all their furniture and equipment."

I turned on the television to find recent news, switching channels again and again until I located two decent channels, each appealing to a single portal of comprehension: a French-language channel with a good picture; an English-language channel with a bad picture. The English-language channel's picture was so distorted that Yassir Arafat consisted of a series of lighter and darker squares. Darker squares made up his eyes and his mouth, which moved in response to an interviewer's questions. Still, if I couldn't see anything, I could listen to the voices. A reporter said: "The carcasses of tanks and armored personnel carriers litter the streets. . . ." A general said: "Any time he puts his armor out in the desert where it's out there, then it's vulnerable." A president said: "At this moment, America, the finest, lovingest nation on earth"–I switched channels for just a second here and then quickly switched back–"triumph of the moral order is the vision that concerns us." A reporter said: "Strong winds are pushing the oil slick away from Saudi Arabia towards Iran."

The fragmentary news lost its novelty after an hour or so, and I determined to start work–whatever that was. I would find the American ambassador and ask him where the chimpanzees were. I dressed, left the room, took the elevator down. This time the elevator music was in English. "What is man without woman?" a man asked. "And what is woman without man?" a woman asked. I didn't know the answer.

I went out onto the street, imagining that the American embassy should not be difficult to find, but I was almost immediately accosted by a man who seemed to be, for no reason I could figure, furious with me.

His face pushed into mine and shouted: "J'ai vous dit, 'Bonjour!' " Perhaps he had said "hello" and was now insulted that I didn't say "hello" in return. I really didn't know. I apologized and kept walking, but he walked right along beside me and, still pushing his face into mine, said again: "J'ai vous dit, 'Bonjour!' "

"Excusez-moi!" I said. "Je ne comprends bien le Français!"

But he wouldn't be mollified. His eyes were bulging with rage now. "J'ai vous dit, 'Bonjour!!!!' "

"Excusez-moi!! Excusez-moi!!" I shouted in return. "Je ne comprends bien le Français!"

I walked fast, but he kept alongside me, half running. "J'ai vous dit, 'Bonjour'!"

I apologized again and kept walking. Finally he dropped away. But the minute he did, someone else appeared, this time a thin man with a loose blue shirt, who pulled a fake gold watch out of his pocket and pressed it in front of my face. "Bonjour," he said, and he started bargaining. The watch is beautiful, he said. It works. How much would I pay for it?

"No, merci," I said. "Je ne le desire. No, merci. Je ne le desire." But my *je-ne-le-desires* had little effect, and my *mercis* were taken as encouragement. He kept on, pushing into me, grabbing my arm, pushing the watch at me, lowering the price. I continued walking until I had gone far enough down the street to see the Soviet embassy.

I turned around and started walking back the other way, still looking for the American embassy, and soon another watch seller was dangling a fake gold watch in front of my face. "Regardez!" he said. "No, merci. No, merci," I said. But my *no* sounded like *yes* to him. He said: It's beautiful. It works well. It's fine. It can be a beautiful gift. Who would I give it to? How much can I pay? A reasonable price will be discussed.

In that fashion, I walked up and down the street until I finally located the American embassy. I felt an irrational relief upon seeing that big white fortress, the big fence around it, the guardhouse to one side, the bristling antennae on top, the painted image of an eagle about to claw the living daylights out of a shield. The guards in the guardhouse were Congolese, and, after they had metal-detected me and looked over my passport, they opened a door and I walked along down a sidewalk to the embassy itself. This was Saturday morning, I forgot to mention, and so the embassy was closed, but someone pressed a button, and a steel portcullis at the front of the building slowly rose with a clanking sound until two glass doors were revealed. From inside, someone unlocked and opened the two glass doors, and I walked through a big metal detector into a closed room with a bullet-proof window at one end. Behind this window stood two marines in uniform—both black, big, friendly, helpful, efficient, and professional, with real American accents. They looked at my passport, listened to my story. The ambassador wasn't in the embassy today because it was Saturday, but since I said he was expecting me, one of the marines agreed to see if he could be reached by telephone. I should call back later in the day, the marine said, and he wrote a phone number on a piece of paper.

With the piece of paper in my pocket, I walked back to the hotel, stepped back into the elevator—the music still in English, this time in a marching cadence with the words: "I want you. I want you. I want you. I want you"—and returned to my room, where I listened to the endless news snippets on television. Late in the afternoon, I reached the ambassador by phone. "Can you sit tight until Monday?" he said. "Jane used to have a person here, but she's gone now. So there's no Jane Goodall Institute infrastructure here right now."

On Monday morning, I searched through clothes scattered around my room to find a clean shirt. Unfortunately, I had just washed my best shirt last night, and it was hanging above the bathtub, still dripping wet. My second best shirt had dark red stains across the front. They looked rather like blood stains, but they were actually liana sap stains. A certain West African liana, when you cut it with a machete, bleeds a red sap that creates indelible stains.

I had only two pairs of pants. I certainly was not going to visit the ambassador in Levi's—that would indicate disrespect—but my other pants, green gardening pants with many pockets and reinforced knees, also had dark red sap stains on them, as did, I suddenly discovered, my only footwear other than rubber boots: the green sneakers my mother-in-law had given me for Christmas.

The inside of the embassy reminded me of the inside of a ship, and the ambassador's office was upstairs, the bridge of the ship. It had a big flag, a big desk, and a couch on the other side of the desk big enough that I felt small when I sat in it. The ambassador looked just like an ambassador should: tall and comfortably bulky with an aura of sympathetic intelligence and impenetrable respectability, with blue eyes and close-cropped white hair. He was wearing a light tan suit and tasseled loafers. He explained again that Jane used to have a representative in Brazzaville who would have taken care of me, but she left. "As you are probably aware," he said, "the Congolese government is collapsing right now."

"No, I wasn't aware of that," I said.

"Yes. They have been strictly Marxist-Leninist until now, but the people have said they want a democracy. And in the process, everything is up for grabs. Jane's representative would go to various ministers, and no one could do anything. They didn't know if they'd be in the government next week."

Also, he said, it wasn't easy to travel anywhere because the roads were bad and this was the rainy season. The road south, to Pointe-Noire, was probably washed out. He thought the train south might not be running due to a strike. But, he said, I could stay in an embassy apartment in Brazzaville. He picked up the telephone . . . and I wound up inside a chauffeured car. The car drove me back to the hotel. I checked out, put my pack in the back of the car, sat in front, and was driven into a residential district of town and placed inside my own rent-free apartment—upstairs and downstairs, washer and dryer, refrigerator, air conditioning, iron grilles on the windows, three locks on the door, armed guards outside the door day and night, and a telephone. Very nice.

By Tuesday afternoon, I was at loose ends. My money was disappearing fast. I was fed up with Brazzaville, in spite of my wonderful apartment. So I dialed the phone number belonging to the president of Conoco Congo in the southern city of Pointe-Noire. After some difficulties, he came on the line. His name was Roger. Roger said that there had been some riots and strikes in the last few months, and Conoco Congo was forced to scale down operations in the country. "When we had all our people here," he said, "everyone was flying back and forth between Brazzaville and Pointe-Noire on the company jet. You could have come down on the jet. But we're not moving right now. So I'm afraid I won't be able to offer that. Lina Congo has regular flights, though. If you feel like having an adventure, you could take the train. If you come down towards the end of the week, I'll be able to spend some time with you."

An adventure! That sounded just right to me, and so I walked through town looking for train tickets—and soon learned that the train wasn't running. A strike. I went to the airlines office, Lina Congo, and bought a ticket to fly down that evening. This was a prop flight, and the pilot wore mirrored sunglasses and carried a briefcase decorated with a decal of a human skull. But we made it intact to Pointe-Noire, and by the time it was dark I had acquired a room in a cheap hotel—only about $120 a night—not very far from the beach.

My room was small and shoddy, with a paint by numbers, Afro-cubist piece of art on the wall and a one-channel color television set in the corner. I ate a late dinner alone in the hotel restaurant, on one side of a bamboo fence separating the restaurant from the hotel bar. Thus, while consuming thirty-five dollars worth of fish in a cream sauce on rice, I was able to observe a fat, nasty German man trying to chat up a young, attractive American blonde at the bar. "You spent all zis time at za pool, in za afternoons, yes?" he said. He was fat, graying, with a long jaw. She was much too pretty for him.

A second German, with a paunch like a watermelon, stood next to them, bought Coca-Colas for the beautiful Congolese woman on his other side, and told stories about his car getting stuck out in the bush at night.

"You should never drive at night," said the first German.

"This was in the *boosh!* The *boosh!!!*" said the second.

Meanwhile, the Congolese woman, with elevated breasts and blue-tinted hair, kept giving me the eye. Perhaps I would buy her more than Coca-Colas, she may have been thinking. And I was thinking, *If she could speak good English, maybe we could talk.* But actually I was in such a lonely funk by then that I wasn't even in the mood for talking.

After dinner, I went to the bar and asked for a white wine: vin blanche. "Eh?" said the bartender. "Vin blanche?" "Oui," I said. "If you want white wine, why don't you order it in the restaurant?" he said.

I went to bed.

Next morning, I went out to find Madame Jamart. I couldn't remember who told me about Madame Jamart or exactly why I should find Madame Jamart, but she was on my list of people to locate, and I did have an address for her in Pointe-Noire. So I wandered into the city until I found a small electrical supply shop called Congo Electricité. Madame Jamart was a thin and frenetic Belgian. She had black hair streaked with gray, cut in a pageboy style. She took me into her back office. It stank in there—"un scent mauvais," she explained, wrinkling her nose. And then she took me into another room where the stench was overwhelming: three or four cardboard boxes with some animal inside, a porcupine she told me later, but I didn't see it.

We returned to the office, and then a couple of local government officials came in. I don't know why they were there or precisely who they were—or even what Madame Jamart was saying to them in machine-gun French, but I think it was about chimpanzees and I know it was dramatic. As she talked, she sliced the air with horizontal, then vertical strokes. She said something about a baby—"bébé" she said, making a cradling motion. She pounded the desk, made circles in the air, flapped her hands like birds, made a look of disgust, make a look of pride and strength (brushed with her hands to indicate expanded shoulders, chest, and a proud strong look in her face). The local officials left then, and Madame Jamart turned to me. She said, in French, that there were nine chimps at the zoo. Did I want to see them?

She said, "I am waiting my car. Do you understand?"

"Oui. Vous attendez vôtre voiture."

Her truck came, and she drove me out to the zoo: a dreadful place, three small sections of weathered concrete and steel cages, the doors shut with padlocks. It was nothing more than a small, sordid jail for animals. But Madame Jamart knew all the chimps. She slapped hands, tickled, gently groomed a face, fondly kissed outstretched lips.

She introduced me to three adult chimps who lived together in adjoining cages of one part of the zoo. Their names were Gina, Zoe, and Verru, she said. Verru presented his rump to Madame Jamart for scratching, looked at her from between his legs, his mouth open and smiling as she playfully slapped either side of his rump. Verru had yellow irises and a slow, sensitive look. "When we arrived in the zoo," Madame Jamart said, "this one was dying—no water, no food. His skull was bare. Nothing." She played with Verru. He laughed, ran back and forth, slapped his hand against hers. "Because men who are working in the zoo do nothing—and sheet, pee pee—didn't clean. No food. Nothing."

From the cage next to Verru, Gina began playing catch with me, using an orange peel. We tossed the peel back and forth for five minutes. Finally, she lay down, put her feet up, grabbed the bars with her toes, and stuck her clitoris out in my direction. She began stroking it with her hand.

Madame Jamart said there were plans to build new cages, make a better zoo, change the attitudes of the zoo workers. But to build new cages they needed cement. "In the Congo we have a problem with semen," she said. "No semen during one month. So I get the semen during yesterday. Now we can work." She said there had been a series of strikes since October, and now it wasn't clear that the zoo employees would be working at all.

Madame Jamart wanted to know if I had experience with chimps. Was I afraid of them? Would I like to see her *ouse*? She has eighteen chimps there.

So, we got back into her truck and drove across wavy dirt roads through deep puddles and came to a single-story house surrounded by a small yard, a hedge, and a high electric fence. She unlocked a metal gate to the yard, and a half dozen young chimps rushed us. "Vite! Vite!" she said, and we rushed into the yard and through a sliding glass door into the house. The chimps outside were youngsters—elf-sized—but inside the house was a baby wearing diapers, with a pale and soft, pouty face and huge, delicate ears, making little hoo-hoo-hoo-hoo noises. "This is Lucie," said Madame Jamart.

Two other baby chimps were brought in, clasped in either arm of a Congolese housekeeper, a young woman with a patient expression, barefoot and wearing a simple green dress. Madame Jamart and the housekeeper played with the baby chimps on the floor, while all the chimps outside were running around, jumping with a boom-boom-boom on the tin roof, hanging from the eaves and looking in the windows, climbing up on the window grilles and looking in, crowded at the front door and pounding with their fists on the glass.

All of these chimps were orphans, made that way when hunters shot their mothers, Madame Jamart explained, and she wanted to figure out what to do with them now. Perhaps an island could be found? Jane Goodall was planning to establish a sanctuary for orphaned chimps around here, she said, but so far not much had happened.

"In April 1989," Madame Jamart said, "in rear of my house, across the road, an old European man who had big chimp, four or five years, and suddenly this man he died. And my friend—Patricia—and me, we saw this chimp every day walking with his master. And Patricia knows very well this Cuckoo. That was the name of the chimp. We tried during three days to find a solution for Cuckoo. She was raised as a child. She is not a chimp. During three days nobody find a solution. We thought we might take to Cuckoo in the zoo. She escape out the zoo. I think Cuckoo was killed. But my friend Patricia has seen the zoo. She said to me, 'You have to go with me.' I go to the zoo on Saturday, and I see very, very bad things. All chimps are in cages full of shit, nothing to eat, nothing to drink. And they are very, very angry." Here Madame Jamart imitated shaking the bars of a cage in anger. She continued. "Patricia didn't work in an office, and she had many time to pass. So we started bringing food to the zoo, every day, every day, every day. But we didn't know chimps at this time. Except Cuckoo, I never see chimps in Congo."

So, Cuckoo disappeared from the zoo. But another chimp, a very young female named Jeanette, had recently appeared in the zoo—orphaned by a hunter, kept for a short time in a village, passed on to a missionary, finally abandoned at the zoo. "When we go to the zoo for the first time, we see Jeanette dying." The chimp was starving to death. And so, eventually, Madame Jamart and her husband took Jeanette into their house and began raising her themselves. "We very like Jeanette. She's my first baby."

The second chimp they took in was a young male named Yombe. "Patricia returned to France. She tried in France to find a solution for the future, and she met Dr. Bernadette Brezar. She's a doctor, a woman, elle a beaucoup travaillé avec une chimpanzee et une orangutan. And one day, the France decided to give chimp and orangutan to Japan, to a very bad laboratory, and she began to make war on the Japanese. And she lose her work. Because she make too much nose. And Bernadette meet Patricia and decide to find money to go to Congo to see what about chimps and gorillas. When she arrived in Congo she wanted to go into the forêt with Patricia, and she meet Yombe in a village, and she took Yombe, and she tried to save him"— Madame Jamart was momentarily distracted here by the sound of a chimp running across her roof—"he was caught in a trap. When he arrived in Pointe-Noire, his leg was complete. And one day his leg was amputated. He is a good boy, but he is the chief, and when a new person arrive in the home he has to prove he's the chief of all the chimps."

That explained the three-limbed chimpanzee I had seen, and could see now, pounding on the glass of the front door.

After Jeanette and Yombe came, others appeared. The local Water and Forests Department began confiscating illegally held chimps; others were brought in voluntarily. "During five years," Madame Jamart said, "never not one chimp was confiscated. But when I begin to work with chimps: one two three four five."

Nkola was confiscated from an army captain. Toube was brought in with a buckshot wound, his face green. Charlotte was brought in having seizures. Matalila arrived inside an iron box. Emmanuelle was brought inside a bag by two white men. One of them said, "Mrs. Jamart, I cannot love this chimp."

Sophie arrived in the following way. One day, a forestry officer phoned Madame Jamart and asked for a driver and car. "He said, 'There is a problem. A Congolese came to my office and said that one chimp was killed in a ouse.' I went to the office of Eaux et Forêts and was told that a Frenchman, Mr. Levesque, married to a Congolese woman, and 'e 'ad a cheemp. We sink 'e 'ad a chimp, and the man said to Eaux et Forêts that Mr. Levesque changed his ouse and left his chimp locked in the old ouse—the chimp perhaps died. They asked Eaux et Forêts and said you have to go to this ouse to see. We went to his ouse, but couldn't get in, so we started to leave. When we entered in my car, I heard a chimp cry. I said, 'Wait! There is a chimp! But the chimp did not die! The chimp is here! Go and take a chimp!' And I see Sophie. Immediately, we put Sophie in my ome."

But Mr. Levesque had another house, and the Eaux et Forêts officer took Madame Jamart to the second place. "When we arrived at this ouse"—she screwed up her nose into a *scent mauvais* expression—"a very bad smell. We open the door. Flies were flying everywhere. We open the door of the bathroom, and we see the chimp like this—died—like Jesus Christ." She walked over to her window, held the window grille, flattened herself into a crucified posture. "Mr. Levesque, he have no money to pay for the location, and one day he left the ome, but he shut the chimp into the bathroom without food and water, and he died. The man who went to Eaux et Forêts was not for chimp; it was for money. He wanted to be paid. He was the landlord. Mr. Levesque he spent three days in prison. And now he's got problems with his woman, and I saw him very often near my ouse. And perhaps he buys another chimp."

The chimps kept coming. Agatha was confiscated. Marble was confiscated. And so on. "In December, I receive five chimps, all ills. Five malades." But now her house was full—she was waiting for a sanctuary to be built. "Now every day we get up at five. We do forty bottles. C'est une industrie. I ave four chimps dormant in one room. Thirteen in another room. And Lucie by herself. Because Lucie is too very small chimp at the moment. But I don't want to take another chimp because the family is full. And we have too many problems when the new chimp arrives. And now I ope that Jane can build the sanctuary rapidly—and I ope that Congolese stop to kill the chimp."

Meanwhile, all the chimps outside were still pounding on the door, reaching into the windows, running across the roof. Madame Jamart gave me a drink of orange juice—it was a very hot day, and I had developed a powerful thirst—and then she said, brightly: "Do you have fear of chimpanzees? You could go outside and be with them. Would you like to?"

I was too lazy to decline, and soon I had gone out a side door of the house into a high, open shed where about a half dozen young chimps surrounded me. First they went for my glasses—I took them off, put them back in the house, and gamely came out for more. A rope hung down from the structure of the shed. One chimp had grabbed that rope, was swinging back and forth at head height and reaching for my face with a hand. Two other chimps grabbed my shoelaces and pulled until my shoes were untied. Then they started chewing on the laces. Two or three others were plunging hands into my pockets—one reached into my left front pocket and tried to pull out my hotel key. Another was trying to pull the notebook out of my back pocket. Two others began grabbing my right hand. They climbed quickly up my arm, swung out and jumped off. By then I had backed up against the wall, trying to protect the notebook in my back pocket, but the chimps surged around me, and now they were reaching around either side to get that note book. Now a bigger one—perhaps four years old and missing a foot—began trying to bite my leg. He had his teeth around my leg. Which chimp did Madame Jamart say had lost a foot? I pushed him away, and then he grabbed my hand. Madame Jamart, who had also come outside and who, for all I know, may have found my discomfort amusing, shouted out in French: "Close your fist so he can't bite your fingers!" But by then I was ready to go back inside. I reached for the door knob only to find it locked from the inside. Two chimps had already gone into the house and had been thrown out again; the housekeeper must have locked it after them. The chimp who was still trying to bite my hand was pulled away by Madame Jamart. But he came right back, took my hand, and began trying to pry my fingers out one by one and bite them. "Close your fingers! Close your fingers!" Madame Jamart reminded me.

She was farther out in the yard and surrounded by even more chimps than were still milling around me. "Do you want to come over here with me?" she asked after we had been outside for ten minutes. "No," I said. "I think I've had enough, thank you."

I was glad to get out of there.

I returned to the hotel late in the afternoon, thinking to go for a swim in the pool. I did swim, but the area around the pool was so filled with topless Frenchwomen soaking up ultraviolet rays and pretending they weren't topless (or, perhaps, pretending the men at the pool wouldn't notice—or, perhaps, not giving a *merde* whether the men noticed or not—or, perhaps, giving some kind of *merde,* judging from the expensive and frilly cut of their suit bottoms. In any case, the men did notice. Their eyes were like scared mice) that I left right after my swim.

I went into the restaurant for an early dinner and so found myself alone at a table seated two tables away from one other person in the restaurant, a young man with sun-bleached hair combed flat across his head and a chiseled face, with a square jaw and a small rectangular mustache, who was just then talking in English to the waiter. The waiter didn't understand English, so the man spoke loudly and accompanied his words with big gestures. "Can you just go *see,*" he said—pointing to his eyes, "in the *kitchen*"—he pointed toward the kitchen—"if there is spaghetti, *spa-ghet-ti,* for me?"

But the waiter didn't get it. So the sun-bleached man repeated the idea. "Spaghetti? Spaghetti? Not on the menu. In the kitchen. Over there. *Over there!!!*"

Finally, with obvious exasperation, he called over to me: "Can you speak English?"

"Yes," I said.

"Can you speak French?"

"A little. What's the problem?"

"Can you just ask this waiter here where my food is? I knew this would happen! I sensed it at lunch time. I sensed it! I don't speak French, and I wanted to be able to order a good meal tonight. I didn't want to embarrass the waiter or myself. So I said to myself, 'I'll just go see the manager. I'll make my order through him.' Oh, I knew this would happen! The manager says, 'Don't worry. What is it that you want?' 'Spaghetti and vegetables.' The manager says, 'I'll just go in the back: It's boom boom.' And now this waiter don't know fuck-all about it! Wait till I see the manager tonight!" Then he went back to attempting communication with the waiter: "Vegetables. Do you have any vegetables?"

I said, "Try: 'légumes.'"

"Legumes? Do you have any legumes? Carrot? Carrot? You have a carrot?"

But the waiter still didn't get it, and so finally the spaghetti and legumes were given up, and a standard meal was ordered in the standard fashion, i.e., pointing at the menu. The waiter went off into the kitchen, and the sun-bleached man looked at me. "My name is Dave Storch," he said. "I just got off the rig, and I thought I'd have me a few relaxing days in Pointe-Noire, but this is terrible! Nobody speaks English!"

I introduced myself.

"I'm a professional diver," he said. "What do you do?"

"I'm a writer," I said.

"A writer?"

"Yes."

"A professional writer?"

"Just about."

"Are you famous?"

"I will be next year."

I couldn't place his accent, so I asked him. He said he was from Yorkshire, and he dove for offshore oil work. He said oil exploration was just opening here in Africa. He was working for an American oil company out in the ocean on a pipe-laying barge. "Once you get offshore—the offshore world's the same everywhere. It's all the same," he said. Then he added, "Things were pretty good out there on the platform, until the other lads left."

The next morning, I went to Conoco Congo headquarters in downtown Pointe-Noire and met several Congolese and several Texans. The Texans wore Levi's and cowboy boots. They were friendly as hell and introduced themselves with power-squeeze handshakes and one-syllable names: Rick, Mike, Frank, Bill, and Mike again.

My own Texan, a drilling supervisor named Rick, drove me in his Toyota Land Cruiser out to a rig on the Kouilou River. Rick's left back pocket was marked with the circle from a can of chewing tobacco. He had a shaggy mustache, and after lunch, a toothpick jutted out from beneath the mustache.

I enjoyed hearing the Texas accents. I was glad to be among Americans. I liked Rick, who said he had spent one year in college up north until he ran out of money, at Georgetown University, and so he learned a little bit about how other people thought, people he might not necessarily agree with but at least could understand where they were coming from, and he reckoned that everybody should spend at least some time out of their usual environment. He thought it was a damn shame that the Africans were destroying their wildlife so quickly, but of course, to gain some perspective on the matter, you needed to think about what we did in the West just a hundred years ago. "We didn't do a real good job on the buffalo, right?"

Rick liked Africans, he said, and indeed some of the villagers along the road seemed to recognize him. They waved and called out. "I've been over most of the world," he said, "and these people are just like anybody else. There's good people and bad people, just like in your hometown and my hometown."

This road was very rough, with deep valleys, holes, gulleys, so driving with Rick was a series of slow-downs and speed-ups, of last minute twists and evasions. I don't know whether it was the motion; or the weather, which was oppressively humid and warm; or the fact that I had only slept an hour the night before; or a fourth factor, such as the several cups of bad coffee I had foolishly taken with breakfast— but I became convinced that a fundamentally embarrassing event churned in the works, beginning as a hot and acidic knot of coffee and half-chewed stale croissants in my stomach, eventually to end up on the carpeted interior and clean exterior of Rick's brand-new, cherry red Toyota Land Rover. Thus, although I enjoyed Rick's comments and attempts at conversation, I spent most of my time leaning out the window. Meanwhile, Rick would find a good stretch of road, step on the gas and accelerate forward only to discover directly ahead a new crater and lake that required lurching deceleration. And the road was muddy and puddled, since there had been an intense storm last night, so Rick would also slow down to avoid splashing the many pedestrians along the way. He carried on a one-sided conversation with the pedestrians we passed, a conversation they never heard and wouldn't have understood. Such as: "Hell of a load you got there!" And: "Them clean pants are gonna be dirty real soon!" And: "I ain't French—I won't barrel down and splash ya!" (Then, to me: "I guess you can tell—French culture is not my favorite culture.")

"This is one of the best-educated countries in the world," Rick said. "Their literacy rate here is high, it's very high. Higher than in the U.S. The only trouble is, then some of these people start reading, and they begin to realize that things could be different. They see all these countries in East Europe becoming democratic and capitalistic, and they want it too. What they don't realize, maybe, is that it won't happen like that. It might take two hundred years."

We drove for a couple of hours on that dirt road, the sight of the ocean to our left, through miles of green grass fields, a few old clapboard shanties along the road, a few trees, and then more fields. "Right over there," Rick said at one point, "is where the old king used to live. He sold slaves. This area used to be one of the biggest slave trading places in Africa."

Finally, we came to the Kouilou River, crossed a bridge there, and turned down to a big storage lot, a couple of trailers, and a dock. There was a boat at the dock. I was introduced to another Texan, was given a hardhat, a life jacket, and then we all stepped into the boat. The boat took us up past a forested, grass-edged island, up to the rig. The rig was huge and towering and painted as brightly in primary colors as a child's toy.

The rig consisted of two giant steel barges (both consisting of several smaller steel barges jigsawed together), both anchored in the churning river with giant steel legs and connected to each other by a bridge. One large barge supported trailers, eating, sleeping, and overall living quarters for the crew; the other large barge was the drilling rig, supporting a great tower and drill, engines, generators, cranes, and associated systems for punching and clawing a hole two miles down in the earth.

The whole thing seemed like a giant alimentary canal to me, as we climbed here and there, high up across catwalks and steel stairways over the river now, and over the mud pump and the churning mud pit, the degasser—"You can lose weight if you have gas in the mud"— and the flow line cleaners that take out even bigger particles. "That red thing is called 'the gas buster,'" the Texan said. "We don't ever like to use that. If we use that, we're in a well-control situation."

As they drill a hole, I learned, they put pipe in. As they put the pipe in, they reinforce it with cement, and they pump weighted mud down inside the pipe to make sure that if they hit something down there with great pressure, it doesn't suddenly just spew kablooie right up and out the top of the hole. The rig plus barge weighs about eight million pounds, and it's held in place with steel legs, resisting an average river current of about four knots. But there are huge problems and great risks, requiring, for example, a constant monitoring of whatever comes out of the hole. "One big risk is H_2S," the Texan said. "We constantly monitor for the presence of H_2S."

"Can't you just smell it?" I said.

"At ten parts per million you can smell it. At twenty parts per million your nose goes dead. At fifty parts per million you go unconscious. At a hundred parts per million for fifteen minutes, you're dead."

Conoco had been drilling an exploration hole, the Texan said, but they have just decided it was a bust. "This well is dry. Only one well in fifteen is successful. You spend millions of dollars to get to the one that's commercial—this is one thing the American public don't understand. Now we have to pull all this stuff down, take it all apart, take it fifty kilometers up the river, and put it together again. It will take five weeks to break it down, move it, and reassemble. There's normally seventy people out here twenty-four hours a day, and another thirty people at the riverside station."

We had lunch on the living quarters barge, and it was superb—barbequed chicken, chips, salad, soup, everything—and I ate and ate. About a dozen Texans were having lunch in the same room, and the lunch-time conversation took on a certain pattern: one, two, three at the most sentences, followed by guffaws. One, two, three: guffaw. One, two, three: guffaw. One, two, three: guffaw. A Texan sitting nearby explained the situation to me: "We try to keep it as light-hearted as possible out here. After twenty-eight days, it gets kind of crowded out here." But I didn't say much. I felt like an over-educated Yankee with a hypersensitive stomach and not much to contribute, just eating more and more and more, trying to keep the cap on the gas in the mud at the bottom of my own well.

What does a Conoco oil rig on the Kouilou River in southern Congo have to do with chimpanzees? I hoped that Roger, the president of Conoco Congo, would explain it to me soon, before I completely ran out of money sitting in that overpriced hotel. I had met Roger briefly at the Conoco headquarters in Pointe-Noire that morning before leaving with Rick, and Roger had said he would call me that night or, if not, then the next morning.

I returned to the hotel in the late afternoon, my stomach still on red alert, and found the professional diver Dave Storch sitting at a table on the poolside patio with two other men—another diver and an

Italian shipping manager—and being upset with the poolside waiter. Dave's face broke into a sneering smile as the waiter, looking puzzled and vaguely concerned, placed a cup and a pot of tea on the table in front of him. Dave opened the pot and told me to look inside. There were three tea bags in the pot. "You see? You see?" he said. "I knew it! You see? They can't get it bloody right here. I says to the man, 'Could we have three teas, please?' Three! And instead he brings me one tea with three bags in it!" Dave said he didn't even try to ask himself. He had that Frenchwoman over there—the one with pink bikini bottom, elongated nipples, and go-away eyes—who speaks English—explain what he wanted.

The waiter wandered off, but Dave called him back, holding up three fingers. "Three! Three! Three! Three bloody teas!" Ten minutes later, the waiter brought two more cups. "Can you believe this? That's how they do it here! He brings us two more cups, but we still only have one pot!"

But now the waiter was nervously casting his shadow over me, wondering if I wanted anything. I decided to order some tea. "Je voudrais du thé, s'il vous plaît," I said.

But the waiter, looking very worried now, wanted to make sure: "Deux thés?"

"No, du thé," I said, and then, as an afterthought: "Et du lait."

"Deux laits?"

"No! Un thé et un lait!" I said.

Five minutes later he brought tea without milk. Dave looked at me with a sly grin and said: "You see? There you have it! That's how they do it here! That's it! That's it!"

I had an early dinner and then locked myself in my room, waiting for Roger's call. I settled down patiently and watched a movie on television, *Les Pygmées,* that seemed to alternate scenes of real pygmies in the forest with sequences of second-rate Congolese and tenth-rate French actors in a studio. Most of it was in French, but the conversations among the pygmies were translated with French subtitles.

The movie starts with National Geographic-style shots in the rainforest: pygmy net hunters catching and killing duikers for lunch. These are real duikers, really slaughtered and eaten, shuddering for a few seconds as they die. Then two white guys, both French I think, fly an airplane to Africa and ask some Africans to help equip them to go into the forest. A small-change African tyrant with bad manners and a green tie, sitting in front of his mud hut, says he can't equip them to go into the forest to find pygmies. One of the white guys leaves in the airplane. The other white guy (who regularly grimaces and swats at imaginary insects, then dabs the sweat off his forehead with a perfectly folded handkerchief) stands up and curses softly to himself: "Merde! Merde! Merde!" He really wants to find the pygmies. He is wearing red socks. . . .

But when Roger didn't call that evening, a little voice in my head began repeating: *You see? You see? There you have it! That's how they do it here! That's it! That's it!* I went to sleep with that voice inside my head.

Roger had said that if he couldn't call that evening, he would call the next morning. But I waited around in my room the next morning, too, only taking a short break to swim some laps in the pool. No phone call. By then, I absolutely hated that little room. *You see? You see? There you have it! That's how they do it here! That's it! That's it!* the little voice said. At five minutes to noon, my exploration drill punctured a high pressure area and spewed kablooie. I was sick of my room! I was sick of waiting! I called up the airport, booked myself on a flight out of town that afternoon. I packed my bag, and then I called up Conoco headquarters and spoke to Roger. I tried not to sound irritated. I said I was sorry, but I had just decided to leave Pointe-Noire that afternoon. Roger said he had tried to reach me three times that morning. Each time the hotel desk clerk had said I wasn't in my room. He had thought we could spend some time together on the weekend. He was disappointed I was leaving so soon. Did I at least have time for lunch? Could I come in to headquarters?

His secretary called him "President." "Oui, President," she said. The Congolese workers at headquarters called him "the boss." The Texans called him "Mr. Simpson." But Roger, in fact, turned out to be one of the world's nicest guys. He was British—a Celt—pink-skinned, with short brown hair, wide and thin lips, and an extremely pleasant and soft-spoken style.

We had a Chinese meal together, and almost immediately I regretted my feverish lapse into surly impatience. "Hunting is the big problem in Congo, not deforestation," he said. "Although Congo is one of the most underpopulated countries in Africa, in terms of population density, it's very, very urbanized. Ostensibly, this sounds like good news; but actually it's bad. Because many of the urbanized Congolese still prefer bush meat as their protein source, and so professional market hunters go out and kill game to bring to the cities. The cities—

Pointe-Noire and Brazzaville, especially—have become a black hole for
wildlife, just draining wildlife out of the country." He confirmed that
chimps are not eaten in southern Congo. "Although they cheerfully
admit to eating most everything else, they say they do not eat chimps.
'The chimpanzees are our fathers,' is how they put it. So chimps are a
totemic animal. But arboreal monkeys are almost wiped out between
here and the mountains. The Congolese have never before felt the
need to conserve animals because they've never had to. They've never
run out—they've got a relatively large reservoir of forest and a comparatively small population. But now we've got almost industrial-scale
hunting to satisfy the big city markets."

He said that Conoco was working with Jane Goodall and the
Congolese government to create a chimp sanctuary near Pointe-Noire.
"The government is interested and willing to donate land. Conoco
will give support in terms of finance," he said. "I expect the final cost
will be over a hundred thousand dollars. We'll also be providing support in terms of advice to Jane about working with the government,
since we've had a good deal of experience. Jane feels that if we can
basically build it for her, she can do the rest."

After lunch, Roger drove me back to my hotel. As I was stepping
out of his truck, shaking hands, he said, "Oh, by the way, do you
know Brian Hippelwaithe?"

My heart sank. "Brian Hippelwaithe? The journalist? I've never
met him. I'm not sure I want to. Why?"

"He was here last week."

"He was?"

"Yes. We spent three days together."

Brian Hippelwaithe has beaten me again, I thought. Then I thought: *Beaten
me to what?* I was drifting down there in Pointe-Noire, troubled, frag-
mented and frustrated, while the money just continued to drain out of
my pockets. What was I looking for? I had no idea.

I checked out of the hotel in a foul mood.

Pack in hand, I looked around for the diver, Dave Storch, thinking
I would distribute the usual snippets of recessional benediction: goodbye, good luck, et cetera. I found him lying out on a deck lounge at
poolside, wearing only a minor bathing suit, eyes closed and face
pointed toward the sun. His body was perfectly muscled, an anatomy
lesson in repose. He looked peaceful, satisfied, content: everything the

opposite of what I felt. And I suddenly felt envious. I thought that life as a diver, a professional diver, must be the good life: uncomplicated, salaried, washed in the sun and the sea's warm womb, the life of the body instead of the life of the headache, encountering concrete problems in the real world instead of chimerical paragraphs in the abstract world, facing them with the easy bonhomie of comradeship instead of the distressing buzz of solitude, wrestling open-eyed and sharp-witted with a giant squid or two in the Sargasso Sea instead of struggling blind and brainless with sullen snippets in a closed and lonely room.

He squinted open his eyes, shading them with a hand, and said, "I've been thinking. You must have the good life. You're a writer! You get to do this kind of thing all the time, don't you. Me, I only get snippets here and there. Like this snippet. This has been the most relaxing three days of my life. Most of the time, it's bang: out there, twelve-hour days, nothing to eat but chicken and rice for three months. When you do get on shore, it's only these snippets. But then, I can't complain. A lot of people don't even get the snippets."

14

An American Meal

*Hearne, the North American traveller, recommends
a "haggis made with blood, a good quantity of fat
shred small, some of the tenderest of the flesh, together
with the heart and lungs, cut or torn into small skiv-
ers; all of which is put into the stomach, and roasted
by being suspended before the fire on a string. Care
must be taken that it does not get too much heat at
first, or it will burst. It is a most delicious morsel,
even without pepper, salt, or any seasoning."*

–Francis Galton, *The Art of Travel*

So I returned to Brazzaville, thinking I could either travel north and
perhaps find chimpanzees in the woods somewhere, or just fly back to
the States. Happily, the embassy apartment was still at my disposal.

Brazzaville was very hot, of course, a prosperous and troubled city,
with its share of high rises and big hotels with fancy Japanese cars
parked out front—including the pewter Toyota Land Cruiser with two
bullet holes in the driver's door, parked in front of the M'Bamu Palace.
Garbage was piled out on the streets, however, and the Congolese had
the disturbing habit of piling old leaves and branches next to the boulevard trees that had begotten them and then burning the piles, burning
the trees in the process and so gradually killing all the trees so lovingly
planted by colonialists twenty-five years ago.

What I had been thinking about for some time was—should I
admit this?—American food. Back in Brazzaville, therefore, I began

eyeing an American-style hamburger joint called Joburger on one of the main streets of town, right across from the post office building. I wanted an American meal. The works! Fast food hamburger, french fries, Coke, possibly a small salad, the whole nine yards.

I was walking down the street, headed for my apartment (intending to wait there until that evening, opening time for the Joburger), when I saw a boy, perhaps nine or ten years old, who looked as if he were a polio victim: one short, thin, dangling leg. He hobbled with a crude cane fashioned from an old stick and, as I moved his way, reached out with an open hand and a look of great appeal. I reached into my pocket and pulled out a coin at random, which I placed in his hand. But just as I did that—from out of nowhere!—a crowd of perhaps a dozen young boys with missing or withered arms and legs quickly (hobbling industriously on sticks) converged on me with their hands outstretched. I reached into my pocket again and pressed coins into those hands. But several of the boys looked at the coins in their hands with an angry and dismayed expression and then screeched various things I didn't understand specifically but did generally: They wanted more coins. The coins I gave were too small, too pitiful and demeaning.

I was out of coins, though, so I just walked faster. The boys hobbled after me on their sticks, but pretty soon I had outpaced them, and I walked up the street with only their curses still trailing after me. I went back to my apartment, read a book, and waited until dark.

Brazzaville was not well lit at night. Most streets didn't have street lights, so that the Joburger generated and sat in its own well of bluish-white light, with cigarette smoke rising from an outdoor patio and spreading and curling white in the light and then disappearing as it rose higher, into the surrounding darkness. This patio was surrounded by a soft hedge of plants inside large wooden planters. Outside the hedge occasional cars with dim yellow headlights passed by on the street. People passed by as well, quietly moving through the shadows and murk.

I sat in a red plastic chair at a white wooden table on the Joburger patio. A waiter took my order, and I leaned back to relax and enjoy the American experience. A television set played music videos loudly inside the Joburger—more chairs and tables in there—and, since the glass doors were slid open, the music poured outside onto the patio and into my ears. First Michael Jackson did his thing. Then came Madonna. But somehow the Madonna tape became stuck, so it was Madonna making promises for the rest of the time I spent at the Joburger. She promised an awful lot. "Come, come to me now. Baby, you can have everything!"

Several Congolese came into the Joburger and sat at the tables inside and outside, on the patio, but they were all dressed like Europeans. The Europeans there were dressed like Europeans, too.

A bronzed and stringy Frenchwoman in short shorts, with blond hair done in a thick ponytail, red nails, and a hard look on her face, sat at a table near the edge of the patio and smoked Marlboros. She was flanked by two overweight boys, six and ten years old, apparently her own sons. Two gold chains with pendants hung around her wrinkled, sunburned neck. Four rings decorated four of her fingers. The woman and her sons ordered Joburgers.

Two Soviet women, members of the embassy typing pool, so I imagined, sat at another table. The woman facing me had a bovine face, tubular legs, high-heeled shoes, and a low-necklined, plasticized dress with blue and white horizontal stripes. The one with her back to me wore a white nylon blouse and a short navy blue skirt. She was slender with, I could see whenever she turned her head, a thin face and upturned nose. They ordered Joburgers, too.

My Joburger came, along with the french fries and Coke. I ate and then ordered a second Joburger. I was hungry. But while I ate the second Joburger, a young African boy appeared at the entrance to the patio, standing half out in the darkness of the street and half leaning into the soft blue light of the patio. He was leaning on a crooked stick, and his short left leg dangled. He was the same boy I had given a coin to earlier in the day! I didn't want this—didn't wanted to be reminded of him. Madonna sighed and sang: "Come, come to me now. Baby, you can have everything!"

But he wanted to come into the lighted patio and beg. He hesitated, then started to pass through the patio entrance when a Belgian, who had been sitting at a long table with several Congolese women and children, stood up and blocked his way. Finally and very firmly the Belgian pushed the boy out of the patio entrance and back onto the sidewalk. The boy leaned into the light and responded with a dramatic look on his face: at once angry and painfully aggrieved. He looked pointedly down at his leg. He started slapping at his leg, looking up accusingly. Then he looked down at his leg again, and finally he looked up at his persecutor and held his hand out. The Belgian stood there, saying nothing, not moving.

After a few minutes the boy gave up trying to get through the entrance. With his crooked stick, he hobbled around the outside edges of the patio until he came to an opening between the plants of the patio hedge. He reached his begging hand through the opening right in front of the Frenchwoman and her two children. The Frenchwoman scolded him and said, "Go away!" But he stood right there, his hand still out. "I won't go away," the hand signified, "until you place something right here."

The Frenchwoman called the manager, who came over and scolded the boy, who yet continued to hold his hand out through the bushes. At last he left, but only to hobble back around to the patio entrance. He stood there in the light and started spinning around and around on his stick, leaning on the stick and spinning, pausing once every revolution to peer in at the hamburger-eating customers on the lighted patio. Next, he dropped to the sidewalk, mostly dirt, and began rolling around, pausing on occasion to sit up and look into the lighted patio with a dramatic, pleading, beseeching expression on his face.

And all the while, Madonna, hot and running perpetually one step behind ecstasy, kept repeating her sultry promise: "Come, come to me now. Baby, you can have everything!"

15

Paradise

A phone message from the American ambassador said that Mike Fay
and Amy Vedder were in Brazzaville and gave me their room numbers
at the M'Bamu Palace. I didn't know who Mike Fay was or why I
should see him, but the name Amy Vedder excited me. I had never
actually met Amy, but I had had several long phone conversations
with her about gorillas. She and her husband, Bill Weber, studied
mountain gorillas with Dian Fossey and later helped set up the mountain gorilla tourist project in Rwanda. I wanted to see the person who
until then had been merely a pleasant vibration in the telephone.

I went to room 919 at the M'Bamu Palace, Amy's room, and
knocked on the door. No answer. So I tried the other room number
on my list, which was just across the hall. The door was opened by an
intense young man with round, steel-rimmed glasses, who said he was
Michael Fay. He said that Amy was swimming laps in the hotel pool
and should be back soon. I could wait there, he said.

The television was on, and both Mike and I sat down in front of
the glowing tube to watch something amazing. We saw high-altitude
pictures of small spots in a desert. Some cross hairs locked onto one

244

spot, and a projectile that looked, on the screen, like a single-minded mosquito, entered the spot and quietly transformed it into a puff of smoke.

That was a smart bomb, supposed to outsmart Saddam Hussein.

We watched more smart bombs hit their targets with high precision. I was impressed. Mike said: "I'm thinking: 'If only I could have the money it takes to build just one of those bombs.' You could buy a lot of rain forest with that money."

As it turned out, Mike Fay and Amy Vedder were employed by an American organization, Wildlife Conservation International. They were in Brazzaville on business having to do with a forest in the north. Mike said this forest was absolutely pristine, untouched, even unexplored. The forest was known as the Ndoki—a Lingala word meaning "sorcerer." This was a sorcerer's place, an enchanted forest, and Mike was leading an effort to have the Ndoki and a contiguous forest known as the Nouabalé designated as a national park for Congo.

Mike said he'd first gotten interested in the northern Congo forests soon after he went to the Central African Republic in 1980 with the Peace Corps. The Central African Republic (CAR, for short) is just north of Congo, and during the 1980s Fay became involved in establishing a national park in southern CAR. But he kept looking at maps, and the maps kept telling him to go to northern Congo. "Isolated areas have always kind of captured my imagination," he said, "and you know, ever since we arrived in CAR back in 1980, that part of the map has been of special interest just because it's this huge vacant block of forest. I would say even as far back as 1980, as soon as I got to CAR, and as soon as I started looking at even road maps of the area, that Ndoki, that area right there just stands out. I mean it's like—phew!!!— here's this huge block of forest where there's nothing. There are no villages, no indications of people there. It's very obvious. And it just draws your attention right away."

He continued. "The first time I went there I went with [American biologist] Richard Carroll, and we walked over from his camp in CAR, which isn't too far from Congo, and that's the first time it basically happened. You come across that crest, and you know, you're going from forest that has already been exploited to this kind of no-man's land over on the other side. It just felt like you were going into this vast unknown wilderness. And that was a lot of fun. I still remember that. Really neat. And that one foray wasn't even very far. We probably only went in seven Ks, but even so, it was like, 'Wow, this place is amazing.' But we already knew. You could just tell, just by looking at the map. All the surveys that I've done and all the surveys that just about everyone else has done show that elephant densities are the exact mirror opposite of human densities. So you look at a block of forest and there's nobody out there, no villages, you're almost guaranteed that you're going to find elephants, because all of the data point to that. If you're seventy-five Ks away from the nearest village, the elephant density is going to be real high. That's true in Gabon. It's true in Cameroon. It's true in CAR. It's true in Congo. It's true in Zaire. Anywhere. So really, it was pretty obvious."

This forest was so pristine, he said, that the chimpanzees there acted as if they had never seen humans before. Mike called them "naive chimps." They acted shocked, amazed, curious, and appalled at the sight of people. And they didn't run. Virtually everywhere else in Africa (except for the few protected regions where scientists have slowly and carefully habituated chimpanzees to the presence of observers), chimps flee at the first sign of people. They know how very dangerous the human ape can be.

Mike thought that the Ndoki chimpanzees didn't flee because none of them could remember ever being hunted, which may have meant that no humans had stepped into the center of the region for at least one chimpanzee generation—a few decades. In fact, there was so far no indication that people had ever entered the heart of the Ndoki, although two Japanese primatologists were now studying primates at the forest's peripheries.

The whole idea was very exciting to me. Never having seen people, the animals were not afraid of them. They didn't run. Would this be true of all the animals in Ndoki, or just the chimps? The more I thought about it, the more my interests, and my imagination, expanded. I began to conceptualize the place as . . . paradise. True, this general area of Central Africa received a lot of negative publicity some time back when it was featured as the background setting for Joseph Conrad's *Heart of Darkness*. But Conrad's "dark heart" didn't really refer to Africa or Africans anyhow, and it certainly didn't refer to a nonhumanized wilderness. That book focused on the evil effects of Belgian colonialism and the ivory trade, the darkly evil potential of the human, or maybe it was the Belgian, heart.

When I went looking through the English-language books in a Brazzaville used-books store for the linguistically impaired, therefore,

I passed right over Conrad and kept on going until I had reached Milton's *Paradise Lost*. Yes, I really did buy the book. And I looked at it, too. Just long enough to remember how intolerable I have always found that overextended meditation on theology at the stained-glass level. Does it help to know that Satan is the real hero of *Paradise Lost*? No, it does not.

Still, the concept of paradise intrigued me. I had once been to a place I consider very close to paradise: the island of Nosy Mangabe just off the coast of northeastern Madagascar. Nosy Mangabe is an uninhabited and richly beflowered little place, with dolphins dancing in the waters offshore and lemurs cavorting in the trees. What I learned from that small dose of paradise was this: Paradise starts with the physiological. Perhaps with the absence of serious physiological challenge: close to skin temperature, for instance, steady and predictable enough to humor warm-blooded mammals such as we.

But also, I think, paradise would manifest itself in a natural rather than artificial pattern: alinear and often asymmetrical instead of linear and mostly symmetrical. You don't find Adam and Eve all dressed up in plaid golfing pants and striped blazers standing on a Manhattan street corner, do you? Linear and symmetrical are usually more efficient, particularly if the pattern serves or satisfies a single vector. But in nature, patterns are established from multiple vectors, often conflicting and sometimes codeveloping energies. In nature, in other words, design is democratic: the gradual resolution of conflicting purposes. In artifice, design is autocratic.

Paradise for me would also present natural instead of artificial color. Natural color (in a forest, at least) predominates at the short-waved end of the visible light spectrum: green, blue, indigo, and violet. These are also and not coincidentally (since we evolved, for the most part, inside forests) colors of relaxation. Surrounded by them, simultaneously listening to the soft whispers of a warm breeze into leaves, we believe that all is well. The colors of artifice and arousal occur at the other end: red, orange, and yellow. It is true that real forests sooner or later include all the colors—the shortwaved, relaxing ones merely predominate. So maybe a paradisiacal forest is missing altogether, through miraculous intervention, the colors of arousal: the red of blood or an open mouth, an erect penis or a female ape's sexual swelling; the orange and yellow of ripe fruit. For the civilized ape the same sequence holds, of course. Advertising, the art of inducing arousal, would hit us in the eyes at the longwaved end of the spectrum: bright neon signs in international orange or two-foot-high letters in red that scream:

FINAL CLOSEOUT SALE! GET IT WHILE YOU CAN!

Advertising would pass us the red apple while we visit the Big Apple, and sensuality would trip us up via the scarlet woman. But, in our better moments at least, we intend to dissolve our lives within the shortwaved colors of paradisaical relaxation . . . and so we slip our cars through the green light and head for the green-lawned suburb. If we can afford it.

No straight lines. No longwaved colors. No death. No disease. No labor. No taxes. All these negatives are part of the standard positive vision of paradise—but most important, no clothes. Adam and Eve stood there bare nekkid. That's how we know the place was warm, of course, but it seems to me that nekkid is as much a psychological as it is a physical state. The essence of paradise is the memory of a unity with nature. No clothes. Clothes imply, symbolize, and reinforce ego-identity, the psychological separateness from nature. We are familiar with the paradise of Genesis, a place and time of "innocence" without pain or death, but most importantly, with a miraculous peace in nature, a truce between human and animal. The animals weren't named until the sixth day of creation, and so one also has the sense that paradise lies very close to a prelinguistic time in the human dream.

One could consider paradise as a collective memory, or perhaps the memory of a certain phase of cultural development. But it is also possible to imagine paradise—and therefore paradise lost—as an individual memory of growing up, the development of the brain and mind, part of every person's cerebral baggage and psychohistory. Emily Dickinson struggled with an internal conflict between paradise and paradise lost more than any person I know. Virtually all her poems fall on one side or other of the unfortunate lapse, spoken in two voices so distinct they could be two people or expressions from two separate parts of the brain. And the reason is, or could be, that her father preached at her too much while she was growing up.

Paradise physical and paradise psychological intertwine, and our separation from paradise has been at once a physical and a psychological loss. Mythology suggests that this loss we grieve over. We regret our primordial expulsion from the Garden of Eden, and to the degree that paradise exists in the mind, the fall from paradise describes the development of mind. But paradise also, I think, describes a physical place and time. And our construction of a psychological map of paradise (that unremembered, shadowed dream illuminating all dreamers and seekers of untouched nature and wild places) grieves after our destruction of the real paradise in the real world.

I wanted to find an actual place somewhere, deep in the African forest, an undestroyed, untouched place, a place that would prove itself a heart of light, not of darkness, a private and serene place that could serve as, for my own satisfaction at least, the physical location of paradise. A dappled stillness with chimpanzees running around. One I could find on the map and put my finger on. *There,* I would say, *that's where paradise is.*

Thus, after considerable preparation not worth going into here, I took a Lina Congo flight north, across (or was it through?) the Equator, to a small river town called Ouesso on the eastern bank of the Sangha River. From Ouesso, I would take a boat seventy miles upriver to a place called Bomassa.

Mike Fay met me at the Ouesso landing strip, and we stayed in town, waiting for a mechanic and five onlookers to fix an outboard motor. Mike was renting the downstairs of a rotting mansion overlooking the river, built in the old days by a colonial baron of commerce and ivory. Surrounded by high palms and still beautiful gardens, the mansion's two-foot-thick, moss-streaked and lichen-splotched white walls were topped with a tin roof and ventilated with high, Romanesque doors and windows. A demispiraled dual stairway led to the colonnaded veranda, and, through a once grand front entrance, into a wide hall and rooms with fourteen-foot ceilings and black and white checkerboard tiles on the floor. The upstairs was closed off—dark, musty, cobwebby. I went up there one time to look at the gorilla bed, a wooden platform suspended six feet off the floor. The former owner used to keep a gorilla upstairs, Mike said.

The outboard motor worked on Monday morning, and then it didn't work. It worked on Tuesday morning, and then it didn't work.

Tuesday afternoon, we bought some supplies in town and watched the meat truck unload. It was an old pickup truck surrounded by a powerful odor and a big crowd, perhaps sixty people, buying the meat that was being tossed off the back of the truck. I recognized some of the meat being sold—monkeys and duikers, some skinned and smoked and quartered, some not. A man lowered one big monkey by its tail.

Back at the mansion, Mike spread a large satellite photograph of northern Congo across the dining room table. "Here we are: Ouesso," he said, pointing to one spot on the image. "This is the Sangha River," he said, drawing his finger along a wiggling line. "And here is where you'll be going." He pressed into a soft, dark green area. There seemed to be a small river in the green area. "The Ndoki River," Mike said. There was a small splotch of lighter green inside the larger area of dark green. "This is Mbeli Bai—an elephant clearing. The elephants open up these areas to get at the minerals in the soil. It's a saline, a salt lick for elephants. You'll pass through it, and then you'll walk out here, right into the core area of Ndoki."

One thing had been bothering me for some time, and I brought it up now. If this forest was so pristine, if these chimpanzees were so naive, then by going in and finding them I would be making them less naive and the forest less pristine. I would be destroying something, a piece of wildness, an innocence. "Wouldn't it be best just to leave the Ndoki forest alone?" I said.

"You probably could decide," Mike said, " 'Okay, we've got this hundred-square-kilometer area, and no one will ever go there. We will block it off. And it will be an area where no one has ever been or no one will ever go into.' That would be pretty wild, really, but I don't know if that's realistic. And it is something that I think is sad. That's why I want to see that any encounters with naive chimps are kind of recorded somehow, photographically or in writing. Because it's true, five years from now, ten years from now, there will probably not be any chimps in the Ndoki forest that haven't seen humans. They all will have seen humans—but most of them will never have been shot at. Most of them will never have had a violent encounter with a human being.

"It would be nice to say, 'Okay, boom, this is an area where no man will ever go.' But you're never going to be able to keep humans, the human machine, from advancing. And looking at all the grim statistics of demographics, of logging concessions, of road projects and oil exploration and drying climates and degradation of watersheds and advancing colonization, all those things, if you don't put in some kind of land management structure that will preserve the area, you're going to lose it anyway. There's no question about that. All you have to do is look at the satellite image."

We looked at the satellite image and noted, right below the Ndoki-Nouabalé region, a whole network of rectangular, hairline cuts. "These are logging access roads," Mike said. Everything in northern

Congo was given out to logging concessions during the 1980s. Everything, that is, except the Ndoki-Nouabalé–which had been defined as a concession but, probably because it was a little less accessible than the rest, not yet leased. "The reserve we're creating is basically that logging concession. The Nouabalé River is the northern limit, the Ndoki is the western limit. In fact, just a couple of months after we declared an interest in trying to define this as a protected area, an Algerian logging company tried to get the concession. Only because of us the government said 'No.' "

The motor was ready on Wednesday. We attached it to the back of a rubber Zodiac and traded the oppressive heat and stink of the shore for cool river air and a wonderfully rich smell of river grass. We cut a wake north, upriver, threaded our way around shallows and snags and hidden sandbars, plowed against swelling brown water, moving fast. We noticed a few villages along the shore as we traveled, a few houses of mud and sticks and thatch, and once in a while we saw villagers on the shore or energizing a lonely peapod pirogue in the water: two boys standing at either end of their small canoe, bending and stroking with spear-shaped paddles in unison; a woman wrapped in white, slowly poling her gray vessel upriver. Then we passed through long sections of the river with no signs of people at all, nothing but brown and gleaming water, a gray sky and floating dark pillows overhead, and, on either side, a high wall of leafy trees and matted vines hanging over the river's edge, once in a while the forest wall opening up to show dark insides or the flattened gray trunk of a giant kapok.

We stopped the boat at a bare place on shore with a few dozen houses, a settlement named Kabo, center of a logging concession, and drank beers with two Portuguese mechanics living in a riverbank bungalow, the porch of which hung over enough water to fish in. The Portuguese said they thought the logging operation might go bust.

We reached our destination by late afternoon, tied up the boat, and climbed up a bluff to a clearing that contained the start of a national park headquarters: half a dozen stucco buildings, some running showers and flush toilets, generated electricity after dark, a kitchen, a refrigerator.

We were greeted by two people, Matthew Hatchwell and Andrea Turkalo. Matthew Hatchwell was an unflappable Englishman of scholarly appearance who served the project as diplomat and manager.

Andrea Turkalo was an American who normally sat in a blind at an elephant saline in the Central African Republic. She was in Congo now mainly, I think, because she is married to Mike Fay. "Would anyone like a Coke?" she said.

After dinner Andrea talked about elephants. Elephants communicate over long distances with sounds that are below the human range, she said. When people were "culling" elephants at a park in South Africa, elephants many miles away from the shooting knew exactly what was going on and where. She has learned to identify more than fifteen hundred individual elephants at her site; they all know when she is there watching them, but mostly they ignore her as a piece of background. Sometimes they come up to the blind and reach up with their trunks.

Andrea said that some of the local people used to wonder about Mike's real intentions. The idea that someone might want to save a forest or protect animals was foreign to people who have lived on the edge of a great forest and hunted all their lives. "A lot of the locals have never been to Ouesso. Maybe five percent have been to Brazzaville. Most have never seen anything but their forest. The idea that forests are being cut down all over Africa or that the animals might run out is pretty ludicrous to these people."

One rumor considered the link between Andrea, watching elephants up in southern CAR, and Mike, running around in the woods down in northern Congo. People said that Andrea had figured out a magic way to remove elephants' tusks at night, while they were asleep, and that Mike had cleared a path through the forest from his place to Andrea's place. People said they were smuggling ivory along that path.

Mike and Andrea were headed back down the river to Ouesso and from there to Brazzaville. Mike needed a tooth fixed, among other things. He had just come up to Bomassa to see me launched into the forest.

Bomassa was the name of the park headquarters they were constructing and also of a village just a few miles outside the proposed park. Bomassa village represented the biggest concentration of Congolese in the entire area, about 150 people of two ethnic groups, and the plan for a national park included some reasonable impulse to benefit the Bomassans. American Peace Corps volunteers had, in cooperation with the park project, started a school in the village. The park project also provided serious and potentially long-term employment for Bomassa, and it was from that village that Mike and I hired five Congolese to help me in the forest. One was a Bantu named François Nguembo; the other four were Bangome pygmies: Ma, Ande, Bakembe Victor, and Dede Florent. Ma and Ande had last names too, no doubt, but our communication was weak enough that I never learned them.

Mike and Andrea left in a giant dugout canoe on Friday morning. An hour later, Matthew Hatchwell started up a Toyota pickup truck that contained me, the Bantu, the four pygmies, and two weeks' worth of food and supplies. Matthew drove us along thirty-two kilometers of an old logging road outside the southern boundary of the proposed park until we reached the edge of a wet body he called the Ndoki River. I would call it the Ndoki Swamp.

We got out of the truck, said goodbye to Matthew, and then the six of us wandered down into a cave made by trees with a floor of soft black mud punctuated by deep, round, water-filled holes: elephant footprints. We stepped deeply into the mud, pulling out our feet with a sucking sound, and walked through until we located two small, waterlogged dugout canoes. We bailed out the water, dragged the two pirogues through the mud over to the swamp, tossed our things and ourselves in, and set off, poling and paddling.

This swamp was magical. We moved through a dark channel out into sunlight, tall trees, an open passage of water through razor grass, and then back into a shadowed world of giant, ghostly trees. The water looked black at first, but where shafts of sunlight shot through, I saw it was smoky at the top and then glowing blood-red deeper down. Old logs were strewn darkly below us, down in the dark red water, and above us, trees drooped and twisted. Vines snaked everywhere, and high, thin tree roots crinkled and curled and twisted like ribbons in a languid, half-melted style down into the water, into complicated shadows and reflections. Sometimes we paused and hacked a little with a machete. After a while, the channel became wider, and I saw small purple flowers and water lilies, and looked into the blood water and listened to the piping of birds, the splashing of paddles, and my five companions chatting among themselves in a mysterious tongue. "Orga kowa kowa," they said. "Ka se de bama kodo. Tan bongolade tama chimba." Then the channel became narrow again.

It took about an hour to cross the swamp, and then we beached the two pirogues on the other side and thus entered Ndoki. The forest was cool and beautiful, noisy with insects and birds, and I was so pleased to have reached it. We immediately set about making a temporary camp on the edge of the swamp. But I was eager to see some of the forest, and so I left with one of the pygmies—the oldest, Dede—to find something Mike had told me about, the elephant clearing, the saline called Mbeli Bai.

Dede was small, with thin arms and thinner legs and tiny feet. He wore a blue series of rags as a shirt and a casual, wraparound loincloth as shorts. He went barefoot. He wore a small, dark anklet of woven vine around his right ankle. And he carried a machete, held poised with a cocked wrist in his right hand or, occasionally, resting in the crook of his right arm.

Dede and I walked out of camp and onto a meandering elephant trail. The forest here was dry, and a scattered litter of leaves went crunch, crunch beneath our feet while my spirits lifted higher and higher. This was everything I had expected: hypnotically peaceful, cool, serene. Paradise! After an hour, the trail dipped low, lower, until it was underwater. The water was muddy at first and pocked with elephant footprints the size of large dinner platters; it went from ankle-deep to knee-deep and finally to thigh-deep. This was still a trail, though, a trail through water, and it turned right, turned left, passed through a tunnel of vegetation and dappled light, twisted here, twisted there. We waded past a number of false exits and dark corners, and then we walked right into and through a current: fresh, cool, clear water rushing down, crossing our little water trail and passing on. This was a small river. The current creased the water before us and whispered and chuckled. Dede bent over and began splashing water into his mouth with rapid flicks of his hand. I cupped my hands, dipped, and raised the water to my lips: delicious!

We walked out of the water and perhaps half an hour later came to a sunny open space. We paused, squinting in the bright light. "Mbeli Bai," the pygmy said. Mbeli Bai was a big meadow right in the middle of the forest, oval in shape, just about the right size to land a 727. I could even imagine landing a 727 there, the meadow seemed so flat and predictable, but when we stepped out into it I revised that image. My foot, half my leg, sank into hot mud. I looked around, then, and realized the bai consisted of grass and water and mud with elephant footprints in it. Some of the ground was stable, if you stepped right in the middle of a well-established grass clump; if you stepped into a grass clump that was not so well established, you found yourself slipping down into the mud.

The bai looked deserted, and Dede and I laboriously moved out toward the middle of it. We had stepped out of the shade of the forest and into the glare of a burning tropical sun. I was pulling a hat out of my pack when Dede whispered sharply: "Gorille!" He was looking to the far end of the meadow, where there was a small island of trees and brush. I looked over and saw the gorilla, who sat in tall grass in front of the copse. He was far enough away and obscured enough by the grass that I saw mostly a dark blob. The more I looked, the more the blob took on the somewhat rectangular shape of a gorilla, probably an adult male, I thought, given how massive he seemed.

I wanted to move closer to get a better look. "Allons," I suggested.

My companion seemed to agree, and so we started walking through the high grass and deep mud directly toward the gorilla. Gorillas, I mean. I could see two dark blobs now. Gorillas have good vision, however, and we had only walked several yards before they saw us and ran. I watched them bound away with a rolling motion, a blue glare from the overhead sun rolling on their backs.

"Il est parti," Dede said.

We stood for a few seconds in the bai, assessing the situation, and then Dede turned, very abruptly, and led us in a speedwalk right back along the trail, through the water trail, and back to the camp. I followed him, feeling mildly distressed about our encounter with the gorillas. We had scared them off by approaching directly instead of cleverly concealing our presence in the trees along the edge of the bai. *Why hadn't I thought of that? Why hadn't Dede thought of that?*

It was late afternoon by the time we got back. François Nguembo—I called him Franco—was tending a fire. He had been hired as camp manager, translator (since the pygmies knew only a little French), and cook. After some extended discussion about food, Franco started heating a pot of rice for me. Meanwhile, the pygmies were resting on a green tarpaulin and smoking a newspaper-wrapped cigar made out of something sweet. Very sweet, I thought, as gradually I recognized the fragrance of an organic substance not legal where I come from.

The pygmies smoked their marijuana, Franco tended the rice, and I opened a can of peas. Quite thirsty, not quite comfortable with our plastic jug of communal drinking water drawn from the swamp, I drank all the watery juice out of the pea can. It was good! I watched the rice simmer and stew, then observed as Franco, with two sticks, carefully lifted the pot of cooked rice off the fire, began carrying it over to a spot on top of a tree root—twitched once and flipped the pot upside down so that all the rice landed in a heap on the ground.

He grimaced, said nothing, gingerly picked up the pot and began cleaning it. I said nothing, thinking serenely: *I bought twenty-five kilos of rice. We have plenty!* But by the time I had finished my American-style cogitation on this subject, the pygmies had pulled out their wooden spoons and were squatting on the ground around the steaming rice. They ate every grain.

Franco cooked a second pot of rice. When it was done, he carefully pulled it off the fire and presented it to me. I poured in the can of peas and started eating. I was expecting precooked peas in a can, but these peas surprised me by being raw and very chewy, and so I ate some of the cooked rice and raw peas but had no appetite for the rest. I drank a cup of hot chocolate and watched Franco and the pygmies finish off the rice and peas and then cook a huge pot of manioc—what they called "fufu" and stirred enthusiastically with a stick until it was the consistency of bread dough—and a canned sardine and vegetable stew.

It became dark then, and I turned in, at peace and excited all at once. Outside my tent, Franco and the pygmies finished a big dinner, then sat around the fire and talked loudly, in bursts of speech. A parrot traveled overhead through the darkening sky and announced his or her motion with a moving call: ca-caawk, ca-caawk, ca-caawk! And ubiquitous insects stroked their wings or legs back and forth and produced a churning, gentle clacking sort of noise, like a glass engine idling.

In the middle of the night, I heard deep screams echo across the swamp.

The rice, raw peas, and hot chocolate didn't mix very well, and the next morning I had little appetite and thus for breakfast ate only a small portion of Quaker Oats and drank one bitter cup of hot chocolate. Franco and the pygmies ate a huge breakfast, and then we all packed up and started walking.

The plan was to spend this day walking into the heart of Ndoki, to a place where, Franco said, there was good water. The place with the good water would be our base camp. From that base, I would walk out every day, and, with the help of the pygmies, explore this wonderful forest and look for the naive chimps.

The elephant trail wound and curved and tunneled this way and that, and soon I recognized we were following the same trail Dede and

I had taken the day before, to Mbeli Bai. As happened the day before, the trail at one point gradually dipped and went underwater, turned left, then right, then entered a long channel and tunnel, and we crossed the magical spot where a small river ran right across our trail, and we bent over and drank the water. I was by then hot and quite thirsty. The water was, again, delicious. And as we left that spot of water, its freshness and coolness lingered in my mind: liquid proof of good water in this forest. I thought of the place we were headed for. Franco had said it too would have good water, running water. It would be just like this, I thought, cool and delicious.

The trail took us out to Mbeli Bai–this time no gorillas–and beyond. We stopped at the edge of the bai for a cigarette break. The pygmies had all the marijuana, which they smoked at night; I carried all the tobacco, which they accepted as part of their wages and smoked by day.

This was not such a difficult hike, although the pygmies forever put me to shame by the size of the burdens they carried, by the fact that they walked barefoot in this rough and thorny place, by their never getting lost. But I kept up, and though I was getting thirsty, I pretended not to be whenever they passed around the plastic jug full of swamp water.

There were animals all around us, that was certain, and birds, too, not to mention insects. You could hear the birds, a hundred different toots and cries and warbles, but I never saw any that day. They were up there somewhere, but I couldn't make out where. It was hard to see animals, too, as we wove through our meandering tunnel in the vegetation. But every once in a while the pygmy in front of me would stop, stand still and silent, a foot raised and held in mid-step, then whisper in a language I didn't know. He might whisper: "Ngandi!" Something would crackle and then not crackle. And I, having seen nothing except perhaps one dark flicker behind leaves, would be left standing there like a dummy. *Ngandi? Huh? Huh?* I would be thinking.

Once during this walk, we disturbed a tree full of monkeys, high up in a house of leaves. I saw four monkeys appear out of the leaves and leap from one green cluster to a second, which dipped and shook and swayed with their weight. High up, perhaps sixty or eighty feet above us, agitated by our presence, they called out with a chittering cry.

And once, as we moved along the trail over a slight crest, the pygmy in front of me stopped, whispered something incomprehensible, and I saw five tiny antelope-shaped shadows dart silently across to the left and into a thicket. Blue duikers! A few seconds later, to the right, I saw seven more duikers rush into the open, tiny and beautiful, and then toss themselves into a deep shadow and cave of leaves. They moved quickly in a tight herd, with a feint to the left and a dart to the right, like small fish in a dark pool.

Mostly, on this walk, I followed one of the pygmies, but once Franco led the way. He soon became lost. It was just the two of us then, Franco and I. The pgymies were quietly threading passages somewhere behind us. The elephant trail, which perpetually twisted, forked, and converged and diverged with a thousand other elephant trails, turned one way, another way, and then seemed to peter out into nothing. Why had it petered out? We backtracked and turned and backtracked again and turned again. My compass was useless. Since we had already changed directions so many times, I had no idea where we had come from or where we were going. Franco was alarmed, I could see, and he started hooting and calling out to the pygmies. No one called back. He called and called. No answer. Then it started to rain and then to pour. I was thirsty, and the rain reminded me more of water than of being lost. We sat down in the rain, getting soaked, and I just let the rain flow down my face and concentrated on the idea of all that cool water that would be at our camp after we found the pygmies and got to where we were going. Indeed, fifteen minutes later one of the pygmies appeared from out of nowhere, followed, within a few minutes, by the other three. They all sat down and had a quiet smoke in the rain.

The rain stopped after a while, and toward the end of the day we came into a modest clearing, and my companions shrugged their shoulders and let their packs drop. We were there! I dropped my pack, thirsty and eager to find all the clear, delicious water I had been dreaming about all day. I turned to Franco. "Où est l'eau?" I asked him. He pointed at a trail running away from the far side of our little clearing.

I followed the trail as it snaked twenty yards out and terminated at a series of stagnant mud puddles.

I walked back to camp and said to Franco: "L'eau est mal."

Franco was working on a fire. He looked up. "Mauvais?"

"Oui. L'eau est mauvais!"

Franco indicated that there was more water farther out, and he tossed some words in Lingala to one of the pygmies, who without even a glance in my direction, walked out and down the trail. I was expected to follow. We passed the mud puddles and pretty soon found a mud path with elephant footprints in it. After ten or fifteen minutes, the path turned into a dark and narrow swamp with trees and vines drooping tightly overhead and a soft, murky bottom. We waded through the narrow swamp for another ten minutes, over a rotting log, into deeper swamp, through a tunnel of thicket and vine, and out into an open piece of swamp.

"Beaucoup de l'eau," the pygmy said as we stood at the open swamp. Having made his point, he turned around and walked quickly away. I followed him back through the narrow, murky-bottomed swamp and along the meandering mud trail back to camp.

So much for the water. But my fussiness about the communal swamp water in the plastic jug during the day had left me dehydrated and minus an appetite. My mouth was dry, my voice hoarse. I felt weak, tired, and hot. Possibly feverish. When Franco began discussing dinner, I told him I wasn't hungry.

It rained hard during the night, and I woke at dawn to a deep humming sound and the sight, looking up through the fabric of my tent, of many compact and waggling shadows.

I conceptualized the bees as a temporary plague and remained inside my tent for some time, figuring they were attracted to the water on my tent from last night's rain. When I did leave my tent and wander down to wash my face at the nearest mud puddle, I found that last night's rain had turned the puddle into a sluggish but still actual stream.

But the bees were everywhere, swarming over my tent, over Franco's tent, over the big green tarp the pygmies had stretched across a horizontally lashed sapling. Small blankets of bees shivered noisily around the sugary parts of our food cache; they crawled excitedly over clothes and packs and every other artifact we had brought into the forest. I sat down in front of the smoky fire, where Franco was tending a potful of Quaker Oats. Bundles of vibration began flying figure eights around my head, inspecting my eyes, exploring my shoulders and arms, investigating the interior of my shirt, dive-bombing my ears, walking excitedly through my hair and creating sympathetic oscillations among the follicles. "Beaucoup des insects!" I said to Franco.

"Oui," he said. "Abeilles."

"Abeilles! Abeilles!" I said. "Ils sont terrible!"

Two of the pgymies, Ma and Ande, had been hired only to help carry supplies out into the woods, so that morning I paid them, gave them enough food and cigarettes for the two-day return to Bomassa, and they disappeared when I wasn't looking. That left only four of us, and Franco explained how we would operate. He would stay in the camp, he said, and cook meals, while the two pygmies still with us, Bakembe and Dede, would take turns going out with me into the forest every day to find animals. Bakembe would work one day, Dede the next, so they would each be able to rest every other day.

It was Dede's turn to rest, so Bakembe and I went out that morning. I intuitively liked Bakembe. He was young, perhaps late teens or early twenties, and he seemed bright but very shy. He was bigger than Dede. His face was round and boyish, his eyes large, his chin small, his nose pug, his upper lip long with a small mustache across the middle. He walked out into the elephant trails barefoot, wearing dark shorts and an old brown T-shirt that must have been white once, and every few steps he whacked something with his machete. We walked out through the mud puddles, the mud trail, past the narrow swamp and through the big swamp, out onto a trail that wound way back somewhere into the forest. Within an hour, we had stumbled upon gorillas, who knew we were there before we knew they were there.

First, we heard a terrific scream-roar, a bellowing WRAAAA-AAGGGH! That was a go-away scream, I think. Then we heard a thudding gallop and a crackling away through the underbrush. "Gorille!" Bakembe said. I had already figured it out.

We looked up to see, high above us, forty-five-feet up in the trees, a big dark face looking down. The gorilla stood up, still looking down at us, so that we saw a full black body against a white cloudy sky. The ape began climbing higher up a limb, then stopped, paused, and then clapped a solid chest with cupped hands: apocapocapocapocapocapoc!

This gorilla seemed concerned: looking down at us, waving a hand as if brushing away flies, grabbing and throwing a small branch and a couple of bigger branches, and then climbing higher. The branches came crashing down into the underbrush. There was a sound of urinating from high in the trees, and another gorilla appeared up there—very big—who just sat and looked down at us from a perch sixty-feet high.

Pretty soon Bakembe and I had counted six gorillas in the tree, including a toddler and perhaps a young adolescent.

They looked at us. We looked at them. Once in a while, one would let off a volley of chest-claps: apocapocapocapocapoc. And occasionally we heard deep grunts from inside a thicket of vegetation at ground level, perhaps in response to the general anxiety communicated from the tree.

This went on for half an hour. Eventually some of the gorillas in the tree moved away across branches and out of sight. I think they descended to the ground and took off. One very big gorilla stayed put and just looked down at us quietly, as if thinking, while a couple of others kept looking down and clapping their chests. Then there was a terrible scream in the thickets at ground level, then a second, and a third terrible scream. The gorillas in the tree kept looking down, clapping their chests again and again. And now we heard a deep and ominous grunting from inside the bushes, some twenty feet away.

Should we creep closer for a better look? Should we leave, before a hairy locomotive explodes out of the bushes?

We left.

We followed a trail for half an hour before sitting down on a fallen log inside a minor clearing. Bakembe smoked a cigarette while I let myself hear the forest again: a rolling and rattling of insects; a whistling, chirping, warbling, and tooting of birds; the surfy sound of a soft breeze filtering between trees and making leaves brush against each other; and every once in a while an interruption, a startling *crack!* as some branch somewhere succumbed at last to gravity.

"Beaucoup de l'eau ici," Bakembe said, having finished his cigarette. Immediately I became enthusiastic. Water! Maybe this would be a better place to camp. Bakembe led me over to where all the water was: another fetid swamp, not even as nice as the one next to our camp.

We wandered around for another couple of hours. I had no idea where we were, no sense of direction or distance or topography. Any tree, any bush, any thicket and vine maze looked like a dozen other trees and bushes and thickets and vine mazes we had just passed by. Every elephant trail looked the same. Moss didn't grow on any predictable side of any tree. The ground didn't slope in any consistent direction. The sunlight falling between leaves and dappling the floor seemed merely to fall from overhead. My compass was useless. I couldn't even figure out how Bakembe knew where we were—if he did! But at last the trail twisted and deposited us into familiar territory, the swamp near our camp. As we waded through a shallower part of the swamp, Bakembe whacked the water with his machete twice and picked up two small, stunned fish. Then we followed the platter-sized elephant prints along the mud trail.

First I smelled our camp. Wood smoke hung low and traveled out by an atmospheric osmosis, extending itself slowly outward between the trees and vines and faster along the trails. Then I heard our camp: humming. Yes, the whole camp was still swarming with bees, I saw, as I walked in and dropped my day pack. This was a nightmare, a horror show, a Prufrockian thriller by J. Alfred Hitchcock.

I tore off my clothes, ran out and bathed in our puddle, then scampered back into camp, unzipped the hatch to my tent, quickly jumped inside, and quickly zipped up the hatch. A few bees had moved into the tent along with me, so I killed them and placed their bodies in one spot where I would be sure not to step on them. But the rest of the bees were still there, outside, a thousand wandering bizarrely in semicircles over the surface of two tents, four thousand shivering insanely around the sugar and the larger stacks of bagged and canned food, five thousand hovering brazenly in a demihemisphere around our campsite, all humming and buzzing with ten thousand voices merging into one mighty, harmonious, vibrating drone: the Mormon Tabernacle Choir of bees.

Franco was lying in his tent, mosquito netting down, but as I could see through the mosquito net hatch in my tent, the pygmies were out there, ignoring the bees, busy improving their lean-to with the green tarp roof. They constructed a broom from weeds and vines and swept the dirt floor. They cut down several small trees and built two bed frames, lashed into shape with vines. With strips of bark, they wove two mattresses for the beds. Then, with vines and sticks and green leaves, they built walls on either side of the lean-to, and they created a smoky fire inside, right next to Dede's bed.

I read escapist fiction, played solitaire when I was too sweaty to read, and then, toward the end of the afternoon, unzipped the hatch and went out into the bees long enough to eat dinner. I found that if I walked while eating my dinner and drinking my hot chocolate, the bees didn't bother me so much. Motion made them nervous.

Day and night were equal partners here, almost twelve hours each with a quick transition in between.

At six o'clock it was dark, and the bees left. The forest turned cool and haunting. A moon with a hazy halo floated overhead, and moonlight filtered through the trees and scattered a pale laundry onto leaves and branches and down to a dappled floor. Moths rose in a sea of moonlight and swam silently. Fireflies carried soft, trembling beacons in dark places. A Chinese pictogram settled onto my tent.

There were noises at night I didn't understand. A little, lonesome voice went: ooooouuuuu!!! Some other lonesome voice practiced the scales, a hoo hoo hoo hoo hoo hoo hooo down the scale, then up the scale. Things fell at night, leaves and branches, I think, that landed with a plunk or a crash. Sometimes I heard a scream; hoots; the sewing machine sound of a galago interested in sex; the PingggggPingggg-PingggggPingggg of a fruit bat interested in sex. Crickets interested in sex made the sound of a million squeaking mattresses in a million cheap hotels: urge and urge and urge, always the procreant urge. There was heat lightning and distant thunder, but the night insects were everywhere, a gentle corrugation of sound, a soothing, a hypnotic presence that tucked itself down somewhere in the back of your brain so you forgot you were hearing it until you closed your eyes and saw the restful, pulsing chorus as a rippling vision in green and blue.

In my dream I was staying inside an old church inside the forest with a European biologist and his wife, people who used to be friends. He wanted to do some kind of experiment to see how the bees mate. I suggested—joking, of course—that he build a small bower just below the circular hole at the peak of the cathedral's dome (the church had grown by now, arching high above us, shaped exactly like my tent with its ventilation hole at the top), so the bees would be able to mate in the moonlight. He laughed, and then a cat started flying around inside the cathedral. Amazed to see a flying cat, we followed his spiraling progress with the beams of our flashlights until he caught hold of one of the vertical cathedral walls, turned, faced us, and then, in the eerie light of our flashlights, his face grew and was transubstantiated into a black and white satanic mask.

Bakembe and I found gorillas again a few days later. We were walking on a trail past a cluster of vegetation when we heard some cracking sounds. Bakembe stopped instantly, his left foot still in the air, his leg cocked. "Gorille!" he breathed. With a cupped hand, he softly pushed the air toward what we heard, as if to say: *Over there in that general direction.*

But half a minute later he was walking along the trail again, away from the gorillas. I stopped him. "Bakembe," I said. "Allons. Cherchons les gorilles! Allons chercher les gorilles!"

He acted as if the thought had never occurred to him. *Find the gorillas? Okay, I guess.* We turned quietly off the trail and slowly moved in the direction of the sounds we had heard. Pretty soon we saw a couple of dark shapes obscured by vines and branches and leaves. The instant we saw them, they saw us. One big gorilla stood up, let out a roar that sounded like a giant's belch: "BWWAAAAAAAGGH!!!" And then there was a pounding and stomping, a tree fell down, and then a crashing and cracking sound of big animals running away. They didn't run far away or all at once, however, and we followed and moved into a somewhat open area where we could see them, now thirty feet in the distance and moving behind trees and into another thicket. Bakembe said there were six gorillas, but I never saw more than two at a time.

Having moved into that thicket, all the dark shapes and their sounds seemed to recede, except for one big gorilla who held his ground right at the entrance to the thicket and played peeka-boo with us through vegetation. Through a small tunnel in the leaves, I saw massive shoulders and a gigantic jet black face look-ing at me. He started roaring: "BWWWAAAAAAAGGHHH! BWWWAAAAAAAGGHHH! BWWWAAAAAAAGGHHH!" Fi-nally, he turned and left, every thirty seconds letting out another roar as he, too, receded into the thicket.

Gorillas turn out to be bigger than makes sense, bigger than they ought to be, bigger than you remember them being, even when you remember that they will be bigger than you remember. That gorilla was massive! I thought he must have been the silverback of the group.

We turned around and sat at the base of a tree, resting. In follow-ing that small group toward the thicket, unfortunately, we must have accidentally divided a larger group, because right before us now, per-haps twenty-five to thirty feet away and lurking behind trees and brush, hard to see at first, was another gorilla. This one, it seemed to me, was even bigger than any of the others. He must have been the silverback! He stood, huge and rectangular, like a dark house, half obscured still, without a sound. But then he turned and pushed a tree that fell with a great CRASH! and moved into a denser section of brush where we could barely see him. Bakembe and I stood up. I could see that Bakembe was excited, out of breath. But then I heard his breath, ragged, tremulous—and I realized he was scared!

We saw yet another gorilla, a female I believe, who climbed a tree and then—apocapocapocapocapoc—let out a burst of chest-clapping.

They were not going to move.

The chest-clapping in the tree continued. Then the big one on the ground started shaking branches, barking at us with a series of deep belch-barks. These were benthic fulminations, like barks from the biggest dog in history: WOOOOOF! WOOOOOOF! WOOOOOOOF!

The gorilla in the tree moved up higher and started throwing branches down from on high. The one on the ground began galloping sideways inside a green thicket—way to his left, way to his right—with a series of belch-barks, knocking small trees over as he stirred up things, producing a violent boiling effect in the green thicket. He moved out of there, knocked over a big tree—and I could see him clearly now. He was hulking in the open space of an elephant trail, looking like a small mountain.

We walked slowly away from all this commotion, then sat down again where we thought it was safe, only to realize there was a gorilla in a tree directly above us. That one screamed. Then the gorilla back on the trail screamed.

Suddenly, Bakembe had had enough. He jumped up and started running for all he was worth. I knew from everything I had read that running is the worst thing you can do around gorillas. People who run are people who get damaged. Nonetheless, it took only a few seconds of watching my companion run away before I ran too, following and finally catching up with him.

We sat down on a log, with sounds of gorillas some distance away now: a roar, some chest-clapping. We took a cigarette break, and then Bakembe abruptly stood, turned around, and looked down at where he had been seated: swarming black ants.

This was not his day.

Bakembe had not wanted to find those gorillas in the first place, and after that incident, he more clearly than ever did not want to find gorillas. Perhaps that was when the bad feelings began. I don't know exactly when it started, but at some point, Bakembe got completely fed up with me. He may have said to himself: *Why should I risk my neck for this crazy, weak, spoiled, and incompetent white person? He's going to pay me the same amount, whether or not I get killed.*

Although Bakembe and I continued going out into the forest every other day, we stopped seeing animals. Oh, occasionally we would run into a confused sitatunga—a deer—or look into the undergrowth and spy a flock of twenty fat, blue-black guinea fowl, wandering on the forest floor like chickens, walking erratically and cluck-crowing, then fleeing in alarm when at last they saw us. But whenever we came across unavoidable signs of big animals, chimps or gorillas, for example, Bakembe made excuses: *They are way over there. They have already left. They are far away. They went through here and left that huge knuckle print in the sand tomorrow*—meaning, of course, *yesterday.*

Bakembe stopped trying. He stopped leaving the trail, stopped listening very hard. The day we spent only two or three hours walking in the forest and returned to camp while it was still morning, I was furious. "I feel cheated," I said in English, and I stalked off, bathed in the puddle, and then sulked in my tent for pretty much the rest of the day. It was true that I was a crazy, weak, spoiled, and incompetent white person. It was true that I would pay them the same wages no matter what happened. It was even more true that I depended upon Franco and the pygmies for just about everything—for survival, come to think of it, since I couldn't walk more than a few yards by myself in the green labyrinth before the way forward became the way back. The only leverage I had was cigarettes. I possessed all the cigarettes in camp, and everyone depended on me for their daily cancer fix. That day I really sulked: I didn't give out any cigarettes.

Bakembe got the message. The next time we went out into the forest, we still didn't find animals, we still didn't leave the trail very much, but we walked very fast for nearly eight hours. He was trying to wear me out, drive me helpless and undone, twist my arm until I cried uncle. Once as we speedwalked through the forest, I tripped and fell flat on my face. He heard me fall, I'm sure, but he didn't look over his shoulder or even pause in his fast walk. When we did sit down for the occasional break, he sat with his back fully turned to me.

This went on. During the next few days, he always sat with his back to me, and often, during a smoke break, he would make a point of sitting twenty feet away from me, as if I stank of rancid sweat. I did stink of rancid sweat, but so did everyone else.

This behavior was simple rudeness, even (since he was a kid, twenty years younger than me) absurd insolence, and my anger over it slowly turned into a cold and stable animosity. Bakembe's face had what I first thought was a quiet charm but later discovered to be mere youth.

As I came to disappreciate Bakembe, I started to appreciate Franco. When we started out on this trip, I didn't trust Franco. Call it first impressions. Call it intuition. I didn't like his looks or style. His legs, his feet were so big. He seemed so bulky, so clumsy compared with the pygmies. His eyes were narrow, hard to read, his manner impatient and explosive. And, I knew, his brother Jean was an elephant killer, the most notorious elephant poacher in the entire region.

Every night, when the bees were gone, Franco and the pygmies would smoke their marijuana and have long loud talks in Lingala or Bomassa by the fire. Sometimes I sat with them and occasionally interjected some weak French or, when comprehension was no longer an issue whatsoever, English. Even when I listened to these long fireside discussions from inside my tent, I always knew Franco's voice because it was louder than the other two combined. He shouted, he argued, he bantered, he laughed wildly, and sometimes he harangued the pygmies into a submissive silence.

"Carrbea? Ged sa opa primfordia!" he would shout, his voice ringing out through the night air.

The pygmies would say, meekly, "Uh-huh."

"Benga megawabawsa, camba wanoe fwassa kinde? A paredon!"

"Uh-huh."

"Ma tea mateddy compugeda! Mopa buest wa awah!"

"Uh-huh."

But gradually, I came to trust and then to like Franco. If he was loud, explosive, he was yet predictable and reliable. And he worked. He cooked all the meals, cleaned up afterward. To my way of thinking, he became the head counselor of Camp Many Bee, the one person who knew with a Protestant grasp of reality how horrible the bees were, yet simultaneously understood, in the way of Pygmy Zen, that the bees just *were*. These bees didn't usually sting, incidentally. But if you swiped at one with a hand, you might accidentally hit a stinger. In that way, I was stung and found the venom to be remarkably toxic and painful. A stinger was lodged in my finger—and Franco pulled it out. Another venom-saturated stinger somehow became lodged in a remote spot on my back. Franco pulled it out. Who else?

My feelings about Dede varied according to the time of day and phase of the moon. He was almost my age, a fact I appreciated. We were the old men of the camp. I could look at the two hundred hairs on his upper lip, the thirty-seven hairs on his chin, and recognize a small but fair representation of white and gray.

Most important, he worked. While Bakembe seldom left the comfort of the trail, now, Dede seldom followed the trail at all. Most of the time Dede and I would be stalking something, somewhere, following footprints, an old trail of dung, some half-chewed fruit, passing through thorns and thickets or crawling on our bellies through a vine maze.

Once we stumbled across something big and noisy, something snorting in the underbrush, snorting and growling—at least grumbling.

"Qu'est-ce que c'est?" I asked Dede.

"Ncuru," he said.

"Ncuru?" I said. "Qu'est-ce que 'ncuru'?"

Dede tried another language: "Quoisso," he said.

I saw the brown flank of something and then heard a crash and then saw nothing.

Ncuru turned out to be giant forest hog. We found about ten of them, and they seemed confused. They could hear us and were starting to get alarmed, but their vision was bad, I think. They couldn't see us and so weren't sure exactly what to do. They receded slowly and inefficiently, as Dede and I crawled toward them along a narrow passage through vines. Dede was really pleased now, we were so close, and when he got a good sight of them, he raised and aimed his machete as if it were a gun, lifted and put down his thumb, and said, quietly, "Pomb!"

The pigs looked fat and had reddish brown fur.

An hour later something strange surprised us. We had been walking along a trail when suddenly Dede stopped and then slowly moved up to a large tree and peered around the corner of the trunk. He looked at me. "Simpangee!" he whispered.

It was a big surprise, perhaps the only time we ever found apes before they saw or heard us. We must have been impressively quiet on the trail, because these three big hairy creatures never noticed us. They were sitting on the forest floor: in a circle!

I think there were three, but there may have been four. Even though they were close, perhaps fifteen or twenty feet away, with a clear line of sight in between, it was dark where they sat. I was, moreover, busy trying not to be discovered, standing behind the tree and carefully peering around the edge of that big tree trunk, while Dede, bent below me, also carefully peered around the edge of the trunk.

This whole scene had an absurd and childish quality to it, and I felt a child's delight. Dede and I were playing hide-and-seek with imaginary animals. And why were these three big apes sitting on the ground in a circle? They looked as if they were having a quiet tea party. They could have been The Three Bears.

I thought there might be four apes there, as I said, but it was dark in the shadows, and anyway, I was busy noticing two other things. First, these apes were unusually dark-haired for chimpanzees. Chimps are generally more brown than black. Second, these apes looked big, actually quite big. I mulled those two observations over in my mind for a couple of seconds. Dede must have been doing much the same thing, because just then he whispered: "Gorille!" At that, his breathing turned ragged.

We were very quiet, and I thought we had done an excellent job of just peeking around that tree. Somehow, however, the gorillas suddenly realized someone was spying on their party. They started to scramble. Two or three folded themselves into the forest and disappeared, while one turned and began moving erratically in our direction.

Dede called on technology to rescue us.

He whacked the flat side of his machete against the tree, and the noise scared this gorilla enough that he spun around once and evaporated.

At one point Dede and I came upon some chimp nests in a tree. "Simpangee est dormi là-bas. Quatre. Cinq," he said. We counted five nests.

We sat down against the tree, and Dede placed some fingers on the bridge of his nose and began honking: "Meeawwp Meeawwp Meeawwp! . . . Meeawwp Meeawwp Meeawwp! . . . Meeawwp Meeawwp Meeawwp!" This was a duiker birthing call (made by the mother) that the pygmies use as a lure for duikers and duiker predators—in this case, chimps. "Meeawwp Meeawwp Meeawwp!" Dede honked again. But we listened then only to insects and birds. The chimps, wherever they were, didn't take the bait.

We waited. We waited. A bird whistled a geographic argument: Ohio. Ohio. Ohio. Vermont. Ohio. Vermont. Ohio. Ohio. Ohio Ohio. Vermont. Ohio.

"Mange," Dede said at last, and he sat down and opened up his leaf-purse, a big green leaf tied shut with a strip of bark. Inside was his lunch: rice. We were just off the edge of a swamp, with white butterflies dueling in a patch of sunlight. A black and white monkey in a treetop greeted us with a deep, rolling, burp-like call: Buurrrrrrrrrrrp! Buurrrrrrrrp! The light around us took on a greenish tint at midday, with leaves above us illuminated by sunlight.

Later, we came across leftover fruit from a chimpanzee feast. We sat down. "Meeawwp Meeawwp Meeawwp!" Dede called, loud and nasal. "Meeawwp Meeawwp Meeawwp!"

We found chimpanzee knuckle prints, followed them for a while, and came to a spot where Dede squatted, flattening his nose, calling again the duiker call: "Meeawwp Meeawwp Meeawwp!"

Dede and I heard, from somewhere in the distance, a sudden chorus of screams and the booming noise chimps make by drumming on tree buttress-roots.

Dede squatted down, held his fingers on his nose, and went: "Meeawwp! Meeawwp! Meeawwp!"

We waited for perhaps two minutes before, suddenly, they were coming—fast! I heard a low rumbling in the ground, some crackling, and a half-stifled whimpering. They were excited! They could barely contain themselves! Supper was calling! They approached us through the forest fast and unseen, then hit the trees about twenty feet away and climbed just high enough to look out over the brush. I saw three of them. They were big! They saw us and instantly they started screaming. One big male hunched over on a branch, his hair raised in fear or rage. They stared, craned their necks, opened their eyes wide—and screamed!

My heart started pounding.

My vision was interrupted and limited by leaves and branches, but I saw at least five chimps now, perhaps six. One climbed higher, twenty feet up in a tree.

Then suddenly they were quiet. They just stared and stared and stared and stared. Were we visitors dropped down from the clouds? Were we aliens from another planet? Had they ever seen humans before?

Pretty soon they began screaming again.

They must have recognized us as fellow apes—of a strangely different species, of course. But still we had their faces, their hands, their body shape. Our clothes must have confused them. Our bright objects—my yellow pack, Dede's machete, the knife at my belt, my pen and notebook—may have intrigued them. Perhaps they were wondering what to do next. But their moods seem to shift: from curious, puzzled, and confused, to fearful and enraged. They would be quiet, just staring. Then one chimp would start whimpering. He or she would soon be joined by others, and then the whimpers would turn into a sequence of crescendoing hoots and then into screams. Pretty soon they would all be worked into a frenzy, chorusing into an orgy of earsplitting screams and shrieks. If we had been merely chimps from a different social group, trespassing into their territory, they might have attacked and possibly killed us. Jane Goodall once described to me how warring male chimps tear their victims to pieces, mutilate them, even drink their blood.

This encounter was unnerving. We were about their size, and I knew they were quicker, more agile, and several times stronger than any human ape. Even our little pieces of protective magic, my knife and Dede's machete, would probably not save us if they attacked. An image of the attack seeped into my mind: a lightning rush by a dark ape as strong as a bull, teeth to the throat, a single quick grab rendering both Dede and me off balance and helpless. My heart was pounding. I reassured myself with some thin intellectualizing: "No scientific ob-server has ever been seriously injured by a wild chimpanzee." But these chimps did not behave like ordinary wild chimps. They were not afraid.

It seemed to me then that the most disturbing thing about us, for them, was that we didn't act fearful. When chimps threaten other chimps, everyone gets very exercised, starts displaying, screaming, and so forth. These chimps were threatening us and we didn't react at all. We just sat there and stared right back. *It must be very disconcerting,* I thought, *to see apes wearing clothes and not emoting.*

They were quiet. Then they started screaming again and shaking branches, and my pulse started racing. One big male on a branch craned his neck, screamed, and bent over with his back arched high, his arms and shoulders and neck bulked up with hair standing on end, his mouth open in a dark and fanged rectangle, vomiting screams like a gargoyle. After ten or fifteen or twenty minutes back with the rest of the group, he sprang out onto a limb, climbed into a nearby tree, and passed over into another tree and another until he was climbing di-rectly above us.

I had resolved to sit still, not to move. But as this big guy thumped through vegetative passageways directly above us, a branch tested by his weight broke with a deep craaaaaaaaack! At that alarming sound, Dede and I stood up together, as slowly and deliberately as we could manage—stood still, looked at each other and the chimps, and then slowly walked backward fifteen feet.

The moment we stood up, the chimps became quiet. Our un-folded size, our upright stance, may have surprised them.

But the big male in the trees continued approaching us. He threw a branch down, jumped to another tree, broke another branch and tossed it–crash!–and leaped into another tree. While the rest of the chimps remained in the background, a disorganized sort of Greek chorus, that big male was trying to drive us away. He kept coming closer, gradually approaching with stares and screams and raised hair. He climbed across a branch right over us, tore out a huge branch, and threw it at us.

So we stood up again and moved back again, slowly, facing him and them, another ten feet. Then we sat down again. Dede didn't like this. He said something that must have meant: "Shall we go?" I said, in French: "No. Let's stay."

He left, walked away thirty feet down a trail, so that I was sitting there facing the chimps alone, the chimps looking down, sometimes scratching themselves, then screaming, teeth bared. I stood up at last and moved back to where Dede was. The chimps of the chorus, seeing me move off, began moving away themselves in their own direction, climbing into other trees. The big male nearby and low in the trees, seeing he had succeeded in driving us away, climbed down a gray trunk all the way to the ground and turned and disappeared in a blur.

I am convinced there were elephants all over the place, in the en-chanted forest. But as I have already suggested, it was a deep labyrinth. Our trails turned into tunnels, and our vision was limited by thickets and clumps, complicated trees and cascading vines, and, when a storm was coming through, by a bluish, gloomy light, an eerie, twilit, flick-ering quality of being underwater. Sometimes we could see as far as forty or fifty feet before an accumulation of tree trunks blocked further sight, but often our eyes and minds registered only two or three or five or six feet before a gigantic mess of leaves and vines obliterated everything beyond.

Elephants were there, all right. I saw their dung, sometimes fresh and scattered like wet tobacco, sometimes maturing, sprouting little white mushrooms. I saw their footprints. I saw the trails they had worn everywhere through the forest. But the elephants were smarter than we were. They heard us first, knew where we walked when we had not even a clue where they stood, embedded figures in a matrix. While we were tripping over vines and breathing heavily, they paused and magically transformed themselves into a dream of plants and wind, of leaves and ferns flickering or wavering ever so slightly as a current of air passed slowly through.

The elephants were invisible.

They stayed that way, it has occurred to me, because no one seriously wished to render them visible. Once Bakembe and I heard a wheezy snort, like an outburst of steam. "Éléphant!" Bakembe said.

We circled back, climbed a small and densely overgrown hill, waited. Several minutes passed. We heard a kind of heavy, breathy honk. Then we heard a plowing through the brush.

"Allons," I said, thinking to follow the noise.

"Méchant! Elle est méchant!" Bakembe insisted, refusing to move.

Another time, while resting along a trail, Dede and I heard heavy breathing with a slight wheezing effect. With his left hand, Dede pushed some air in the direction of the sound.

"Dede," I said.

"Uh?"

"Qu'est ce-que c'est?"

"Uh?"

"Éléphant?"

"Uh."

Neither of us did anything further about that.

The elephants materialized at night, inside my head. "Elephants are intelligent," a voice explained, lecturing me in an absurd and didactic dream. "When one dies, all the elephants for miles around know it instantly. Elephant communications do not resemble human communications. The waveshape of their voices most resembles the waveshape of a hyrax communication, whereas the waveshape of a human communication most resembles the waveshape of a mouse communication." I floated inside the great dark barrel of an elephant's body, intending to become and understand an elephant. I was trying to look out the egg-sized eyeholes, but whatever pale image I saw through those two orifices was flickering, flickering, flickering. In a flash of insight, I realized the problem was that elephants have eyes on either side of their heads, giving no visual overlap, whereas humans and other primates have eyes in the front of their faces, with considerable overlap in the visual field. My little primate brain hadn't adjusted to the problem of seeing through elephant eyes. Thus the flickering. I realized it would go away as I more fully adjusted to elephant episte-mology. I saw a child, then, and a child-sized horse.

In the middle of the night (or was it early in the morning?) I was awakened by a deep drumming, so deep I wasn't sure I heard it. Perhaps it was the deep trumpeting of elephants from very far away. It might have been distant thunder, but perhaps it was more like a deep feeling from my own heart. It could have been a dozen chimpanzees drumming wildly on trees somewhere inside a green arabesque, but perhaps it was more like a dozen chimpanzees drumming softly from a paradise inside my own head.

I woke up all the way then and suddenly, swept back into the quotidian fever I sometimes call reality, I thought, *Paradise?* For the last two weeks I had been so busy dodging bees and dealing with swamp water, bad feelings, confusing trails, screaming gorillas, raging chim-panzees, and hiding elephants, I hadn't even entertained a single naive thought about paradise. I saw the clearing light of dawn and listened to the bees gathering in the forest and approaching my tent. Pretty soon their little shadows would be spinning and buzzing on the nylon tapestry above my face. This place was beautiful and mysterious, all right. It was an enchanted forest, all right. I loved the Ndoki forest—in the abstract. Perhaps it was a paradise . . . for chimpanzees! For me it was more like purgatory, or, worse, one of those endless circles in the hot place.

Paradise? My ancestors left their chimp brothers in the forest many years ago and took off for the savannas.

I began organizing my things and packing my bag.

Acknowledgments

My Chimpanzee Travels were not traveled alone.

Even before I packed my toothbrush, in fact, many people encouraged and supported me, and even helped plan my trip. Most particularly, I want to thank Geza Teleki, director of the Committee for Conservation and Care of Chimpanzees (3819 Forty-eighth Street, NW, Washington, D.C., 20016), who sat me down with a map of Africa and an amazing address file and advised me on what to do and how to do it. I will also thank Jane Goodall, who was always there as friend and mentor. There is no one I admire more. Thanks to my brother, Dwight ("Pete") Peterson, who encouraged me in my folly, even to the point of lending money. And to my wife, Wyn Kelley, and my children, Britt and Bayne, who did everything possible to sustain and encourage me; at the same time, they made me reluctant to leave and eager to return.

Many of the people who helped me in Africa are named in the chapters of this book, but they should also be thanked now. In Zambia: David and Sheila Siddle at the Chimfunshi Wildlife Sanctuary; also, Bruce, and Cephas Masuku. In Tanzania: Alex on the *Liemba*; Polly Boom in Kigoma; and Gerry Ellis, Hank Kline, Halid Kuwe, Ken Pack at Gombe, and Stephan Qoli. In Burundi: Mimi Brian, Paul Bunda, André Niokende of the INECN, and Charlotte Uhlebroek; also Matt, Rob, Rose, and the fourth person whose name I forgot, from the U.S. Peace Corps. In Kenya: Gerry Ellis, again, and Mike Garner of Mike Garner Safaris. In Uganda: Tim Holmes at the Entebbe Zoo, and Amazing Grace, B.J. (Joseph Basigara), Kevin Hunt, Peter Tuhairwe, Richard Wrangham of the Kibale Forest Research

Project and Steve at the U.S. Embassy. In the Gambia: Eddie Brewer and Dr. Camara of the Wildlife Conservation Department; Philippe Bussi, Janis Carter, Boiro Samba, and Jim Zinn of the Gambia's Chimpanzee Rehabilitation Project. In Ivory Coast: Christophe and Hedwige Boesch of the Centre Suisse de Recherches Scientifiques and the University of Basel in Switzerland; Denis Lia and Paul and Natalie Marchesi of the Centre Suisse. Elsewhere in West Africa: Abu and others. In Gabon: Michel Fernandez and Caroline Tutin of the Lopé-Okanda Forest Reserve, as well as Josef Maroga, M'Guema, Rebecca, and Lee White. In Brazzaville, Congo: Ambassador James Dan Phillips and Lucie Phillips. In Pointe-Noire, Congo: Aliette Jamart, Rick the drilling supervisor from Conoco Congo, Roger Simpson of Conoco Congo, and Dave Storch, the diver. In northern Congo: Michael Fay, Matthew Hatchwell, and Richard Rugiero of NYZS, the Wildlife Conservation Society; Marcellin Agnagna, Gerome Mokoko, and Daniel Shodja of Project Nouabalé-Ndoki; and, from Bomassa, Ande, Ma, Dede Florent, François Nguembo, and Bakembe Victor.

Back home, while I was writing *Chimpanzee Travels*, Frank Fox, owner of Marcella's in Porter Square, Cambridge, generously donated many, many cappuccinos on those mornings when my brain needed a kick start. I am grateful for his generosity, and for that of several people who read parts of the manuscript, commented, and otherwise provided helpful suggestions and insights, including: Janis Carter, George Morgan, Mark Savin, Richard Wrangham, and Phil and Carol Zaleski.

As ever, Peter Matson of Sterling Lord Literistic helped with the most difficult part of book writing, finding the right publisher; and Bill Patrick demonstrated, as editor, that Addison-Wesley was that.

This book is nonfiction but in those few instances where I felt issues were politically sensitive, I changed names and otherwise disguised identities. I did, in addition, use my poetic license to pretend there were two trips to Africa, to protect the Unity of Time. In reality, most of the final chapter describes a third trip, to Brazzaville and from thence to Bomassa and Ndoki, taken a couple of years after the second.

Most of my background material is named in the text and obvious. Sources that may not be so obvious include the following: Chapter 2: Amin, Willets, and Matheson, 1986; Crowther, and others, 1992; 1977; Naipaul, 1979; 1978; Chapter 3: Collins, 1967; Hepburn, 1987; McCutcheon, 1993; McLynn, 1993; 1992; Moorhead, 1960; and

Severin, 1973; Chapter 4: Collins, 1967; McLynn, 1993; 1992; Moorhead, 1960; and Severin, 1973; Chapter 10: Linden, 1986; Chapter 11: Gavron, 1993; Smith, 1967.

Bibliography

Amin, Mohamed, Duncan Willets, and Alastair Matheson. *Railway Across the Equator: The Story of the East African Line*. London: The Bodley Head, 1986.

Carter, Janis. "Freed From Keepers and Cages, Chimps Come of Age on Baboon Island." *Smithsonian,* June 1988, 36–49.

Collins, Robert O. Introduction to Richard F. Burton, *The Nile Basin,* and James Macqueen, *Captain Speke's Discovery of the Source of the Nile*. New York: De Capo Press, 1967.

Crowther, Jeff, and others. *Africa on a Shoestring*. Berkeley, Calif.: Lonely Planet, 1992; 1977.

Diamond, Jared. "The Great Leap Forward." *Discover,* May 1989, 50–60.

Forester, C. S. *The African Queen*. New York: Random House, 1940.

Galton, Francis. *The Art of Travel*. Introduction by Dorothy Middleton. Harrisburg, Pa.: Stackpole Books, 1971; 1872; 1855.

Gavron, Jeremy. *The Last Elephant: An African Quest*. London: HarperCollins, 1993.

Goodall, Jane. *In the Shadow of Man*. Boston: Houghton Mifflin, 1971.

Hepburn, Katherine. *The Making of The African Queen, or, How I Went to Africa with Bogart, Bacall and Huston and Almost Lost My Mind*. New York: Alfred A. Knopf, 1987.

Hyams, Joe. *Flight of the Avenger: George Bush at War*. New York: Harcourt Brace Jovanovich, 1991

Linden, Eugene. *Silent Partners: The Legacy of the Ape Language Experiments*. New York: Time Books, 1986.

Naipaul, Shiva. *North of South: An African Journey*. New York: Simon & Schuster, 1979.

McCutcheon, Shaw. "African Queen: Does the Old Girl Still Have It?" *Boating,* February 1993, 66.

McLynn, Frank. *Hearts of Darkness: The European Exploration of Africa.* New York: Carroll & Graf, 1993.

Moorehead, Alan. *The White Nile.* New York: Harper & Brothers, 1960.

Sacks, Oliver. "An Anthropologist on Mars." *The New Yorker,* December 27, 1993, 106ff.

Severin, Timothy. *The African Adventure.* New York: E.P. Dutton, 1973.

Smith, Cyril Stanley. "Materials." *Scientific American,* September 1967, 69–79.

Swift, Jonathan. *Gulliver's Travels.* Edited and introduced by Paul Turner. New York: Oxford University Press, 1971.

Temerlin, Maurice K. *Lucy: Growing Up Human.* Palo Alto, Calif.: Science and Behavior Books, 1975.

Waal, Frans de. *Peacemaking Among Primates.* Cambridge, Mass.: Harvard University Press, 1989.